Introducing
Microsoft®
Windows® CE
for the Handheld PC

Robert O'Hara

Microsoft Press

PUBLISHED BY
Microsoft Press
A Division of Microsoft Corporation
One Microsoft Way
Redmond, Washington 98052-6399

Library of Congress Cataloging-in-Publication Data
O'Hara, Robert P.
   Introducing Microsoft Windows CE for the Handheld PC / Robert O'Hara.
     p.   cm.
   Includes index.
   ISBN 1-57231-515-6
   1. Microsoft Windows (Computer file)   2. Operating systems
(Computers)   I. Title.
QA76.76.O63O3438 1997
005.4'469--dc21   97-833
                                           CIP

Printed and bound in the United States of America.

1 2 3 4 5 6 7 8 9 MLML 2 1 0 9 8 7

Distributed to the book trade in Canada by Macmillan of Canada, a division of Canada Publishing
Corporation.

A CIP catalogue record for this book is available from the British Library.

Microsoft Press books are available through booksellers and distributors worldwide. For further
information about international editions, contact your local Microsoft Corporation office. Or contact
Microsoft Press International directly at fax (206) 936-7329.

Acquisitions Editor: Stephen Guty
Project Editors: Stuart J. Stuple and Saul Candib
Manuscript Editors: Laura Sackerman and Saul Candib
Technical Editors: Linda Rose Ebenstein and Roslyn Lutsch

CONTENTS *at a Glance*

TABLE OF CONTENTS

Foreword

In 1993 a group of people were sitting in a small, windowless room (what an irony) at the Microsoft campus in Redmond, Washington, thinking up a code name for a new product. The planned product was fascinating— a tiny computer that would cost a fraction of what desktop PCs cost. It would allow people to create information, access information, and connect to the rest of the world through wireless and wired data networks. The group decided on the code name Pulsar, and one of the most unique adventures that I have had the privilege to be part of had begun.

The mission of that group of people, later to become the Consumer Appliance Group, was (and still is) to build an operating system and applications for a device that could be carried in a person's pocket. However, unlike a typical electronic organizer, which has limited capability for expansion, this system would be a computing platform. It would offer a rich development environment that would allow software developers to unleash their creativity and ingenuity on this to-be-named device.

Creating an operating system that was a subset of Microsoft Windows might have seemed to be a reasonable plan. After all, Windows is ubiquitous, with lots of tools and support. However, the challenge of squeezing even a subset of Windows into the constrained set of devices we had in mind seemed too fantastic. Also, it turned out that the hardware and the architecture to create the sort of tiny PC we wanted were not available at that time. The more we looked at the problems, the more difficult they seemed. That was actually very good news, since the problems attracted some of the more creative, challenge-hungry folks at Microsoft.

The product plan evolved, the Pulsar team merged with the WinPad team, which was working on a similar device, and the Windows CE train started its journey. During the next three years we would define a hardware reference platform, recruit some of the most creative hardware makers in the world, build a software community, and build a processor-independent version of the Windows operating system that can live in about 500 KB of memory, powered by two AA batteries.

Creating this new machine—the Handheld PC—was the goal the group set for itself, and indeed we become so obsessed with the device that we stopped talking about the software only. We referred to the Handheld PC as "our device," although we did not build a single machine. As we designed the software, it became apparent that Windows CE would be able to power not only pocketable devices but also information appliances that would be found in people's living rooms, clipped to their belts, and in their cars. The opportunities are almost boundless.

Windows CE can power most of the credible processor architectures today. It allows hardware manufacturers to make the design tradeoffs they need and to work with the partners they like to build their devices. It allows software makers to leverage their experience in developing applications for Windows. Windows CE connects devices to the Internet by allowing the devices to interact using the known data types and object types that were built for the PC. And people get to use devices with an operating system that is familiar to them.

This book, written by Robert O'Hara, one of the early members of the Consumer Appliance Group, covers Windows CE and the Handheld PC. Reading this book will allow you to understand the principles of the newest, smallest member of the Windows family.

Harel Kodesh
General Manager, Consumer Appliance Group

Acknowledgments

This book describes my colleagues' and my work in producing a new version of Microsoft Windows and a new category of computers. The Microsoft Windows CE team is the finest I have had the privilege of being associated with in the nearly 25 years that I've worked in the computer industry. That Windows CE was produced nearly from scratch in less than two years is amazing, I think.

The words in this book are mine, and I typed them all! So all the errors are mine as well. That there are relatively few of them (I hope!) is due in no small part to my colleagues on the Windows CE team. Ido Ben-Schachar, Jeff Blum, James Chen, Neil Fishman, Jim Floyd, Jossef Goldberg, George Hu, Greg Keyser, Cathy Linn, Laura Martinez, Mark Miller, Chad Schwitters, Scott Skorupa, Garrett Vargas, Dave Wecker, Charles Wu, and Sarah Zuberec all reviewed manuscripts. Ido, Chad, and Laura, in particular, were most thorough in their reviews and comprehensive in their feedback.

Many of the tips and tricks in this book came from colleagues and others who suffered through early versions of Windows CE, along with sometimes temperamental prototype hardware. Thank you all!

If you could see the difference between the manuscript I handed the folks at Microsoft Press and the finished work you hold in your hands, you would appreciate the skills of the team that produced this book. Stephen Guty got me started, and Stuart Stuple led the editorial team and drove back and forth in the rain to get the latest updates. Laura Sackerman and Saul Candib tuned my prose; Linda Ebenstein and Roslyn Lutsch made sure I told the truth, the whole truth, and nothing but the truth; and Bill Teel edited screen captures. Jean Trenary and Katherine Erickson at Frog Mountain Productions composed the pages, and David Holter created the illustrations. It was a pleasure to work with all of you.

Finally, to my family, who put up with an 8-month project that stretched into 13 (well, it was a programmer's estimate), a very big thank you. Michael and David showed far more patience than one should expect from either an 8-year-old or a 5-year-old. And most of all, to my wife, Maureen: you make all the difference for me.

Introduction

Microsoft Windows CE is the newest and smallest member of the Microsoft Windows family of operating systems. It is designed to run on computers that are much smaller than traditional desktop PCs or laptop PCs. Over the coming years you can expect to see Windows CE showing up in all kinds of devices. The first version of Windows CE runs on a new category of computer, the Handheld PC, or H/PC.

A Handheld PC is a miniaturized version of your desktop PC or laptop PC. It is small enough to fit in your hand, yet powerful enough to run the Windows operating system and special versions of Windows-based programs with which you are probably familiar. Handheld PCs are small and light enough to carry with you most anywhere.

How To Use This Book

This book is a much more comprehensive user's guide than that included with your Handheld PC. Although that user's guide will get you started, this book shows you alternative ways of accomplishing various tasks and has more tips and tricks to help you become as productive as possible with your Handheld PC.

You certainly don't need to read this book from front to back. Browse through the table of contents, and then read those chapters that interest you or dip into chapters as the need arises. Be sure to read Chapter 1, "The Handheld PC in Action," and Chapter 9, "Windows CE in Action: Tips and Tricks." These two chapters suggest ways of using your Handheld PC that you might not otherwise have thought of. Appendix B, "Programs for Windows CE," introduces you to a wide variety of programs that you can install on your Handheld PC.

If you don't have a Handheld PC, this book will give you a pretty good feel for what an H/PC is good for and how it works. The information in this book can help you decide whether one of these devices is right for you or your organization. Appendix A, "Handheld PCs," offers you capsule summaries of each of the first generation H/PCs. Reading this appendix will give you an overview of the features of each device. Then, if you decide to buy one of them, you'll be able to jump right in and be immediately productive.

If you are considering developing software for Windows CE, this book provides a comprehensive description of the environment in which your proposed program will run. Chapter 10, "Inside Windows CE," outlines the system services your program can use and describes the Visual C++ program development environment.

Other Sources of Information

Beyond this book and the documentation that comes with your Handheld PC, the Microsoft Windows CE page on the World Wide Web is *the* source for additional information, updates, more tips and tricks, and free add-on programs for your Handheld PC. Updated versions of H/PC Explorer and Pocket Internet Explorer are periodically available from this Web page. I strongly recommend that you install these updated versions. The Web page also includes pointers to the Web sites of H/PC manufacturers and vendors of Windows CE-based programs. You can visit the Microsoft

Windows CE page either from your desktop computer or from your Handheld PC. The address is http://www.microsoft.com/windowsce.

There are many other resources available on the Internet. Here is what I found as this book went to press.

Each of the seven hardware manufacturers of the first generation of Handheld PCs has a Web site:

Company	Handheld PC	Address of Web Site
Casio	Cassiopeia	http://www.casiohpc.com
Compaq	PC Companion	http://www.compaq.com/us /common/prodinfo/handhelds
Hewlett-Packard	Palmtop PC	http://www.hp.com/handheld
Hitachi	Handheld PC	http://www.hitachi.com
LG Electronics	GP40M	http://www.lge.co.kr
NEC	MobilePro H/PC	http://www.nec.com
Philips Electronics	Velo 1	http://www.velo1.com

There are several Web sites that offer more independent information about Windows CE and Handheld PCs:

Web Site	Address	Features
HPC.net	http://www.windowsce.com	Lots of links to other sites about Windows CE
Hot Pocket	http://hotpocket.com	"Everyone's guide to the world of pocket and handheld computers"
World Wide Windows CE	http://www.ziplink.net /~maxm/windowsce	More news and gossip than some of the other sites

There are two regularly published magazines available on the Web that are relevant. They feature articles, news, reviews, and usage tips:

Magazine	Address	Description
Mobilis Magazine	http://www.volksware.com /mobilis	This monthly magazine, published by Volksware, Inc., is billed as "the mobile computing lifestyle magazine." It covers all small handheld computers and includes both technical and general articles.
Mobile Worker Magazine	http://www.microsoft.com /windowce/hpc/mobile	This monthly magazine is published by the Windows CE group at Microsoft. Although you won't get unbiased reviews or criticism here, this magazine provides a lot of useful information.

Then there are the Usenet newsgroups. The two that seem to have the most activity related to Windows CE are comp.sys.handhelds and comp.sys.palmtops. Both of these cover handheld computers in general, not just Handheld PCs running Windows CE. These two newsgroups are not moderated, and their discussions are wide ranging. If you mention that you are interested in Windows CE, some people will praise you and others will claim you're a jerk for even considering it.

A good way to find information about Windows CE on the Web is simply to use your Web browser to search for *Windows CE* or *Handheld PC*. Because Windows CE and Handheld PCs are new, more developments and announcements are made almost weekly.

Finally, there are the traditional magazines that are published on real paper and mailed to you. These include:

Magazine	Publisher	Description
Handheld PC Magazine	Thaddeus Computing, Inc. 57 East Broadway Fairfield, IA 52556	This is a new magazine, focused exclusively on Handheld PCs running Windows CE. It is aimed at general users, providing information to increase the effectiveness and utility of Handheld PCs. Expect to read lots of reviews of hardware and software products.
Handheld Systems	Creative Digital, Inc. 293 Corbett Ave. San Francisco, CA 94114-1842	This is a journal for programmers and developers of products for handheld computers. All the major handheld platforms are covered, including, of course, Windows CE.
Pen Computing Magazine	Pen Computing, Inc. 88 Sunnyside Blvd. Suite 203 Plainview, NY 11803	This magazine covers mobile computing and communications devices and software, including Windows CE, Newton, Pilot, Zaurus, and Magic Cap.
Windows Magazine	CMP Media, Inc. 600 Community Drive Manhasset, NY 10030	This magazine covers all versions of Microsoft Windows, and just started a column covering Windows CE.

As you can see, an entire industry is springing up around Windows CE. This is pretty impressive for a product that has been around for less than a year. I predict a long, productive, and interesting future.

A Final Note

As this book goes to press, the first wave of Handheld PCs have reached the stores. Casio and Compaq have had their machines out since late 1996, and NEC machines have been available since the beginning of 1997. Handheld PCs from Hewlett-Packard, Hitachi, LG Electronics, and Phillips Electronics are just now becoming available. All these machines are running the same version of Windows CE, with the same base set of built-in programs. This book applies to all these Handheld PCs. The Hewlett-Packard machine has a wider screen than the others—640 pixels rather than 480. If you're using a Hewlett-Packard Handheld PC, your screen will look a little different than the screen illustrations in this book. Details about the H/PCs from all these manufacturers are found in Appendix A

Throughout this book I use the term desktop computer. By this I do not mean to exclude laptop computers or notebook computers. In this book, *desktop computer* refers to any PC running Microsoft Windows 95 or Microsoft Windows NT version 4.0.

The Basics

Chapter

The Handheld PC in Action

This chapter is an admittedly contrived scenario intended to show a busy person using her Handheld PC with a variety of programs and services. All the situations described here are drawn from the real experiences of early Handheld PC users. Everything described here does work, although it all probably wouldn't happen to the same person on the same day. The goal here is to paint a picture of the many ways a Handheld PC might increase your productivity and effectiveness.

Some of the programs mentioned in this chapter are built into Microsoft Windows CE, and some must be installed separately. The programs are described at greater length in the rest of this book. Despite the newness of Windows CE, there are already a great many programs for it available. Those mentioned in this chapter are merely representative of their categories. For each of the tasks described, there is usually more than one program available.

Maura is a marketing manager for a Fortune 500 corporation. She sometimes feels that the pace of life in the nineties increases daily. Some days she seems to be working and living in "Internet time," which compresses deadlines and places higher demands on her time and talents than ever before. But she has a tool that helps her stay in control and connected so that she can work away from her desk, stay on top of her commitments, and keep in touch with the people in her life.

At her desk she has a PC with Microsoft Windows 95 and the usual set of programs installed: a word processor, a spreadsheet, an e-mail program, and so on. Her company uses Microsoft Outlook for group scheduling of appointments and meetings. Over the last year, Maura has become quite comfortable using Windows 95, so when she saw the first Handheld PCs she was immediately attracted to them. "I like that I don't need to learn anything new to use it," she told a colleague. So now her Handheld PC travels with her on every business trip.

"Mommy, wake up!" sounds the little speaker of Maura's Handheld PC. "Better than the buzz of an alarm clock," she thinks as she surveys her hotel room. She had recorded her children's voices on her home PC and brought the sound file in to work, where she then downloaded it to her Handheld PC. Now when she travels, she always uses the recording as the alarm sound of the World Clock.

An hour later Maura is driving to the office of a potential customer. But finding it is difficult since the map she picked up with her rental car does not have enough detail. Fortunately she used Microsoft Automap Streets Plus to download the map for the area before she left on her trip. With Pocket Automap Streets on her Handheld PC, she just types in the address of the company, and the map immediately appears on the screen. The zoom feature lets her display just the right amount of detail to find her way.

During the customer meeting Maura refers to two documents she previously downloaded to her Handheld PC: a spreadsheet containing product availability and price information, and a document summarizing the competitive situation her company faces with this customer. She has found that having such information available for discreet reference during negotiations is a great asset. When Maura needs to take quick notes she sometimes finds that the tiny keyboard of her Handheld PC slows her down, so she uses her stylus to write electronic "ink" in QuickNotes from Communication Intelligence Corporation, a note-taking program. It's great for jotting down information when there is no time to type.

Soon she is back at the airport waiting for her flight home to board. Maura enters the information from the business cards she collected at the meeting into the Contacts program. Then she uses Microsoft Pocket Word to transcribe some of the notes she took using QuickNotes, list customer questions, and detail several action items for her staff. Suddenly her SkyTel 2-Way pager buzzes. Ah, a marketing strategy meeting has been called for this afternoon as soon as she gets back to the office. Maura quickly composes a reply confirming her attendance. She also pastes the action items from the customer meeting that she had jotted down in Pocket Word into another message for her team. Since she has both Pocket Word and the Inbox running (as she does most of the time), it's easy to switch between the two using their buttons on the taskbar. She connects the pager to her Handheld PC, and the SkyTel Messenger for Windows CE mail service sends the messages just as boarding commences.

Level at 37,000 feet, Maura opens up her Handheld PC and finishes her expense report in Microsoft Pocket Excel. She really likes the fact that her Handheld PC is not weighing down her carry-on luggage and that she can comfortably use it on the airplane even when the person in front of her has the seat fully reclined. (Maura usually flies coach.) Also, the batteries last far longer than any flight she's ever been on. She takes a few minutes to flesh out her notes from the customer meeting into a brief trip report. As her mind moves from her business life to her personal life, she creates two projects in Tasks: a dinner on Saturday evening that she and her husband are hosting and her son's upcoming birthday party. Soon she has each project filled with a list of things to do.

It turns out she's already seen the in-flight movie, so she plays a few games of FreeCell. It and Chess are her favorites from the Microsoft Entertainment Pack for Windows CE, although her daughter is partial to Space Defense. After finally winning a game, Maura peruses her task list. She updates it and marks a couple of tasks completed as a result of the day's meetings. While she's reviewing her tasks, an idea for a great birthday present for her husband comes to mind, so she adds it to her "gifts" project in Tasks.

A couple of hours later Maura is at her office. She doesn't even get to sit down but instead heads directly to a strategy meeting, pausing only to pull her Handheld PC out of her pocketbook. As the meeting is getting under way, she uses infrared transfer to "squirt" the new contacts from her trip to a colleague. Her trip report is quickly uploaded to a laptop connected to the large-screen TV in the conference room, since her Handheld PC can connect as a guest to any PC on which Microsoft H/PC Explorer has been installed. Now Maura can summarize her customer visit to the group, and they can move on to planning their business strategy.

Back in her office after the meeting, Maura sets her Handheld PC in its docking cradle, where it immediately begins synchronizing her contacts, schedule, and tasks with Outlook on her desktop computer. By the time she has finished checking her phone messages, the synchronization is complete. Now she has but one thing to do before heading home: using H/PC Explorer, Maura drags her expense report from its folder on her Handheld PC to the desktop of her office PC. H/PC Explorer automatically converts it into a desktop Excel document, which she opens. From Excel on her desktop PC she quickly reviews the expense report and then prints a copy so that she can submit it for reimbursement. Then, at last, it's home to her family.

No, a Handheld PC is not the greatest thing since sliced bread. But by making it easier to take data with you when you need it, your Handheld PC can be a useful tool that helps make you more productive.

Exploring Your Handheld PC

This chapter begins by walking you through setting up your Handheld PC (H/PC) so that it is ready to use. There are lots of tips to help you get started on the right foot. Then it explains the main differences between using Windows 95 and using Windows CE. Finally, you'll find out how data is stored on an H/PC and how to keep your data secure. If you don't yet have a Handheld PC, read this chapter for a vicarious "out of box experience." Who knows, you may be so excited you'll want to run right out and buy one!

Setting Up Your Handheld PC

After you take your Handheld PC out of its box, the first thing to do is to follow the instructions that come with it and put both the main AA batteries and the backup battery in the device. Then you can turn it on. When you turn on your Handheld PC for the first time the Welcome Wizard appears on screen.

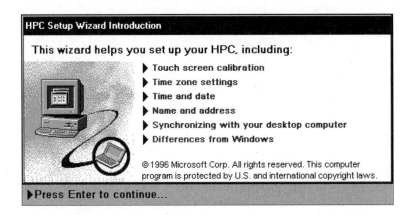

This program walks you through setting up your Handheld PC.

TIP If you have turned on your Handheld PC but it does not look like it's on, or if you are having trouble reading the screen, you probably need to adjust the contrast. Some models have a small wheel, like the volume control on a radio, that you use to adjust the contrast. If you have one of these models, watch out when you have the H/PC in your pocket or bag because the wheel can sometimes be inadvertently moved. On other models, you hold down the ALT key and press the < and > keys to adjust the contrast. Check the hardware section of your H/PC user's guide to learn how to adjust the contrast on your particular device.

In Windows CE, instead of clicking with the mouse, you tap with the stylus. This is discussed in more detail in "Tapping Instead of Clicking," later in this chapter.

It will take you just a few minutes to go through the Welcome Wizard. If you are using your Handheld PC for the first time, I strongly recommend doing this. If you're in a real hurry, you can bypass most of the Welcome Wizard by typing *pegasus* while the first screen of the wizard is displayed. You can't skip calibrating the touch screen, so the calibration screen will immediately appear. When you finish the calibration, the Windows CE desktop will appear. If you choose to skip the Welcome Wizard, be sure to run through it later. You can run it by tapping the Start button, tapping Programs, double-tapping the Accessories folder, and double-tapping the Welcome shortcut.

Completing the Welcome Wizard

As you can see from the previous illustration, it's a good idea to customize several settings before you start to use your Handheld PC:

- Calibrating the touch screen ensures that when you touch a certain spot on the screen, Windows CE and you agree on just where that spot is.

- Indicating your home city sets the time zone for the World Clock.

- Telling Windows CE the current time and date allows the alarms and the Calendar to work correctly.

- Entering your name and address personalizes your H/PC.

The rest of the Welcome program gives you a very quick overview of some of the features of Windows CE. Press the ENTER key to get started.

Calibrate the touch screen

Although you can use your finger to touch objects on the screen, the initial calibration is best done with the plastic stylus that came with your Handheld PC. Be sure that you are not touching the screen with your other hand while performing the calibration. The calibration screen looks like this:

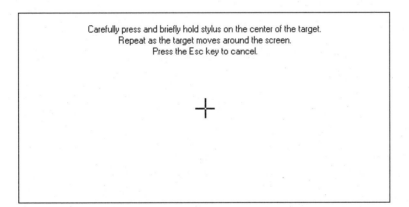

Touch the + target with the stylus, hold it there for a second, and then lift the stylus. It is OK to move the stylus about until it is centered over the target, because it is the point at which you lift the stylus from the screen that is recorded. After you lift the stylus, the target moves to the next position. Repeat the procedure for each successive position of the target.

You don't need to press hard: the screen is sensitive to where you touch it, not to how hard you press against it. If you feel you did not touch the targets accurately, press the ESC key to restart the calibration process. When you have touched the target in all five positions, press the ENTER key to record the calibration settings.

 TIP Over time the calibration of the touch screen might drift. If you find you are having trouble tapping buttons or selecting objects on the screen, double-tap My Handheld PC, double-tap Control Panel, double-tap Stylus, and recalibrate your Handheld PC. A quicker way to bring up the calibration screen is to press CTRL+ALT+=. That is, hold down the CTRL and ALT keys while pressing the = key. You can remember this because the + key, which looks like the calibration target, is on the same key as =.

Set the time zone

Next you need to specify your home city. Windows CE uses this information to set the time correctly when you switch between your home and visiting cities.

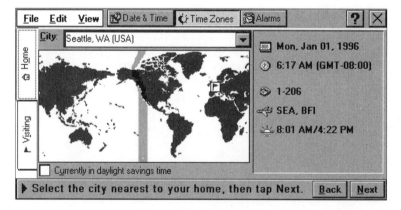

The default city is Seattle, Washington, because that is the closest large city to where Microsoft is located (in Redmond, WA). Tap the downward-pointing arrow to the right of the City field, and a scrollable list of cities appears.

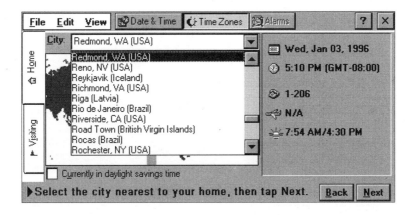

TIP   If you try tapping the arrow and nothing happens, or if you tap the Next button and nothing happens, it means the touch screen calibration is off. Press CTRL+ALT+= to return to the calibration screen, and recalibrate the touch screen. When you complete that, you will return to this screen to continue setting up your Handheld PC.

If you don't find the city you want, you can add it to the list of cities. Also, the Visiting tab on the left side of the screen lets you identify a city you are visiting. Both of these topics are covered in the "World Clock" section of Chapter 3.

You can easily scroll through this list by pressing the first letter of the city you want to find. For example, pressing the R key displays *Raleigh, NC (USA)*. Then pressing the DOWN ARROW key twice moves the selection to *Redmond, WA (USA)*, which is where I live. Press the ENTER key to pick the selected city, or just tap the selected city with the stylus.

Before you leave the time zone screen, make sure the box in the lower left is checked if it's currently daylight savings time in your home city. Then tap Next to continue on.

Set the date and time

You need to set the date and time so that the alarm clock will wake you up when you ask and so that the Calendar can accurately notify you of your appointments.

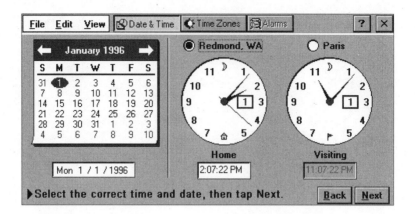

You can also set the date by tapping the calendar. Tap January to get a list of months, tap "1996" to get a list of years, and then tap the current date in the calendar.

You can also set the clock by touching the clock hands with the stylus and dragging them to the proper positions.

To set the date, tap the first number (the month) in the box below the calendar, type today's date, such as *7/19/97,* and press ENTER. This first version of Windows CE supports dates only in the format month/day/year.

To set the time, tap the box below the home clock, type the current time, such as *12:40p,* and press ENTER. Windows CE supports 12-hour time and 24-hour time, so you can enter 1:15 P.M. as *1:15p* or *13:15*. Tap Next to move on to entering your name and address.

Enter your name and address

To fill out the form, tap a field, and then start typing. There's room for your name, company, address, and work and home phone numbers. Be sure to fill in the area codes for your work and home locations if you plan to use your H/PC to communicate over phone lines; the information is needed to determine if the number you are dialing is a local or long-distance call.

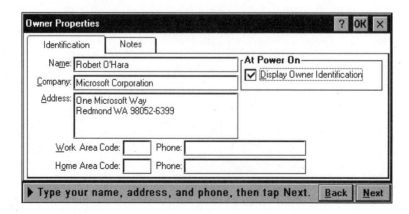

If you wish, Windows CE will display this information whenever you turn on your Handheld PC. Selecting the Display Owner Identification check box sets this up. If you later change your mind, you can go to the Control Panel, double-tap Owner, and select or clear this check box.

Tap Next, and read the information in the rest of the Welcome program if you want to. When you're done reading the final screen, tap Done. I'll cover the information on these screens in greater depth throughout the other chapters in this book.

Using Windows CE

If you've used Windows 95, Windows CE will look familiar to you. Using the two programs is very similar, but there are a few differences in how to take certain actions. If you're in a hurry, you can probably skim the rest of this section and simply figure out the differences between Windows CE and Windows 95 as you go.

Tapping Instead of Clicking

Don't rush your double taps—open the Stylus program in the Control Panel, and adjust the double-tap speed. For more details, see the "Control Panel" section of Chapter 3.

With your desktop PC, you probably use a mouse to point at, click, and double-click objects on the screen. With your Handheld PC, you use the stylus to touch, tap, and double-tap objects instead. When you're using Windows 95, you can click an object with the right mouse button to display its shortcut menu, and you can hold down the right mouse button while dragging to make a copy of an object. To accomplish the same things in Windows CE, hold down the ALT key while you tap or drag the object.

Tapping the screen harder does not help. Instead, tap gently and slowly—hold the stylus on the screen for a split second.

Instead of the stylus you can use your finger, but I've found this usually ends up leaving smudges on the screen. When I am without a stylus I turn my hand so that I can use my fingernail. This seems to give greater accuracy and avoids smudges. A pencil eraser, a retracted plastic ballpoint pen, the plastic cap to a pen, or any soft, plastic, pointy object will work fine. Stay away from pencils, open pens, or any metal object that might scratch the screen. Also, don't run with scissors, and be sure to exercise in moderation and drink plenty of liquids.

Selecting Objects

Selecting objects in Windows CE works the same way it does in Windows 95. To select an item, tap it. To select multiple contiguous items, hold down the SHIFT key while tapping the first and last items. If you want to select several items but they are not next to each other, hold down the CTRL key and tap each of the items.

In this book I usually describe how to use the stylus with the programs on your H/PC, but I have found that much of the time I use the keyboard. See the tips and tricks in Chapter 9 for more information.

As in Windows 95, you can use the keyboard to select and operate on items. You use the arrow keys to select an item, and you press the ENTER key to open it. Hold down the SHIFT key while pressing the arrow keys to extend your selection to multiple adjacent items. To select multiple items that are not necessarily adjacent, hold down the CTRL key while using the arrow keys to move the dotted selection rectangle, and then press the spacebar to select an item.

When you are editing text in a program, tapping moves the insertion point—the blinking cursor that marks where the next character typed will go—to the spot where you tapped. You can select a string of characters by holding the stylus against the screen and then sliding it across the text.

Dragging and Dropping

Dragging and dropping works just as it does in Windows 95 except that you use the stylus instead of a mouse. To drag an object, touch it with the stylus, and hold the stylus against the screen. Slide the stylus across the screen, and lift it when you want to drop the object. If you hold the CTRL key down while dragging, in most cases a copy of the object is made. You can tell whether you are making a copy of an object or moving it because when you're making a copy, a small plus sign (+) appears with the icon of the object being dragged. If the plus sign is not there, you are moving the object.

Using the Desktop and the Windows CE Explorer

On some Handheld PCs the desktop has additional shortcuts to programs that have been installed. The ones shown here, and described in this book, are the ones common to all Handheld PCs.

The Windows CE desktop looks like this:

Yes, I know it doesn't look like a real desktop, but then neither does the one in Windows 95. However, it functions like one. And if you have used Windows 95, you've already noticed the similarity in appearance.

I'll describe how to create shortcuts on the desktop in the "Windows CE Explorer" section of Chapter 3.

The Windows CE desktop is never more than a tap away. If you tap the button of the current program on the taskbar, the program is minimized, and the desktop is displayed. Therefore it is quite useful to place shortcuts to the programs you most frequently use on the desktop. For your convenience, shortcuts to Pocket Excel, Pocket Word, Calendar, Contacts, Tasks, and Inbox are already there.

Also located on the desktop are two special icons, Recycle Bin and My Handheld PC. The Recycle Bin works as it does in Windows 95. If you want to know how much space the files in the Recycle Bin are using, display its shortcut menu by holding down the ALT key and tapping the Recycle Bin icon. Then tap the Properties item. The Recycle Bin Properties window appears.

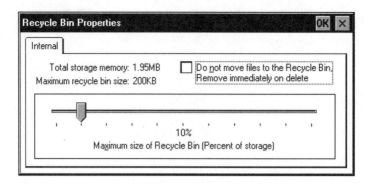

From this window, you can control the Recycle Bin. You can specify how large it is to be allowed to grow, or you can disable it entirely, which means that any file you delete is really deleted immediately, with no possibility of recovery.

The second special icon, My Handheld PC, opens Windows CE Explorer to display all the data on your Handheld PC, whether it is stored in RAM in the H/PC or on a storage card in the PC Card slot.

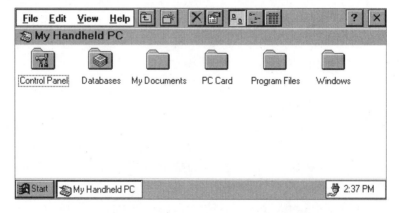

Up One Level

My Handheld PC works basically the same way My Computer does in Windows 95. When you double-tap one of the folders, it opens and displays its contents. In this manner you can move down into folders and subfolders. When you tap the Up One Level button, you move back up to the previous folder. The first few levels of folders and their contents look something like this:

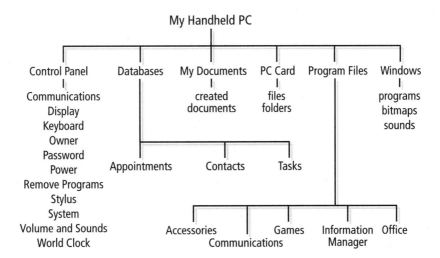

Windows CE Explorer is described in more detail in Chapter 3.

You'll be navigating these folders when you use Windows CE Explorer and when you tap the Open command on the File menu in Pocket Excel or Pocket Word.

Using the Taskbar

At the bottom of the desktop is the taskbar.

It's kind of like the dashboard of your car, because from here you control the operation of your Handheld PC.

At the right side of the taskbar is the status area, as in Windows 95. In the previous illustration, the current time is displayed at the right of the status area, and the power state of the Handheld PC is displayed at the left. The little plug picture indicates that the Handheld PC is plugged into a wall outlet. When the H/PC is running on batteries, a picture of a battery appears instead. Other pictures will join these two from time to time, and I'll explain them as needed throughout this book.

As in Windows 95, these status indicators are more than just little pictures to look at. You can double-tap them to activate the corresponding program. For example, double-tap the current time in the status area, and the World Clock starts. Double-tap the battery, and the Power Properties window appears, which will tell you the condition of your main and backup batteries.

At the left of the taskbar is the Start button, which opens the Start menu, just as in Windows 95. I'll cover the differences in the Start menu commands in the next section. Between the Start button and the status area are buttons that correspond to the programs that are currently running on your Handheld PC. You switch between programs using these buttons the same way you do in Windows 95.

Using the Start Menu

When you tap the Start button, the Start menu opens.

Windows key

Pressing the Windows key on the Handheld PC keyboard does the same thing as tapping the Start button.

From the top of the Start menu, let's look at each of the commands in turn.

Explore

This command starts Windows CE Explorer, opening the My Handheld PC folder. Double-tapping the My Handheld PC icon on the desktop gives you exactly the same result.

Programs

In Windows 95, this command takes you to a series of submenus that give you access to all the programs installed on your computer. Windows CE does not use submenus, so this command instead starts Windows CE Explorer and opens the folder that contains all the built-in programs of Windows CE.

When you install additional programs, new shortcuts are added here, or in the folders displayed here.

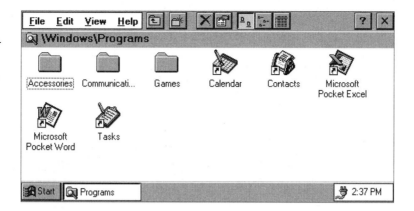

Several of the shortcuts here duplicate those on the desktop. These are shortcuts to the main built-in programs of Windows CE. The three folders—Accessories, Communications, and Games—contain the additional built-in programs. The Accessories folder has shortcuts for the Calculator, the Welcome Wizard, and the World Clock. The Communications folder has shortcuts for Inbox, PC Link, Remote Networking, and Terminal. The Games folder has just a single shortcut, Solitaire.

Documents

This command starts Windows CE Explorer and opens a folder that contains shortcuts to documents you have recently worked on. The documents themselves are, in general, stored in the My Documents folder. As in Windows 95, if you delete a document from My Documents, the shortcut stored here is not removed. However, Windows CE shows you which documents have been deleted by displaying them with the generic Windows icon (instead of with the Word or Excel icon, for example).

Settings

This command starts the Control Panel. I'll cover it in detail in the "Control Panel" section of Chapter 3.

Help

This command launches Help. This is described more fully in the "Getting Help" section, a little later in this chapter.

Run...

This command opens a dialog box into which you can enter the name of a program you want to run. It works essentially the same way it does in Windows 95.

Suspend

Tapping this command is just the same as pressing the Off key. Windows 95 has the Shut Down command instead of the Suspend command. Windows CE has Suspend because you never really shut down your Handheld PC—you just suspend it until the next time you use it. Any reminders or alarms you have set will wake Windows CE back up to sound the alarm and flash the light as you have set them. Programs remain in their suspended state whenever you turn off your Handheld PC, and they pick up right where you left off when you next power it on.

Getting Help

Sometimes you just want to know "what does this button do?" In Windows 95, when you hold the mouse pointer on top of a button, a ToolTip appears that explains what the button does. Although Windows CE does not use a mouse pointer, it does provide ToolTips for the command bar buttons in most programs. (Unfortunately, Windows CE Explorer does not provide ToolTips.) To display the ToolTip for a button, touch the stylus to the button and don't lift it from the screen. The ToolTip appears.

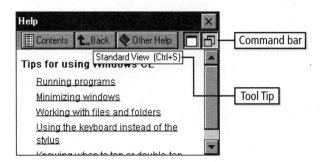

When you slide the stylus off the button (without lifting it), the ToolTip disappears, and you can lift the stylus from the screen without performing the button's function.

When the previous illustration was made, I was holding the stylus on the second button from the right in the command bar. The ToolTip proclaims this to be the Standard View button and reminds me that it has a keyboard shortcut of CTRL+S.

Windows CE comes with a modest context-sensitive Help system. It is not as comprehensive as the Help system in Windows 95, nor will you find an online tutorial. What you'll find are tips, reminders, and basic information about how to use Windows CE and its programs. A printed user's guide also comes with every Handheld PC.

Help

Most Windows CE programs have a Help button on the right side of the command bar. Those programs that do not, like Solitaire, usually have a button labeled *Help*. In either case, tap the button to get help with that program. To get help with Windows CE in general, tap the Start button, and then tap the Help command. The following window appears:

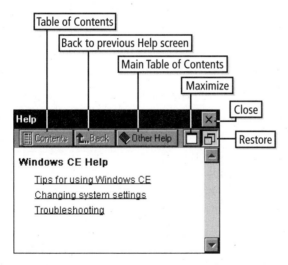

Help is one of the few Windows CE programs that does not occupy the entire screen. By not covering the entire screen, Help lets you see the program (or in this case, the desktop) to which the Help text is referring.

The Contents button takes you to the table of contents for the particular program you are in. If it is disabled (gray instead of black), you are already at the table of contents. The Other Help button takes you to the master table of contents for the entire Help system. If you want to browse through all the available Help, this is the button to tap. If you have installed additional programs on your Handheld PC, their Help contents will appear in the master table of contents as well.

Data Storage and Security

To use your Handheld PC effectively, it helps to know where your documents and programs are stored, the options for adding storage, and how to keep your data secure.

Where Your Data Is Stored

Your Handheld PC stores all the data you enter into it in computer chips called RAM (Random Access Memory). This is different from PCs that store your data on a magnetic disk. A disk retains the information stored on it even when the power to the computer is turned off. Memory, on the other hand, loses its data when the power is cut.

In Handheld PCs, power is always supplied to the memory chips. So even when you turn off your Handheld PC, a little bit of battery power is being used to keep the memory intact. Very little power is used, so the batteries can keep the memory powered for months if the H/PC is not being used. When you need to replace the main batteries, a small backup battery keeps the memory powered and your data intact. The backup battery can last many months, or even years, before needing to be replaced, especially if you don't let the main batteries run down. This technique of using RAM as a permanent storage medium is called battery-backed RAM.

See Chapter 6 for more details about H/PC Explorer and backing up your data.

Since your Handheld PC must be powered for your data to survive, keep it plugged in when you are not using it. As with any computer, be sure you regularly back up all the data on your Handheld PC. H/PC Explorer makes this so easy that you have no excuse.

Storage Memory Versus Program Memory

In your Handheld PC, the memory is used for two purposes. One is to store your data, as just described. Memory used for this is called storage memory. The other is to run programs. This memory is called program memory. The memory of your Handheld PC is shared between these two uses. You can see this graphically by double-tapping the System icon in the Control Panel and then tapping the Memory tab.

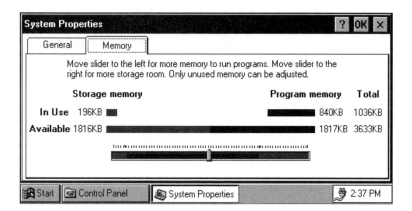

In the middle of the Memory tab is a slide control. You can "grab" it by touching it with your stylus, and then you can slide it from side to side. Moving it to the left decreases the amount of memory available for storage of your data and increases that available to programs. This means that you have less room to store appointments, documents, contacts, and so on, but you can run more programs at the same time. (The advantage of running more than one program at a time is that you can more quickly switch between them.)

Conversely, moving the slider to the right allocates more memory to data storage and less to running programs. You'll be able to store more appointments, documents, contacts, and such on your H/PC, but you might have to close down one program before running another. As you gain familiarity with your Handheld PC, you can adjust this setting to the best position for you. If you find that you want to have more programs running at the same time *and* that you want to store more appointments, documents, and contacts, you'll need to expand the storage capacity of your device. Doing this is described in "Additional Storage," later in this chapter.

IP   As in politics, extremes of the left or right do not work so well. If you move the slider as far to the left as it will go, you won't have room to create documents, appointments, or contacts. If you move it as far to the right as it will go, you might not be able to run some programs. In general, on a device with 2 megabytes of RAM, leave the slider somewhere in the middle. On a device with 4 or more megabytes of RAM, leave at least 1 megabyte of program storage.

Where the Built-in Programs Are Stored

The programs that come built into Windows CE are stored in ROM (Read-Only Memory). ROM chips are manufactured with the data already included, and in this case, the data is the programs of Windows CE. The big advantage of ROM is that, unlike battery-backed RAM, it retains its information even without power. So the programs that make up Windows CE can never be accidentally lost. All Handheld PCs have at least 4 megabytes of ROM.

Additional Storage

The use of PC memory cards is described in more detail in Chapter 3.

Windows CE supports additional storage for your documents on flash or SRAM PC memory cards. These are solid-state cards that are formatted as if they were disks. You can store files and programs on these cards, but you cannot place databases such as those used to store your appointments, tasks, contacts, or electronic mail on them. Windows CE formats the cards in the industry-standard FAT file system, so they can also be used with most laptop computers.

To use a PC Card, just insert it in the PC Card slot of your Handheld PC. On some H/PCs, the PC Card slot is housed in a modular add-on to the base device.

Almost any PC Card placed in your Handheld PC will consume power from your H/PC batteries, so you won't get the same battery life that you would with no card in the slot. In fact, some PC Card modems will drain the pair of AA batteries in a few minutes. PC memory cards, however, use very little power, so their effect on battery life should be negligible.

Some Handheld PC devices can have their RAM expanded by purchasing additional memory. Check with your manufacturer for details.

Security and Privacy

How safe is the information you store on your Handheld PC? Well, let's compare it to the similar information you might store in a paper-based appointment and address book.

- If you leave the address book on a shelf for a couple of years, all the information in it will still be there. But if you leave your Handheld PC next to it, unplugged, both the main and backup batteries will have run out of power, and your information will be lost. Of course, you would have an up-to-date backup of all your information on your desktop PC, right?

- If you drop your address book to the sidewalk, it will most likely survive undamaged. Your Handheld PC is less likely to survive a four-foot plunge to concrete.

- If you lose your address book, anyone who finds it can easily read all the information in it. If your Handheld PC is lost, as long as you set the password protection feature in Windows CE, you know your data is still private. (Files stored on a PC Card are the exception to this; they're easily read on any PC with a PC Card slot.) Also, if you have regularly backed up the data on your Handheld PC, you can restore that data to your replacement unit. This is much more difficult with a paper address and appointment book.

 IP   I keep my Handheld PC in the nice leather cover of my old appointment and address book. Now that it's not full of paper (because I've removed the calendar and address book pages), there is lots of room for my Handheld PC.

Pressing CTRL+ESC is another way to open the Start menu.

So the key to keeping your private data private is to set a password. To do this, tap the Start menu, and then tap the Settings command. The Control Panel appears. Double-tap the Password icon to display the Password Properties screen.

IP Don't forget your password! Kiss your data goodbye if you do. And don't write your password on a piece of paper that you tape to the back of your Handheld PC. (Don't laugh; it's been done.) You should probably avoid obvious passwords such as your name and the names of your spouse, pet, child, and so on.

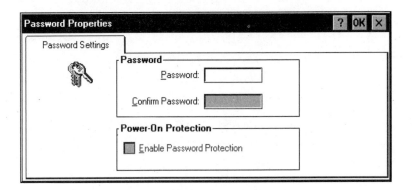

Here you can enter (or later change) the password needed to access your Handheld PC whenever it is powered on. Type your password, press TAB to move to the Confirm Password field, and type it again. The password is not displayed, in case someone is peeking over your shoulder. Then select the Enable Password Protection check box, and press the ENTER key. Your Handheld PC is now password protected. Turn it off and turn it on to try out your new password.

What's Next

This chapter covered only some of the ways in which you can set up your Handheld PC so that it best meets your needs. There are more things you can do to customize it according to your own preferences. Most of these are accomplished from the Control Panel, which is covered in the next chapter.

Using Windows CE Explorer, World Clock, Calculator, and Control Panel

This chapter starts with more information about using Microsoft Windows CE Explorer, which was introduced in Chapter 2. You'll learn how its options differ from those of Microsoft Windows 95, how to use infrared transfer to move documents between Handheld PCs, and more about using PC Cards for extra data storage. Next is in-depth coverage of the World Clock, the Calculator, and customizing Windows CE with the Control Panel. The chapter wraps up with a look at one of the most popular games for Windows: Solitaire.

Windows CE Explorer

It is not the goal of this book to teach you the basic concepts of files and folders or to cover information that is familiar to people who have used Windows 95 on a desktop or laptop computer. If all this is new to you, I strongly suggest that you turn to any of the great Windows 95 books available, which can give you the needed grounding in these ideas. So, assuming that you are comfortable with using Windows Explorer, you'll find Windows CE Explorer very familiar.

As mentioned in Chapter 2, you can launch Windows CE Explorer from the Start menu, or you can double-tap My Handheld PC on the Windows CE desktop. Explorer opens and displays the contents of the My Handheld PC folder:

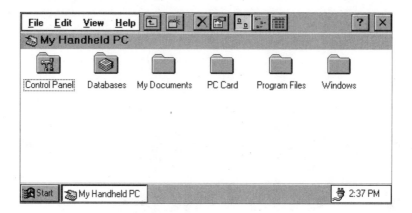

The command bar at the top of the screen contains a set of familiar buttons and menus:

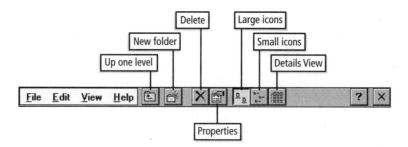

The New Folder button is the only one of the buttons that isn't also found in Windows 95. It creates a new folder in the current folder. The Large Icons, Small Icons, and Details buttons give you different views of your files and folders, as in Windows 95. The Up One Level, Delete, and Properties buttons have the same effects as in Windows 95.

Windows CE Explorer does not have several of the buttons found in Windows 95. These are Map Network Drive, Disconnect Net Drive, Cut, Copy, Paste, Undo, and List. Windows CE does not support network drives, nor does Windows CE Explorer have a List view. The functions of the other buttons are available through the menus; there is just not room for all of them on the command bar.

The menu to the left of the buttons is very similar to that in Windows 95. The File menu contains two additional options: Send and Receive. These allow you to exchange files with another Handheld PC via infrared transfer, which is covered in the next section of this chapter.

You can display a shortcut menu for a particular file or folder by holding down the ALT key while tapping its icon.

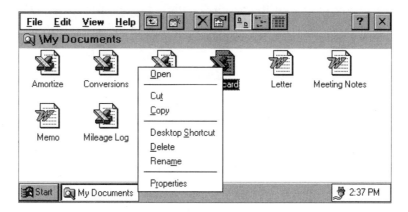

This menu is similar to that in Windows 95. If you want to create a shortcut to the selected file or folder and place it on the Windows CE desktop, just tap Desktop Shortcut.

A common way to move or copy files and folders from one place to another in Windows 95 is to open two instances of Windows Explorer, display the source folder in one and the destination folder in the other, and then drag and drop the files or folders from one window to the other. In Windows CE this does not work, because although you can have two instances of Windows CE Explorer open, you can't view them both at the same time. Each occupies the entire screen.

There is a neat workaround, however. Open two instances of Windows CE Explorer from the Start menu, just as you would in Windows 95. In one instance, move to the folder containing the files you want to move or copy—the source folder. In the other, move to the folder in which you want the files to go—the destination folder. Now go to the instance of Windows CE Explorer that is displaying the source folder, drag the files to the destination folder's button on the taskbar, and holding the stylus on the button, wait for the folder to open. When the destination folder opens, drag the files into the window displaying the folder. Lift the stylus, and the files are moved or copied to that open folder.

Sending and Receiving Files via Infrared Transfer

You can wirelessly transfer one file at a time between one Handheld PC and another through their infrared ports. The Windows CE team refers to this as a "data squirt." To send a file, use Windows CE Explorer to open the folder in which the file is located. Tap the file to select it, and then tap the Send command on the File menu. The following dialog box appears:

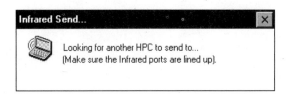

To receive the file on the other Handheld PC, start Windows CE Explorer on that H/PC and tap the Receive command on the File menu. This dialog box appears on the receiving H/PC:

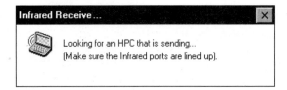

Bring the two machines within 3 feet of each other, and hold them so that their infrared ports are aimed at each other. When the two machines recognize each other, each will emit a brief sound to confirm the connection. Dialog boxes on each machine will then update you as to the progress of the data transfer. The sender will see a message like the one in the following dialog box, and the receiver will see a similar message.

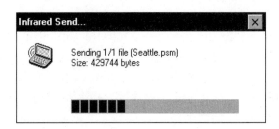

IP   If you have trouble making the connection, move the two machines closer together. This will help especially if the ambient lighting is very bright, as when you are outside on a sunny day.

When the transfer is complete, each machine will emit a second sound and display a final message.

On the receiver's machine, the file is always placed in the My Handheld PC folder, regardless of where the file resided on the sender's machine. From this folder, you can easily move the file to the place you want it. Simply tap the file to select it, press CTRL+X to cut the file, move to the folder where you want the file to go, and press CTRL+V to paste the file there.

CPU stands for Central Processing Unit, the "brain" of a computer.

One restriction on file transfer is that you cannot transfer executable program files (those files that contain the instructions that make up a program and are identified with .exe, .cpl, or .dll extensions) between Handheld PCs. This is because Handheld PCs built by different manufacturers use different CPUs, and the executable file that runs on one H/PC might not run on another. See Appendix A for details about different H/PCs and which CPU each uses.

 IP   If you know that the executable file you want to transfer will run on the other machine—for example, if both machines are made by the same manufacturer—you can get around the executable file restriction by renaming the file to another name with an extension other than .exe. Then squirt the file as described previously. The receiver will need to rename the file to its original name, including the .exe extension.

By default, Windows CE Explorer does not display filename extensions. Tap the Options command on the View menu to open a dialog box that lets you choose to have filename extensions displayed.

Using PC Memory Cards

PC memory cards are solid-state devices that act as if they were tiny hard disks. They are also known as flash memory cards and SRAM (static RAM) cards. You can use them to increase the storage capacity of your Handheld PC. Since many laptop PCs have PC Card slots, you can also use them to exchange data between your Handheld PC and a laptop. Windows CE can work with ATA type II flash memory cards and SRAM cards.

OTE   By default, some laptops will use SRAM cards as additional memory, not as a tiny hard disk. Make sure your laptop sees the memory card as a disk if you want to use it to exchange data with your Handheld PC. Also, don't use compression if you format the memory card on your desktop or laptop PC. Windows CE cannot work with file compression on a memory card.

When you insert a PC Card memory card into your H/PC, Windows CE creates a folder called PC Card in the My Handheld PC folder. You can open the folder and the files it contains and use them as you would any other folder and files on your Handheld PC. If your Handheld PC is running on battery power when you insert the card, the following message will appear:

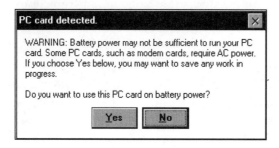

It is safe to disregard the warning and tap the Yes button when you are inserting a PC Card memory card, as they draw very little power from the Handheld PC.

You can move and copy files to and from a PC Card memory card, but you cannot move or copy folders. You can, of course, create folders on a PC Card memory card. Both Microsoft Pocket Word and Microsoft Pocket Excel can work with files on PC Cards. You cannot place any of the Windows CE databases (Appointments, Contacts, and Tasks) or the Inbox on a PC memory card. They can reside only in the RAM of your Handheld PC.

 ARNING   Files you store on a PC Card memory card are not protected by the password you might have established for your Handheld PC. If someone removes the PC Card memory card, it is easily read on any other PC that has a PC Card slot. Don't store sensitive information on a PC Card memory card.

Before you remove a PC Card memory card from your Handheld PC, be sure to close any programs that have files open on the memory card. Then turn off your Handheld PC. Finally, you can unlock and remove the card. Turning off your H/PC before removing the memory card ensures that the file system on the card remains intact.

See Chapter 6 for details about H/PC Explorer and about file conversion when moving between your desktop PC and your H/PC.

There are some other implications of using a PC Card memory card. Obviously, if you want to use a PC Card modem, you'll have to remove the PC Card memory card before you can insert the modem card. If you use the PC Card memory card to move files between a desktop or laptop PC and your Handheld PC, keep in mind that no data conversion is performed. For example, Microsoft Word and Microsoft Excel files must be converted to Pocket Word and Pocket Excel files when moved to your Handheld PC. You can't just copy an Excel file to the memory card when it's in your laptop and then expect to open it when the memory card is in your H/PC. And of course, the same holds true in the other direction. In contrast, when you use H/PC Explorer to move files between two machines, the appropriate data conversion is done in both directions.

On the Windows CE Web site, Microsoft has made available Word and Excel converters that you run on your laptop or desktop PC. With these installed, you can convert a Word or Excel file into Pocket Word or Pocket Excel format and copy it to a PC Card memory card. Then you can place the PC Card memory card in your Handheld PC, where the file is accessible from Pocket Word or Pocket Excel. The address of the Windows CE Web page is http://www.microsoft.com/windowsce.

World Clock

You can use the World Clock to keep track of the date and time and to display useful information about cities around the world. The clock lets you easily switch between two time zones, and it has five alarms, which help to make your Handheld PC a worthy traveling companion.

The easiest way to start the clock is to double-tap the current time displayed in the status area at the lower right corner of the screen. When the clock opens, Date & Time view is displayed. On the clock faces, a small sun icon at the 12 o'clock position indicates A.M. and a small moon indicates P.M. At the 6 o'clock position, a small house icon reminds you that this is the time in your home city; a small flag icon denotes the clock for the city you are visiting.

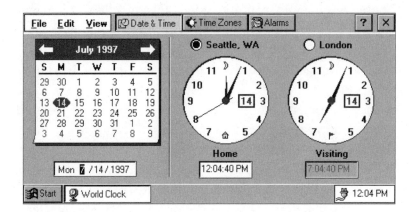

In Date & Time view, you can set the current date and time for both your home city and a city that you are visiting. Set the date by simply tapping the month in the date displayed under the calendar page and typing the current date. Or tap the month on the calendar page to get a list of months to choose from, tap the year to get a list of years, and then tap the day. This is exactly the same way you set the time when you completed the Welcome Wizard, described in Chapter 2.

To set the time, simply drag the clock hands to the desired positions. If you drag the hands past midnight, the date will change to the next or previous day. Another way to set the time is to tap the time displayed below the clock face and then type the correct time in 12-hour or 24-hour format. Again, this is the same as setting the time in the Welcome Wizard.

The View menu allows you to set several options.

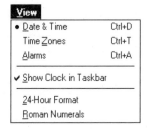

The first three commands on this menu just duplicate the three buttons on the command bar—they select which view is currently displayed. The next command lets you control whether the current time is displayed in the status area. The command after that allows you to choose whether the time is displayed in 12-hour or 24-hour format. The last command lets you choose the elegance of Roman numerals over the more pedestrian Arabic numerals on the clock faces.

Traveling with the Clock

Setting alarms is described later in this chapter. Setting appointments is described in the "Calendar" section of Chapter 4.

The idea behind the two time settings—Home and Visiting—is that you always set alarms and appointments for the local time at the location you'll be when the alarm or appointment occurs. For example, if you have an appointment in Chicago for 9 A.M. tomorrow, create it for 9 A.M., regardless of what time zone you are currently in. When you arrive in Chicago, select Chicago as your visiting city, switch to your visiting city settings, and you'll get the reminder for that 9 A.M. meeting at the correct time.

NOTE Of course, if you're visiting Chicago and you want to be reminded to call in during a meeting that's happening at 1 P.M. back home, you will have to adjust the time of that appointment for the Chicago time zone.

You select a visiting city in the same way you selected your home city in the Welcome Wizard. Tap the Time Zones button to display Time Zones view.

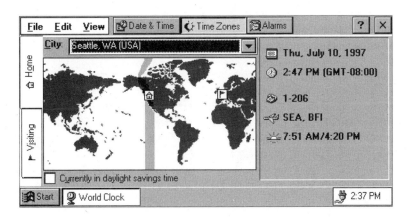

Tap the Visiting tab on the left side of the screen, tap the down-arrow to the right of the City field, and select the city you are visiting from the list. You can scroll to a specific part of the list by typing the first letter of the city name.

 NOTE   It's possible to select cities by tapping the world map in Time Zones view, although you need a good knowledge of geography to do this since the continents are so small. For fun, you can also make a little game out of Time Zones view. Tap the right or left edge of the world map repeatedly, say 10 or 12 times. The world keeps spinning, and for each tap a new city is displayed. Try to predict the city.

CTRL+S is the keyboard shortcut for the Save command.

When you arrive in the city you're visiting, tap that city's name above the Visiting clock face in Date & Time view. Then save the World Clock settings by tapping the Save command on the File menu. When you return to your home city, just tap its name above the Home clock face and save the clock settings again to change back to your home settings.

If you'd like more information about a city you're visiting, look at the Visiting tab in Time Zones view. Windows CE comes with nearly 500 cities in its database. When you're visiting one of these cities, the World Clock displays the current date and time in that city, its telephone area code, the abbreviations of the airports that serve the city, and when sunrise and sunset will occur today. If you just want to display this information about some city, select the city from the list. When you exit the World Clock, you will be asked if you want to save the changes you have made. Tap No since you were just looking at a city and don't want to save it as your home or visiting city.

 TIP   To measure the distance between any two cities in the database, set one city as your home city and the other as your visiting city. The distance between the two is displayed on the Visiting tab. When you are done, close the World Clock without saving the settings.

Adding cities to the database

If your favorite city or town is missing from the built-in database, you can easily add it. First you need to go to an atlas, find your city, and write down its latitude and longitude, offset from GMT (Greenwich Mean Time) in hours, telephone area codes, and airport codes. Then, in Time Zones view, tap the Edit menu, and tap the Add City command. The Choose Nearby City dialog box appears.

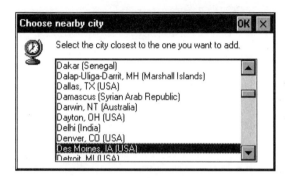

From the list of cities, choose the city closest to the one you want to add, and then tap OK. The Add City dialog box appears.

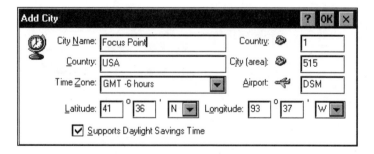

Type the information in the appropriate fields. If you are not sure of the GMT offset, find another city in the same time zone, and temporarily select it as your visiting city to view its GMT offset. Then pick the same value for the city you are adding.

IP You can update one of the cities in the built-in database (say, to add a telephone area code) by tapping the Edit City command on the Edit menu and then simply updating the information about that city.

The cities that you add to the database are stored in a file named usrcity.dat, which is a hidden file in the Windows folder. You can share the cities you have added with friends who have Handheld PCs by squirting them this file. When they receive the file, they will have to move it to the Windows folder on their machines. If they have made changes of their own, their added cities will be replaced by yours; there is no capability to merge two usrcity.dat files.

Setting Alarms

You can tap the Alarms button on the command bar to switch to the Alarms view of the World Clock.

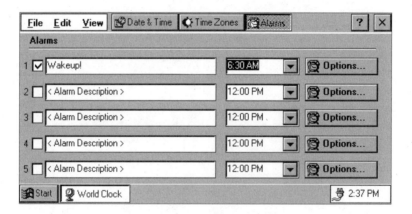

Here you can set up to five alarms, each with a different description and different notification options. When activated, each alarm goes off daily.

Setting an alarm is quite simple. Just type some text in the Alarm Description field, and then set the time you want the alarm to go off. You can tap the Options button to choose how you want Windows CE to notify you of the alarm. You can be notified in three ways, and you can choose any combination of the three.

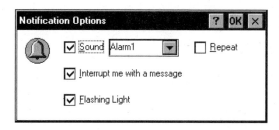

 OTE Not all Handheld PCs support all three modes of notification. Some might not have a flashing light, for example. In this case, the option would not be displayed.

If you select Sound, Windows CE plays the specified sound to notify you when the alarm goes off. It plays the sound only once unless you select the Repeat check box, in which case it repeats the sound for about 12 seconds. To turn off the sound immediately, you can tap the Alarm icon in the status area, or on some Handheld PC models, you can press a button on the case. If you've selected Interrupt Me With A Message as well as selecting Sound, tapping the OK button or the 5 Min Snooze button on the message box also turns off the sound.

To choose a sound, tap the down-arrow in the Sound field, and a list of sounds appears. If you use the DOWN ARROW key on the keyboard to scroll through the list, each sound is played as it is selected. (This can be entertaining if you do it quickly.) Or you can use the stylus to scroll through the list until you see the sound you want, and then you can tap the sound name to select it. The sound will play to confirm your selection.

If you select Interrupt Me With A Message, a message box displaying the text of the alarm pops up when the alarm goes off. You dismiss it by tapping the OK button or the 5 Min Snooze button on the message box. Selecting Flashing Light causes the light on the Windows CE case to start flashing when the alarm goes off. You turn off the light in the same manner you turn off an alarm sound.

Keep in mind that after you turn off an alarm, it is still active, and it will go off again the next day at the same time. If you want to deactivate an alarm without deleting it, just clear the numbered check box to the left of its description.

UN   There are some special alarms hidden in Windows CE. You can trigger them by entering a certain phrase as the description of a specific alarm. Try entering any or all of these phrases: *run backwards* in alarm 1, *run flashing* in alarm 2, *run shrinking* in alarm 3, or *run sounds* in alarm 4.

Calculator

The Calculator program is designed to work just like a real calculator. You can use it when you need to make quick calculations. For anything complicated, Pocket Excel is a better choice. The Calculator is located in the Accessories folder. To start it, tap the Start button on the taskbar, tap Programs, double-tap the Accessories folder, and then double-tap the Calculator icon.

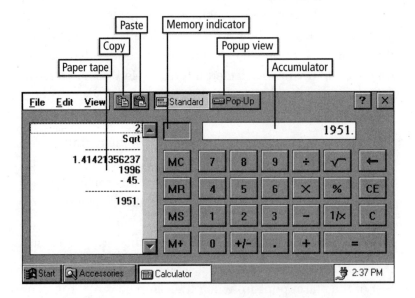

In Standard view, the Calculator displays a paper tape that keeps a record of your calculations. The Calculator buttons are fairly large, so here is a place where using your fingers to touch the Windows CE screen works really well.

You can enter numbers and perform operations either by tapping the buttons on the screen or by pressing the numbers and operators on the keyboard. Here are the keyboard equivalents of the on-screen keys:

Button on Screen	Key on Keyboard	Function Performed
0 through 9 and .	0 through 9 and .	Enters digit; enters decimal point
MC	L	Clears memory
MR	R	Recalls memory, replacing accumulator contents
MS	M	Saves accumulator contents to memory, replacing memory contents
M+	P	Adds accumulator contents to memory
+/-	S	Changes sign of accumulator contents
÷	/	Performs division
X	X or *	Performs multiplication
–	–	Performs subtraction
+	+	Performs addition
√	Q or @	Calculates square root of accumulator contents
%	%	Calculates percentage
1/x	I	Inverts accumulator contents (divides 1 by accumulator contents)
←	DELETE, DEL, or BACKSPACE	Deletes last digit (or decimal point) entered into accumulator
CE	C	Clears last number or operator entered
C	ESC	Clears calculator, except for memory
=	= or ENTER	Performs calculation
(none)	E	Enters exponent
(none)	RIGHT ARROW or DOWN ARROW	Scrolls down through paper tape
(none)	LEFT ARROW or UP ARROW	Scrolls up through paper tape

Square Root

The Calculator remembers your calculations when you close it. The next time you start it up, the last calculations you made are displayed.

You use the Windows CE Calculator the way you would any calculator. For example, enter *3+2=,* and *5* is displayed. Enter *2q* (or tap 2 followed by the Square Root button), and *1.41421356237* is displayed. If the result is too large to be displayed in the accumulator, the Calculator uses scientific notation to display it. For example, using *x=* as the shortcut for squaring a number, enter *999999999x=* (that's nine 9s followed by x and =). The result is displayed as *9.99999998e+017,* which means 9.99999998 times 10 to the 17th power. You can also enter values using the same scientific notation, although there is no on-screen button for *e.*

 NOTE   The Calculator performs its calculations in binary (base two) numbers but takes the numbers you type and displays results in decimal (base 10) numbers. During the conversion to and from binary numbers, some rounding errors occur. These rarely affect the displayed result, as the results are calculated at a greater precision than that displayed, but occasionally the rightmost digit or two might be off in numbers that have many digits to the right of the decimal place.

If you use any operator other than x, such as +, −, or /, the Calculator assumes you meant x and multiplies the numbers.

To calculate the percentage of a number, enter the number, enter the multiplication operator (x), and enter the percentage you want to calculate, and then press the % key. For example, enter *50x25%,* and *12.5* is displayed.

The four memory buttons let you store values to and retrieve values from the Calculator's memory. Tap the MS button to store the current contents of the accumulator in memory, replacing any previous value that might have been in memory. An *M* is displayed in the memory indicator to remind you that a value is stored in memory. Tap M+ to add the current contents of the accumulator to the value in memory. This is useful if you want to calculate a grand total from several intermediate calculations. The MR button replaces the contents of the accumulator with the value from memory, and the MC button clears memory.

Paper Tape and Clipboard

The paper tape records the last 100 lines of your calculations. It is very useful when used with the clipboard. For example, to save a permanent copy of your calculations you can copy the contents of the paper tape to the clipboard, open a document in Pocket Word, and then paste the clipboard contents into the Word document. You can also select some lines in the paper tape, copy them to the clipboard, and then paste them into the accumulator. This causes the Calculator to reinterpret the lines as if you had just typed them in. If you press the Copy button when no line is selected in the paper tape, the contents of the accumulator are copied to the clipboard.

Pop-up View

To switch the Calculator to Pop-up view, you tap the Pop-Up button on the Calculator command bar. The Calculator changes to look like this:

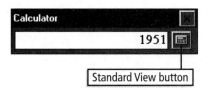

The idea behind this view is that you might want to perform some calculations on numbers that reside in some other document. When the Calculator is in Pop-up view, you can touch the title bar of the Calculator window and drag it around on the screen to a location in which it won't be in the way. If you touch the other program (perhaps to scroll the document you are viewing), the Calculator is covered up by the other program. To get the Calculator back on top, tap its button on the taskbar.

To switch back to Standard view, tap the Standard View button. The paper tape is still working, behind the scenes, when the Calculator is in Pop-up view. Thus any calculations made in Pop-up view are preserved on the paper tape.

Control Panel

The Control Panel is the place to go to adjust the settings of Windows CE. Here you can customize and personalize your Handheld PC. To display the Control Panel, tap the Start button, and then tap the Settings command. The contents of the Control Panel folder appear.

Some H/PCs have additional programs in the Control Panel to control special features of those machines.

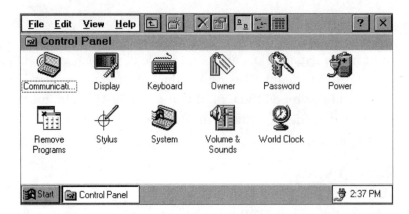

The Control Panel folder holds several small programs, each of which lets you control a different aspect of Windows CE. To open one of these programs, double-tap its icon. In this book, I will describe only the Control Panel programs that come built into Windows CE. If you install additional programs or hardware devices such as PC Cards, you might see additional Control Panel programs. The programs are displayed in alphabetical order, and that is how they are described in this section.

Don't be shy about trying out different settings. You can always change them back. (You might want to record the original settings just in case.) Think of it as adjusting the seat in a new car: it takes a while to get it right for you, and you should try it in different positions before deciding what feels best.

 TIP The settings in the Control Panel programs are organized on tabs. You can switch to a particular tab by tapping it, or you can press CTRL+TAB to move to the next tab.

Communications

The Communications program lets you adjust the settings used when your Handheld PC communicates with another H/PC via its infrared port or with other computers via a modem. The communications settings are arranged on three tabs.

Device Name

The first tab, Device Name, lets you name your Handheld PC.

Communicating with other computers is covered in Chapter 7.

When your Handheld PC sends files to another H/PC, this name is displayed very briefly on the other machine. You might enter something like *RPO_HPC* for the device name. You can't use spaces or most symbols in the name, and it can be no longer than 15 characters. The device description can be up to 50 characters long, and it can include spaces and any other characters. You don't need to fill in this field; the information you enter is displayed there simply for your own amusement.

Dialing

The Dialing tab is where you set things up so that you can connect to other computers via a modem.

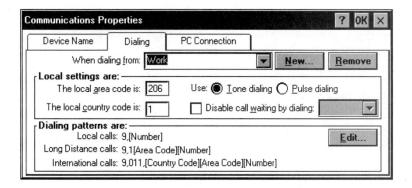

If you don't use a modem with your Handheld PC, you can forget about this tab.

The idea here is that you can define different locations from which you place calls, since the rules about dialing a given phone number differ depending on where you are. For example, from my house, I first dial 70#

to disable call waiting, but when I'm in my office, I first dial 9 to get an outside line. Perhaps the places in which you live and work are in different area codes. You can specify all these settings on this tab.

Two dialing locations are predefined, Home and Work. You can see the existing names by tapping the down-arrow at the right of the When Dialing From box. If you don't like an existing name, select it and tap the Remove button. To create a new dialing location name, tap the New button, type the name, and press ENTER.

To set up a dialing location, select that location in the When Dialing From box. Then fill in the settings. Enter the area code and country code for that location. (The country code for the United States is 1.) Then tap either Tone Dialing or Pulse Dialing. You use pulse dialing only when you are calling from somewhere that has only rotary-dial telephones. If you have call waiting on the telephone line you are going to use, select the Disable Call Waiting By Dialing check box and enter the code that disables call waiting. Call waiting is when an incoming call can interrupt an existing call, which is fine when you are talking to Aunt Meg but bad if your Handheld PC is communicating with another computer. If you don't know the code to disable call waiting for a particular phone line, the local phone company can tell you.

At the bottom of the Dialing tab is a section in which you can specify prefixes needed to place phone calls from this location. The default Work location settings prefix telephone numbers with a 9. This means that Windows CE will dial a 9 and then wait for 2 seconds before dialing the rest of the number, which is what you need to do from most business telephone systems.

If you tap the Edit button, you can customize these patterns.

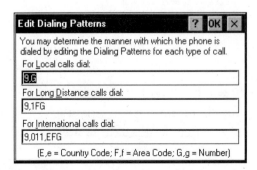

You can automate a great deal of your dialing in this way. For example, you can set things up so that Windows CE dials your long distance carrier, enters your credit card number, and then dials the computer to which you want to connect. Windows CE uses the same dialing codes that Windows 95 does, so if you have set up a laptop computer to dial from a particular location, you would set up your Handheld PC the same way. The dialing codes are as follows:

Code	Effect
0 through 9	Dials the digit
ABCD	Dials the digit (tone only, used for special control on some phone systems)
E	Dials the country code; displayed as (Country Code) in patterns
F	Dials the area code or city code; displayed as (Area Code) in patterns
G	Dials a local number; displayed as (Number) in patterns
e	Dials the country code; displayed as (CC) in patterns
f	Dials the area code or city code; displayed as (AC) in patterns
g	Dials a local number; displayed as (#) in patterns
*#	Dials the digit (tone only)
T	Causes the following digits to be tone dialed
P	Causes the following digits to be pulse dialed
,	Pauses for a fixed time, typically 2 seconds
!	Has the same effect as putting a telephone receiver on the hook for ½ second and then removing it from the hook for ½ second. This is known as "hookflash," and it allows transfer to another telephone extension
$	Waits for the credit card tone ("bong")
W	Waits for a second dial tone (typically used after $ to detect a dial tone after a credit card tone)
@	Waits for "quiet answer" (typically, 6.5 seconds of silence following the call ringing, which indicates the call has gotten through)
?	Asks for input before dialing continues

The codes e, f, and g display an abbreviated place-holder in the dialing string.

Unfortunately, there is more to be done before you can actually connect to another computer via a modem. That will be covered in Chapter 7.

PC Connection

The PC Connection tab lets you adjust the settings used when you connect your Handheld PC to your desktop PC.

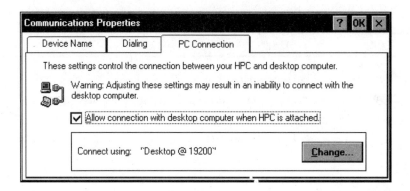

The synchronization program synchronizes the data on your Handheld PC with that on your desktop PC. See Chapter 6 for more information.

The check box lets you turn on or off the desktop connection capability of your Handheld PC. If you have another device that connects to your Handheld PC via the serial port, clearing this check box prevents the automatic launch of the synchronization program when you plug in the device. For most people this will not be a problem, so it is safe to leave the box selected.

The Change button lets you specify how you connect to the desktop PC. By default, connection is via a serial cable and at a speed of 19,200 bits per second. Before you can change these settings, you have to set up a new connection. That will be covered in Chapter 6.

Display

The Display program lets you customize the desktop background, just as you can in Windows 95. It also has an aid to help you adjust the contrast of your Handheld PC screen for maximum readability.

Background

The Background tab lets you choose a bitmap to be displayed as the background of the Windows CE desktop.

The default bitmap prominently displays the Windows CE logo, as you can see in this illustration. To see a list of the other built-in bitmaps, tap the down-arrow at the right of the Image box. The first item in the list is "None," in case you don't want to have a background bitmap displayed. When you select one of the bitmaps, the new background appears on the tab so that you can see what it looks like.

If you select the Tile Image On Background check box, the background bitmap is displayed repeatedly until it fills the entire screen. Except for the default background, all the built-in bitmaps are designed to be tiled.

One of the fun things you can do with your Handheld PC is to display a bitmap of your own. Using H/PC Explorer, which is described in Chapter 6, you can download a bitmap from your desktop computer. Then you can tap the Browse button here to find and select it as your background bitmap. Whether you pick a built-in or custom bitmap, to confirm your choice, tap the OK button. If you don't want to make a change, tap the Close button and things will stay as they were.

Contrast

The Contrast tab contains a "test pattern" that shows the four colors Windows CE can display.

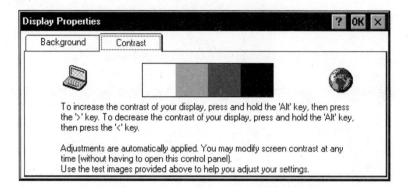

This test pattern helps you adjust the contrast on your Handheld PC. On most Handheld PCs, you adjust the contrast by holding down the ALT key and pressing the < or > key. Some H/PCs have a dial on the side of the case that you use instead. Adjust the contrast so that the black is as dark as possible but not so dark that you can't make out the different shades of gray. You can adjust the contrast at any time: you don't have to be in the Control Panel to do it.

Keyboard

Although the Handheld PC keyboard is too small to use for any serious typing, you can adjust some settings in the Keyboard program to optimize it for the way you type.

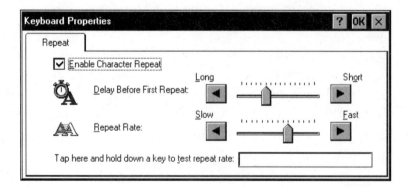

The Enable Character Repeat check box allows you to choose whether a key that is held down repeatedly enters a character. If you select the check box, you can specify how long the delay is before the repeating begins and at what rate the character is repeated. To adjust these settings, drag the sliders or tap the arrow buttons at the ends of the scales. After you have set these parameters, tap the field at the bottom of the screen, and then hold down a key to test your settings. When everything is set the way you want, tap the OK button to save your new settings.

Owner

The Owner program contains the same Owner Properties form you filled out when you completed the Welcome Wizard, which was covered in Chapter 2. You can use this program to update the owner information at any time.

Password

The Password program allows you to protect the data you keep on your Handheld PC by setting a password for the device. This was described in Chapter 2. You can use this program to change your password at any time.

You might find that the password protection can become annoying. For example, let's say you are in a meeting where you use your Handheld PC to take notes or to refer to downloaded information. The machine automatically shuts down to save power after a period of inactivity (by default, 3 minutes). When you press the power switch to restart the machine, you'll have to enter the password again.

To work around this, just clear the Enable Password Protection check box. (You'll need to enter the password to do this.) Then tap OK. Now the machine will not prompt you for a password when you turn it back on. Don't forget to re-enable the password protection when the meeting is finished.

Power

The Power program helps you monitor and control the power usage of your Handheld PC.

Battery

The Battery tab reports the status of the main and backup batteries.

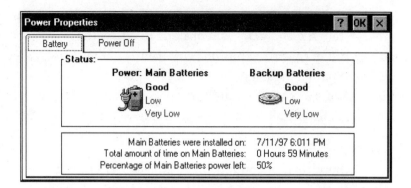

A small picture of two batteries is displayed in the status area. This represents the main batteries. As the batteries drain, the color drains out of the picture. Thus you always have a quick visual indication of the state of your batteries.

Power Off

The Power Off tab allows you to control the Handheld PC's power time-out.

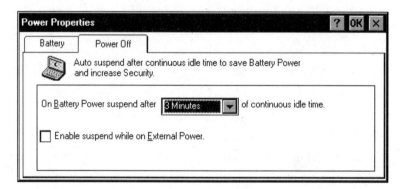

To maximize battery life, Windows CE suspends the machine after a specified interval of inactivity. The timing of this interval, of course, is a trade-off between conserving power and annoying you. The default interval is 3 minutes. You might want to try out other values to determine the one best for you.

When you plug your Handheld PC into its AC adapter, there is no need to conserve power, and thus the power time-out is not really necessary. But if you want your Handheld PC to suspend after the specified idle period even when it's running on external power, select the Enable Suspend While On External Power check box. You might want this to happen if you leave your Handheld PC on your desk for periods of time and you use the password feature. This way, when the machine powers off, the password must be entered to use it when it is powered on again, and your data is protected. As always, tap the OK button to confirm your changes.

 IP Turn off your Handheld PC when you are not using it. This sounds obvious, but it is easy to forget when you are in a meeting. Because your H/PC is ready to go within a second of your turning it back on, there is really no reason to keep it running if you are not actively using it.

Remove Programs

If you never install any additional programs on your Handheld PC, you'll never need to use Remove Programs. Its purpose is to let you remove programs that you installed onto your Handheld PC from your desktop PC.

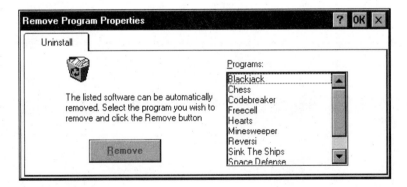

Perhaps you are running low on storage but you want to copy some additional documents to your Handheld PC. You might remove a program that you won't need for a while. Then later, when you no longer need those documents and have removed them, you can reinstall the program from your desktop PC.

To remove a program, select it from the list of installed programs and tap the Remove button. A confirming dialog box appears.

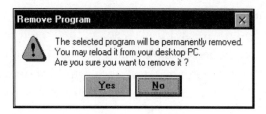

If you tap Yes, the program you selected is removed from your Handheld PC.

Stylus

You need to use the Stylus program only if you are having trouble with the stylus. Here you can recalibrate the touch screen and adjust the double-tap parameters.

Calibration

The Calibration tab opens the same calibration program you used when you completed the Welcome Wizard in Chapter 2. Remember that you can always access the calibration program by holding down the CTRL and ALT keys while pressing the = key.

Double-Tap

If you are having trouble double-tapping objects, you can reset your double-tap parameters on this tab.

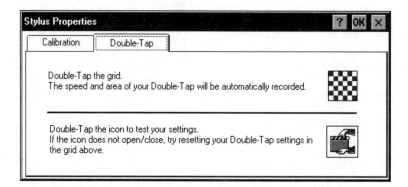

Just double-tap the checkerboard grid. You might want to do it a few times, until you land a double-tap that is representative of the way you regularly do it. In fact, you may want to try to be a little clumsy about it: if you increase the distance between the points where your two taps land, you won't need to be as precise when you are double-tapping later. Double-tap the clapboard icon to try out your new settings. If your double-tap is recognized, the clapboard will open or close.

 TIP If you use your Handheld PC while standing up, set the double-tap parameters while on your feet. Hold the Handheld PC the way you regularly use it. This will ensure the parameters you set here work for you.

System

The System program gives you some information about your Handheld PC hardware and allows you to control how the memory in your H/PC is used.

General

The General tab lists which version of Windows CE your H/PC is running, which type of processor your H/PC has, which type of PC Card is installed, and how much memory (RAM) your H/PC has.

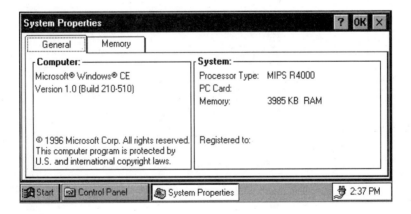

Memory

The Memory tab was described in the "Storage Memory Versus Program Memory" section of Chapter 2, so I won't repeat that information here.

Volume & Sounds

You interact with Windows CE by tapping objects on the screen. But because you are simply tapping a glass screen with a plastic stylus, there is no opportunity for the kind of tactile feedback you get from real buttons or knobs. When you manipulate real buttons, you can feel when the button is pressed down, and when you turn a knob, you can feel that you are turning it. Since Windows CE can't duplicate these forms of tactile feedback, it uses sounds instead.

Your Handheld PC can play standard Windows sound files. Like Windows 95, Windows CE has a large set of events for which sounds can be played. And as in Windows 95, you can control all this in excruciating detail. Thus the Volume & Sounds program is a little bit complicated.

Volume

The Volume tab lets you control the loudness of the sounds Windows CE plays and lets you specify when those sounds should be played.

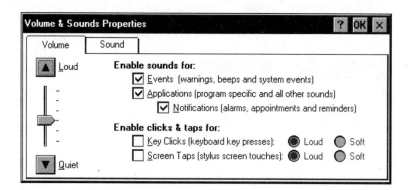

There are five categories of sounds that Windows CE emits. You can turn each of these sound categories on or off by selecting or clearing the appropriate check box.

You can assign different sounds to different events on the Sound tab, which is described in the next section of this chapter.

■ Enabling sounds for events means that Windows CE will make a sound to alert you when certain things happen on the screen. The sound's purpose is to draw your attention to the message that is displayed. Examples of events are warning and error messages, infrared communications beginning or ending, and programs opening or closing.

From the Microsoft Windows CE Web page you can download a "mute" button that lives as an icon in the status area. This makes it very easy to keep your Handheld PC quiet during a meeting.

■ Enabling sounds for applications means that your programs can play sounds. Most of the programs built into Windows CE do not make any sounds. The two exceptions are Solitaire, which plays a "splat" sound as the cards bounce off the screen when you win a game, and the World Clock, which plays a ticking sound if you set a special alarm. Other programs (especially games) that you might install on your Handheld PC do make sounds, however.

■ Enabling sounds for notifications means that your Handheld PC can make a sound to let you know about an alarm, an appointment, or a task reminder. You might want to turn off notification sounds while you're at the opera and then turn them back on afterward so that you'll be reminded to go to the tractor pull, for example. Notification sounds are considered to be program sounds, so if you want sounds to play for your notifications, enable sounds for applications too.

■ Enabling key clicks means that Windows CE sounds a little click to let you know when you've successfully pressed a key on the keyboard. This can be useful because the keys are so tiny you might not be sure when you've pressed one. If you are trying to take notes at a meeting, the clicks can be annoying, and you can disable them. You can tap Loud or Soft to set the volume for the key clicks.

■ Enabling screen taps means that Windows CE sounds a click when you tap the screen. You might want these click sounds on most of the time but off at meetings while you're playing Solitaire. As for key clicks, you can set the volume by tapping Loud or Soft.

The volume control on the left controls the loudness of all of the sounds. You will probably want to try some positions for the slider to determine which volume is best for you.

Sound

The Sound tab allows you to select different sounds for different system events. It is very similar to the Sounds program in the Control Panel in Windows 95.

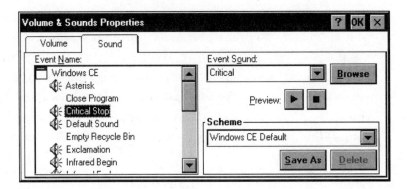

On the left side of the screen are all the events for which sounds can be played. You select an event by tapping it. Then you select a sound to assign to the event by tapping the sound in the Event Sound list or by tapping the Browse button. The Browse button allows you to browse through all the files on your H/PC. After you have selected a sound, you can listen to it by pressing the Play button (shaped like a right-pointing arrow) to the right of the Preview label. When a sound has been assigned to an event, it plays whenever the event occurs.

Since there are 19 events, following these steps to assign a sound to each event is rather tedious. Fortunately, sounds are collected into schemes that let you set many sounds at once. Tap the arrow at the right of the Scheme box, and the available sound schemes will appear. Windows CE comes with a single scheme, plus the choice of using the default sound for each event or no sounds for any events. You can download other sound schemes from the Windows CE Web site (http://www.microsoft.com /windowsce/). Once you have selected a scheme, you can augment it by adding, removing, or changing sounds. Then you can save the modified scheme with a new name.

If you have a sound file (with a filename extension of .wav) on your desktop PC, you can download it to your Handheld PC and then use it here. See Chapter 6 for more details. Sounds are a way to personalize your Handheld PC, so have some fun!

World Clock

This is the same World Clock program that was described earlier in this chapter. The World Clock icon in the Control Panel is just another way to get to the clock.

And Now It's Time For a Break

More than any other game, Solitaire is the game associated with Windows. And since Windows CE is a member of the Windows family, it is not surprising that it comes complete with an implementation of Solitaire. I've found it relaxing to play while waiting in airports, while riding the bus, or when I just need a simple diversion from a busy day.

To play the game, tap the Start button, tap the Programs command, double-tap the Games folder, and double-tap the Solitaire shortcut. A new game begins. Here's a game in progress:

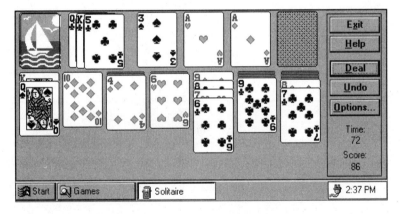

Just use the stylus to drag a card from place to place. If you want to drag a stack of cards, "grab" it by touching the topmost card of the pile. After you've made a move, if you want to take it back, tap Undo. This reverses the effect of the last move made. Once you have pressed the Undo button, it is grayed out so that you can't press it again until you first make another move. So if you realize several moves later that you made a mistake, it's too late, and you will have to deal a new game. The Options button displays a dialog box that lets you configure Solitaire to play the way you want.

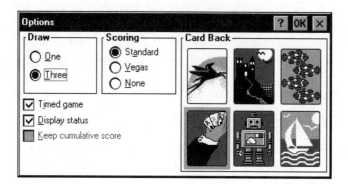

One of the card backs has a picture of a winged horse. This commemorates the code name of the Windows CE project: Pegasus.

You can choose from one of six card backs, four of which are animated. You can choose to draw one card or three cards at a time. If you want to race the clock, select Timed Game, and select Display Status if you want to have the game time displayed. If you want to keep score, you can choose Standard or Vegas scoring. (Las) Vegas scoring is where you buy the deck of cards for $52 and then win money for each card you success-fully discard. Vegas scoring also limits you to three passes through the deck if you are drawing three cards at a time or to one pass if you are drawing one card at a time. You can select Keep Cumulative Score if you want to keep track of your winnings (or losses) between games.

 OTE   There is a way to cheat in Solitaire. Don't read this if you don't want to be tempted. If you have selected Vegas scoring and you are drawing three cards at a time, press CTRL+ALT+SHIFT while tapping the deck to draw a card. You'll get one card at a time, but you can still go through the deck multiple times.

I've never won any money after playing more than a couple of games, and so I never play Solitaire with real money when I am near a casino. I figure this alone has more than covered the cost of my Handheld PC.

When you do win a game by getting all 52 cards up to the discard piles, you will be treated to a cascade of cards for your amusement. Be sure to have program sounds enabled (in the Control Panel Volume & Sounds program). At any time during the cascade, you can stop it by tapping the screen or by pressing a key. If your H/PC is running on batteries, it makes sense to do this, as all of that screen redrawing and noise-making uses a lot of power.

UN   When you go to a movie, the list of credits scrolls by at the end. Software developers take pride in hiding their list of credits somewhere in the program. In Windows CE, the credits are in the Solitaire game. To see them, get the ace of hearts up on the top row, and then hold down the ALT key and tap the ace. For 10 minutes or so, the list of contributors to Windows CE will bounce by in random order. I recommend that you have your Handheld PC plugged in to AC power while you do this.

Using Contacts, Calendar, and Tasks

In this chapter, you'll learn how to use Contacts, Calendar, and Tasks—three of the built-in programs in Windows CE. Together, these programs can replace your Rolodex, business card file, calendar, appointment book, to-do lists, and more.

Contacts, Calendar, and Tasks were designed to be companions to Microsoft Outlook, which is part of Microsoft Office 97, or Microsoft Schedule+, which is part of Microsoft Exchange. If you already use either of these programs on your desktop PC, you're all set. If you don't use a Personal Information Manager (PIM), you're still in luck, because Schedule+ is included on the Windows CE CD-ROM that came with your Handheld PC. See Chapter 6 for more information about this.

If you use another PIM on your desktop PC, you can either import its data into Schedule+ or Outlook and then, from either of those programs, synchronize your data with your Handheld PC, or you can purchase an alternate synchronization program such as Desktop To Go or Intellisync. These programs are described in Appendix B.

Contacts

Before I got my first prototype Handheld PC, I kept an address book in my appointment book and another in a desk at home. I would regularly find myself needing an address or phone number that was in the book that wasn't at hand. Now I keep all my addresses on my Handheld PC, synchronized with the Contacts section of Microsoft Outlook on my desktop PC. I've replaced the address book in my desk at home with one I print using Microsoft Word, which can import addresses from Microsoft Schedule+ and print them in any format one might desire.

No, you don't have to type the entire contents of your Rolodex on that tiny keyboard! If you want to store a lot of addresses on your Handheld PC, use your desktop or laptop computer (and its bigger keyboard). Enter the addresses into the Contacts section of Schedule+ or Outlook, and then use H/PC Explorer (discussed in Chapter 6) to synchronize them with the contacts on your Handheld PC.

You launch Contacts by double-tapping its icon on the Windows CE desktop. It always opens by displaying the contacts list, scrolled to wherever you last were when you used the program. If you haven't entered any contacts yet, the contacts list will be blank.

Creating Contacts

New

The keyboard shortcut for the New command is CTRL+N.

To create a new contact, tap the New button or tap the New command on the File menu. A blank contact card appears:

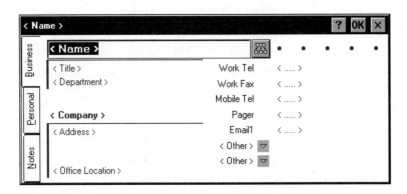

On the left side are three tabs, Business, Personal, and Notes. On the Business tab, you'll find fields to record the information you typically find on someone's business card. On the Personal tab is information you would keep regarding a friend or relative. The Name field is common to all three tabs.

If you are entering the contact information for a company, store, or other institution, leave the name blank and just fill in the company name.

Type the name of the contact, and then either press the TAB key to get to the next field or just tap the field you want to go to. You must fill in either the Name field or the Company field. If you enter text in the Name field, Contacts splits up the name into its appropriate components. For example, if you enter *Mr. John Smith, Jr.,* Contacts splits up the name as shown in the Confirm Name dialog box:

Confirm Name	? OK ✕
Mr/Ms/Dr: Mr. ▼	First: John
Suffix: Jr. ▼	Middle:
	Last: Smith

Confirm Name

If Contacts is unsure how to split up the name you enter, this dialog box appears when you leave the Name field. You can display it at any time by tapping the Confirm Name button to the right of the Name field. The Confirm Name button appears only when the Name field is selected.)

The Address field works the same way as the Name field. Just enter the address as you would on an envelope, and Contacts splits it up into the appropriate components. You can tap the Confirm Address button (located to the right of the Address field when the Address field is selected) to confirm and, if necessary, correct the way the address is split up.

Most of the other fields are pretty straightforward. Contacts doesn't split up the text you enter in them, so type whatever you want. Contacts automatically adds the default area code to the phone number fields. (You set the default area code in the Options dialog box; see "Customizing the Contacts List," later in this chapter, for details.) You can type over the default or use it, as appropriate.

At the lower right corner of the screen are two fields labeled Other. In these fields, you can fill in all sorts of other information about this contact. The Contacts program can store many fields of information for each contact, but there isn't room to present all the fields on the screen at the same time. Instead, the most commonly used fields appear on the contact card, and the two Other fields give you access to all the other available fields.

If you tap one of the Other fields, a list of available fields pops up:

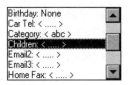

Scroll through the list until you find the field you want to fill in. Tap it, the pop-up list disappears, and the Other field is replaced by the field you selected.

Now you can enter the appropriate information in the field. This field and its value will remain displayed in place of Other. You can repeat this process for the second Other field. In either of these fields, you can repeatedly select additional field names and then enter values for them. The last field you select is the only one that will be displayed, but all the data is recorded. Simply tap the field name to see a pop-up list of all the field names and values you have entered. If you want, you can then change which field is displayed by selecting it from the list.

If you tap the Notes tab at the left side of the screen, you can enter any information that does not fit well in any of the predefined fields. I find it useful to copy information from other documents to the clipboard and then paste it on the Notes tab.

When you are finished entering information about your contact, tap the OK button. The contact card is closed, its data is saved, and the contacts list appears. If you don't want to save a new card you have started, press the ESC key or tap the Close button. You are not prompted for confirmation; the new card is silently discarded. If you pressed the ESC key, a new contact card is displayed. If you tapped the Close button, the contacts list appears.

TIP Don't limit your contacts to people. I have contacts for taxi cab dispatchers, the library, airline reservation phone numbers, the roof repair company, the video store, and all sorts of other people and things.

Finding, Editing, and Deleting Contacts

When you have some contacts entered, the contacts list looks like this:

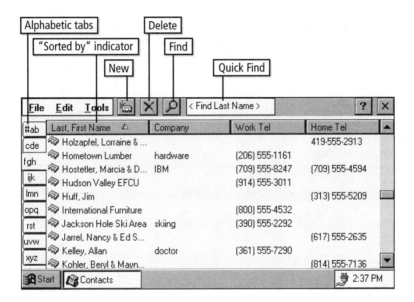

All your contacts are displayed in this sorted list, with four fields shown for each contact. By default, the fields are name (last name first), company, work telephone number, and home telephone number. The list is sorted by last name. You can sort the list by any of the other three fields simply by tapping its column title. You can tell which column the list is sorted by because that column has a small triangle (or up-arrow) to the right of the column name. Unfortunately, when the list is sorted by name, it is sorted by only last name, not last name then first name as you would expect. This flaw in Contacts is probably one of the worst shortcomings of the programs in Windows CE. You can change the size of the columns by touching the boundary between two of them and dragging the line to the left or right. Even if you make room for another column, Contacts displays no more than four.

Finding a particular contact

ALT+UP ARROW *and*
ALT+DOWN ARROW *are
the equivalent of*
PGUP *and* PGDN *on
other keyboards.*

You can scroll through the contacts list in the usual ways—by using the scroll bar or the keyboard arrow keys. To jump quickly to a particular spot in the list, tap one of the alphabetic tabs on the left side of the screen. Tapping the IJK tab, for instance, moves you to the first contact whose last name starts with *I, J,* or *K.* If you have sorted the list by a different column, say Company, tapping the IJK tab moves you to the first contact whose company name starts with one of those letters. If you are sorting the list by a field containing numbers (such as work telephone or home telephone), the tabs are disabled.

I have found that the quickest way to find a particular contact is to use the Quick Find feature. If you have the contacts sorted by last name, just start typing the person's last name, and Contacts immediately scrolls to the entry for that person. This works very well unless you have a couple of pages of Smiths, or in my case, O'Haras. You can't continue the search with the person's first name. After you get to an entry with a matching last name, you must scroll manually through the list. Quick Find operates on whichever column the list is currently sorted by.

Finally, you can easily search all the contacts to find one that has text you specify in any of its fields. Press CTRL+F or tap the Find command on the Tools menu to display the Find dialog box.

Type the text you want to search for (case is not important), and press ENTER or tap the Find Next button. Contacts displays the card for the next contact that contains the text you entered or displays a message box informing you that the text could not be found. Press ENTER again to continue the search, or press ESC to dismiss the Find dialog box. After you have dismissed the dialog box, you can restart the search at any time by pressing CTRL+I.

The Find dialog box "floats" above the Contacts program and does not prevent you from tapping or typing text into fields in the contact card below. You can even close the current card and return to the contacts list, leaving the Find dialog box displayed and ready for further use. You can touch the title bar of the dialog box and drag the box to a corner of the screen where it is not in the way.

Editing contacts

I've actually done very little editing of contacts on my Handheld PC; I usually do this in Outlook when I'm back at my desk. However, there have been times when, returning from a business trip, waiting for the plane to take off, I've pulled out the business cards of the people I've just met and entered them into the Contacts program on my Handheld PC.

To edit an existing contact, select it in the contacts list and then double-tap it or press ENTER. The contact card is displayed, and you can modify the existing fields, add new data, or delete data. You can also make a copy of a contact card. This is useful if much of the data in the new card is the same as in another. In the contacts list, select the contact whose information you want to copy. Then tap the Create Copy command on the Edit menu. A copy is created just after the original in the list. Double-tap it or press ENTER to open the contact card, and make any changes you want.

Deleting contacts

Delete

In the contacts list, select one or more contacts you want to delete, and tap the Delete button or press SHIFT+BACKSPACE. A dialog box appears to warn you that when these contacts are deleted they are gone for good and are not placed in the Recycle Bin. Remember that you can select multiple contacts by holding down the CTRL key as you tap the contacts.

Any contacts you delete from your Handheld PC will be deleted from Schedule+ or Outlook the next time you synchronize with your desktop machine. See Chapter 6 for more information about this. You don't need to keep every contact you have stored on your desktop PC on your Handheld PC. In Chapter 6, you'll see how to select just those contacts you want to have downloaded to your Handheld PC.

 OTE   When I talk about the BACKSPACE key, I'm referring to the key that appears on the upper-right of the keyboard. On some H/PC models, this key is actually labelled DEL, but it still works by deleting the character to the left of the insertion point (just like the BACKSPACE key on a desktop PC keyboard). When you press SHIFT+BACKSPACE, you delete the character to the right of the insertion point.

Sending and Receiving Contacts via Infrared Transfer

This is fun. If you know someone who also owns a Handheld PC, you can wirelessly transfer up to 25 contacts at a time between your two Handheld PCs through their infrared ports. The sender selects the contact or contacts to send by highlighting them in the contacts list or by tapping Select All on the Edit menu. Then the sender taps the Send command on the File menu. The receiver opens Contacts and taps the Receive command on the File menu. The rest of the process is the same as for transferring any files between H/PCs. For more information, see "Sending and Receiving Files via Infrared Transfer" in Chapter 3.

Customizing the Contacts List

If you tap the Options command on the Tools menu, a dialog box appears in which you can customize the columns displayed in the contacts list.

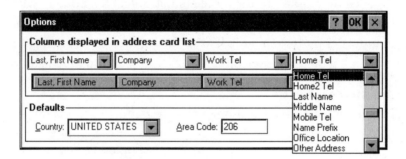

Here you can set how many columns are displayed and which field is displayed in each column. The leftmost column is reserved for first and last name; you can choose to have the last name or the first name displayed first. In the other three columns, you can display any field you choose. Pick < None > to remove the column from the contacts list.

You cannot display the same field in more than one column. If you want to "move" a column to the left or right, you must first change the field of the column you want to move; then you can pick that field for the other column. For example, in the previous illustration, if you want to have Company be the third column, you must first change the field displayed in the second column from Company to some other field. Only then can you choose the Company field for the third column.

At the bottom of the dialog box, you can set a default area code and country. When you select one of the telephone number fields on a new contact card, the default area code is automatically inserted. If most of the contacts you add on your Handheld PC are in one area code, set it as your default, and you won't have to type it each time you enter a contact. In the same manner, the default country is set for new addresses you create.

The following table lists all the available fields for a contact card. It also lists the name under which the field appears when synchronized with Schedule+ on your desktop PC. If that column in this table is blank, the field cannot be viewed or edited in Schedule+. Don't worry, it is stored in the Schedule+ database; you just can't get to it from within Schedule+. Thus the Schedule+ database acts as a backup to the Contacts database on your Handheld PC.

Property	Description	Contacts Usage	Outlook Name	Schedule+ Name
Anniversary	anniversary	Personal tab	Anniversary	Anniversary
Assistant	assistant	Other field	Assistant's Name	Assistant
Assistant Tel	assistant's telephone	Other field	Phone, Assistant	Assistant Phone
Birthday	birthday	Personal tab	Birthday	Birthday
Car Tel	car telephone	Other field	Phone, Car	
Category	delimited categories	Other field	Categories	
Children	children's names	Other field	Children	
Company	company name	Business tab	Company	Company
Department	department name	Business tab	Department	Department
Email1	primary e-mail address	Business tab	Email	User 1
Email2	secondary e-mail address	Personal tab	Email2	
Email3	tertiary e-mail address	Other field	Email3	
First Name	given name	Name field	First Name	First Name

continued

(continued)

Property	Description	Contacts Usage	Outlook Name	Schedule+ Name
Home Address	home address, parsed	Personal tab	Home Address	Home Address
Home Fax	home fax machine number	Other field	Phone, Home Fax	
Home Tel	home telephone	Personal tab	Phone, Home	Home Phone
Home2 Tel	second home telephone	Other field	Phone, Home 2	Home 2 Phone
Last Name	surname	Name field	Last Name	Last Name
Middle Name	middle name	Name field	Middle Name	First Name
Mobile Tel	mobile (cellular) telephone	Business tab	Phone, Mobile	Mobile Phone
Name Prefix	Dr., Mr., Ms., etc.	Name field	Title	First Name
Notes	notes text	Notes tab	Notes	Notes
Office Location	office or building number	Business tab	Office	Office
Other Address	other address, parsed	Personal tab	Other Address	
Pager	pager telephone number	Business tab	Phone, Pager	Pager Phone
Spouse	significant other's name	Personal tab	Spouse's Name	Spouse
Suffix	PhD., Jr., III, etc.	Name field	Suffix	Last Name
Title	business title	Business tab	Job Title	Title
Web Page	Web page address (URL)	Other field	Web Page	
Work Address	work address, parsed	Business tab	Business Address	Business Address
Work Fax	business fax machine number	Business tab	Phone, Business Fax	Fax Phone
Work Tel	business telephone	Business tab	Phone, Business	Business Phone
Work2 Tel	second business telephone	Other field	Phone, Business 2	Business 2 Phone

(continued)

Property	Description	Contacts Usage	Outlook Name	Schedule+ Name
[Home, Work Other] Address City	city	Address field	Address City	Address City
[Home, Work Other] Address Country	country	Address field	Address Country	Address Country
[Home, Work, Other] Address Postal Code	zip code or postal code	Address field	Address Postal Code	Address Postal code or Address ZIP code
[Home, Work, Other] Address State	state	Address field	Address State	Address State
[Home, Work, Other] Address Street	street	Address field	Address Street	Address Street

The following fields in Schedule+ are not synchronized with your Handheld PC: Private, User 2, User 3, and User 4. The data in these fields remains on your desktop PC and is not lost. Outlook has many other fields available for each contact, too many to list here. Those not listed in this table are not synchronized with your Handheld PC; the data in these fields remains on your desktop PC and is not lost.

Using Contacts with the Inbox

If you don't plan to use the Inbox in Windows CE, you can ignore this section. But if you do, you'll want to know how the Inbox uses information stored in Contacts. The Inbox Internet mail service uses the Email1, Email2, and Email3 fields in Contacts. If you want to be able to easily address electronic mail to people in your contacts list, be sure one of these e-mail fields contains the person's e-mail address.

Other mail services you might install use these fields as well, or perhaps others. For example, the SkyTel 2-Way messaging service uses the Pager field. This and other mail services are described in Appendix B.

Calendar

During the development of Windows CE, I was not a big user of my desktop computer-based appointment book, Schedule+. My real appointment book was the paper one I carried with me at all times. The computer version was filled mainly with appointments created by others through the group scheduling capabilities of Schedule+. I would (usually) transfer these appointments over to my paper appointment book. Of course, sometimes I forgot to do this and therefore missed meetings. And I never kept track of my tasks in Schedule+; I had them in my head or on scraps of paper about my office.

When I received my first prototype Handheld PC, all this changed. Now by just plugging my Handheld PC into my desktop computer I suddenly had my schedule with me when I needed it; no more double entries. Now I can't imagine going back to a paper-based system. So give it a try; you might have the same experience.

You don't have to enter all your appointments directly on your Handheld PC. Instead, at your desktop PC, enter them into Schedule+ or Outlook, and then use H/PC Explorer to synchronize them with your Handheld PC. You'll learn how to do this in Chapter 6.

To start the Calendar program, double-tap the Calendar shortcut on the Windows CE desktop. The Calendar always opens in the view in which you left it, or if this is the first time you're using the Calendar, it opens in Day view.

Day View

Day View looks like this:

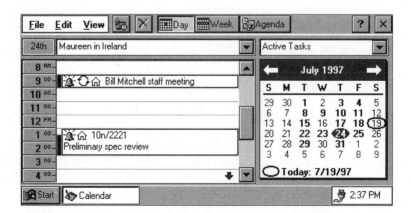

It is designed to display the appointments of a business day and to let you quickly jump to other days. If you have used Schedule+ or Outlook, you'll find it quite familiar, and in general, it works just the way the Day View in those programs works.

Appointment area

If you wish, you can display the day's schedule in half-hour increments. This has the advantage of giving more room for each appointment, but then not as many hours are displayed at once. You can switch between displaying half-hour increments and displaying hour increments by tapping the Half-Hour Slots command on the View menu.

The day's appointments are displayed on the left side of the screen. The time is shown at the far left of the appointment area; at the right is a scroll bar with which you can move through the hours of the day. In the previous illustration there are two appointments. The second starts at 1:30 P.M. and ends at 3:00 P.M. Although the text for the appointment makes it look as if the meeting starts at 1:00, the black bar at the left of the appointment shows the actual starting and ending times. Sometimes this can be a little confusing, so always check the black bar for the actual time of an appointment. After showing up a half hour early for a few meetings, you will have no trouble remembering to do this.

There are three icons in the description of the first appointment. In order, they indicate that a reminder is set for this appointment, that this is a recurring appointment, and that the Location field has data in it. The second appointment has two icons. In this case, there is a reminder set for the appointment, and the Location field has data in it. Since the second appointment has two lines available, the first line shows the location information. The second line is the appointment description.

If you highlight a time and start typing, a new appointment will be created for that time. You highlight a time by tapping that time in the appointment area. If you want to highlight several hours, touch the stylus to the first hour and then drag it down through the other hours you want to highlight. If you move the stylus down off the appointment area, the area will automatically scroll.

The small, downward-pointing arrow at the lower right corner of the appointment area indicates there are more appointments later in the day that are not currently visible. If there were appointments earlier than the first one displayed, a similar upward-pointing arrow would be displayed at the upper right corner of the appointment area.

Date picker

The right side of the screen displays the month, with the current day (the one being displayed in the Calendar) highlighted. Today's date is circled in the appropriate month.

This is called the date picker, and you can use it to select dates in the World Clock as well as in the Calendar. At the bottom of the date picker, today's date is displayed, which will be different from the currently selected day if you've moved from today to check appointments on another day.

The date picker lets you move to any date you want to display in the years 1900 through 2999. If you tap a day in the date picker, it jumps to that day. If the day is in the next or previous month, it jumps to that day and month. To move to the next or previous month, tap the arrows to the left or right of the month name. To jump to another month in the current year, tap the name of the month at the top of the date picker. A list of the twelve months pops up, and you can then tap the month to which you want to jump. Likewise, to jump to another year, tap the year at the top of the date picker. A list appears, with the current year highlighted. If the year you want is shown, just tap it, and then press ENTER. Otherwise, type the year you want, and when you press ENTER, the date picker jumps to that year.

When you want to return to today, tap today's date at the bottom of the date picker. If the day displayed as today is wrong, now is a good time to go to the World Clock and fix that. You can get there quickly by double-tapping the time in the lower right corner of the screen.

Creating Appointments

To create a simple appointment—that is, one that does not repeat—follow these steps:

1. Use the date picker to move to the day on which you want the appointment.

   If the appointment is for today and if you are currently viewing another day, you can press CTRL+T to jump to today. Or you can press CTRL+G, which pops up a small dialog box in which you can type the date you want to go to.

2. If necessary, use the scroll bar in the appointment area to move the starting time of the appointment into view.

3. Select the hours in which the appointment falls.

   For example, if you want to create an appointment that runs from 9:00 A.M. to 11:00 A.M., touch the 9:00 A.M. line and drag down until the next hour is highlighted. If the ending hour is not visible, the appointment area will automatically scroll down (or up) to bring hidden hours into view. Simply lift the stylus when the hour you seek is in view. If you go too far, just drag the stylus back up until just the right hours are selected.

4. Start typing the description of the appointment. The Appointment dialog box will appear, and the text you are typing will be displayed in the Desc field. When you have finished entering the description, press TAB to move to the Location field, and enter a location.

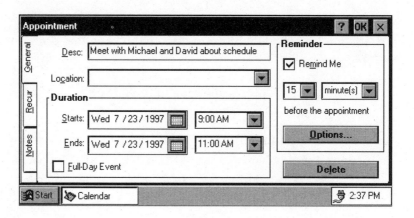

> **TIP**   If you tap the down-arrow at the right of the Location field, several of
> the locations you have previously entered are displayed. To save yourself
> some typing, you can tap the one you want.

5. Adjust the starting and ending times, if necessary.

   For example, what if the appointment starts at 9:30 instead of
   9:00? Tap the arrow at the right of the starting time field, and a
   list of alternate times drops down. Tap the time you want. If the
   appointment starts at a time that's not listed, such as 9:17 (for an
   airplane departure, for example), just tap the starting time field
   and type the correct time. Use the same techniques to adjust the
   ending time of the appointment. When you open the ending
   time list, both the ending time and the appointment duration
   are displayed.

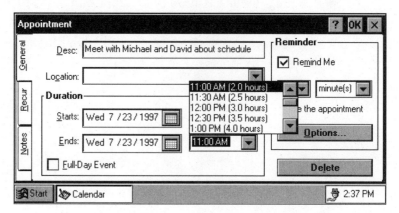

Setting reminders

One of the most popular features of the Calendar is appointment reminders. Having Windows CE remind you of upcoming appointments is especially useful because you probably have the Handheld PC with you, so you'll be able to hear the reminders when they go off. In the previous illustration, the Remind Me check box is selected, and Windows CE will notify you of the appointment at 8:45 A.M., 15 minutes before the appointment is due to start. You can tap the Options button to choose the methods Windows CE will use to notify you of the appointment.

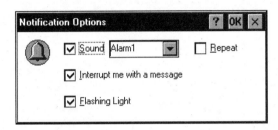

These options are the same as those for alarms in the World Clock, which were discussed in the "Setting Alarms" section of Chapter 3.

You can set your own defaults for the reminders of new appointments you create. To do this, tap the Edit menu, and then tap the Reminder Defaults command. Here you can specify how long before each appointment you are to be notified.

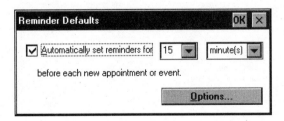

The Options button displays the same Notifications Options dialog box shown previously. You can set default values for the sound, message, and flashing light options.

Creating Recurring Appointments

You probably have several appointments that repeat on a regular basis: the weekly staff meeting, the monthly planning meeting. Instead of entering the same appointment repeatedly, it is far easier to create a recurring appointment. Start by creating a one-time appointment, as described previously. Choose the starting and ending time of the appointment, type the description, enter the location if you want, and set the reminder to your liking. These settings (times, description, location, and reminder) will be the same for all occurrences of the appointment, although after you have created the recurring appointment you can make exceptions to the recurring pattern. Creating exceptions to recurring appointments is covered in "Modifying Appointments," later in this chapter.

Options for recurring appointments are on the Recur tab of the Appointment dialog box. Tap the Recur tab, and specify the frequency of the recurrence by tapping the appropriate option in the upper left corner of the tab. In the box to the right, you'll then be able to specify details of the recurrence pattern. Setting recurring appointments can be a little tricky at first: sometimes the appointments don't repeat the way you intended. It's not a bad idea to spend a little time in the Calendar trying out the various recurrence patterns.

When you create a new appointment, Once is the default frequency of occurrence.

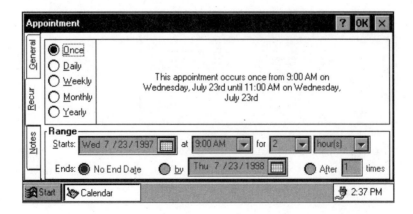

This, of course, just confirms that you have created an appointment that does not (yet) repeat.

The Daily option lets you create an appointment that that repeats every day, every two or more days, or every weekday (Monday through Friday).

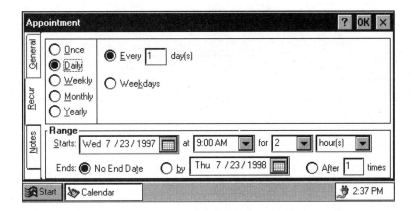

If you want the appointment to be every two or more weekdays (such as Monday, Wednesday, and Friday), you need to use the Weekly option, which will be described shortly.

For all types of recurring appointments, you can specify the first and last occurrence of the appointment. In the previous illustration, you can see that the default is that the appointment has no ending date; the appointment repeats forever. (Well, actually it repeats until the last date that Windows CE can handle, which is December 31, 2999.)

There are two ways to set the ending date for a recurring appointment. You can specify that the appointment end by a certain date. That is, any appointments that would have fallen after the date are not scheduled. You can also specify that the appointment end after a certain number of times. If you know the appointment will recur three times, this is the easiest way to specify that.

The Weekly option lets you specify an appointment that occurs on a certain day or days of the week.

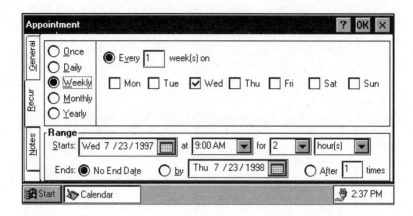

For example, you might specify that the appointment occur every Thursday or every other Monday. Or, if you wanted an appointment for every Monday, Wednesday, and Friday, you could select the Mon, Wed, and Fri check boxes.

Use the Monthly option to create an appointment that repeats on a specific day every month or every two or more months.

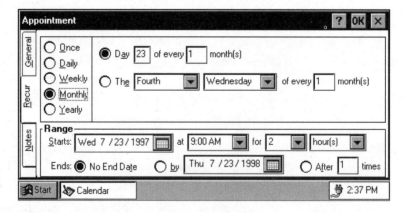

The day can be a specific date, such as the 1st or 15th. Or you can specify a certain day of the month, such as the first Friday, the last day, the last weekday, or the last weekend day. Try creating some sample appointments, and you will see that there is a lot of flexibility here.

The Yearly option is very similar to the Monthly option.

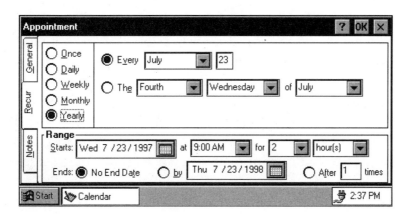

The difference is that here you select the month of the appointment. Again, you can specify a specific date, such as July 4 or April 15. You can also create an appointment for the first Monday in September (Labor Day in the United States) or the last Monday in May (Memorial Day in the United States). Unfortunately, you can't create appointments for more complicated special days like election day in the United States (the first Tuesday after the first Monday in November).

Creating Appointment Notes

I find it convenient to use the Notes tab of the Appointment dialog box to take notes during a meeting.

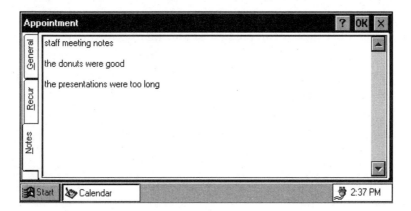

Although the Notes tab does not have the outlining capability of Word, I like that the information is automatically copied back to my desktop PC the next time I connect the Handheld PC and synchronize them.

A single appointment's Notes tab can contain up to 4095 characters of text. For recurring appointments the story is more complicated. No single note in any of the individual appointments that make up a recurring appointment series can be more than 4095 characters of text. In addition, the sum of all the notes of all the appointments in the series can be no more than 64,000 characters of text. For most people in most situations this is not a problem. However, let's say you have a recurring appointment for a daily staff meeting, and each day you copy the agenda onto the Notes tab for that day's appointment. At each meeting, you also record the notes of the meeting on the Notes tab. If you stored 1000 characters on each Notes tab (which is quite a lot of text), in about 3 months you would run out of space.

Schedule+ does not share these restrictions. If you use Schedule+ to create an appointment with a note containing more than 4095 characters, when you synchronize your schedule with your Handheld PC you will receive a message warning you that the data in the note will be truncated. You can choose to skip synchronization of the appointment if you want to retain the long note.

Modifying Appointments

Often you will need to need to change an appointment after you have created it. Fortunately, this is very easy to do. Simply double-tap the appointment. The now-familiar Appointment dialog box appears, and you can modify any of the particulars of the appointment. You can flip back and forth among the three tabs, changing any or all of the values, including changing a recurring appointment to a one-time appointment or vice versa. When you are done, tap the OK button to save your changes, or tap the Close button to discard your changes, leaving the appointment as it was.

One of the most common changes to an appointment is simply moving it to another time. Perhaps you just received a call, and tomorrow afternoon's meeting has been moved from 2:00 P.M. to 3:00 P.M. Just go to tomorrow in Day view, touch the appointment, and drag it to its new time. If the new time is not visible on screen, drag the appointment to the bottom or top of the screen, and the appointment area will scroll to bring it into view. If you tap an appointment, the appointment is selected. You can drag the triangular "ears" of a selected appointment to change its duration.

To display Day view with half-hour time slots, tap the Half-Hour Slots command on the View menu.

You'll learn about Week view later in this chapter.

There are limits to the changes you can make to an appointment by dragging it. You can move it only to a time that is one or more hours earlier or later than its current time, unless you are displaying Day view with half-hour time slots. In that case, you can move it to a time that is one or more half hours earlier or later. In Week view, you cannot drag the appointment to another day. Finally, you can extend or shorten an appointment's duration only by multiples of an hour or half hour, depending on whether you are displaying half-hour time slots. To perform finer-grained changes, open the appointment and change the appropriate values in the Appointment dialog box.

If the appointment you modify (by dragging it or by changing values in the Appointment dialog box) is a recurring appointment, a confirming dialog box appears. This dialog box asks whether you want the changes you are making to apply to just the single instance you selected or to all instances of the recurring appointment. You can change just this instance of the appointment (the weekly staff meeting is moved to 3:00 P.M. today but will meet next week at the usual time), or you can change all instances of the appointment (the weekly staff meeting will be at 3:00 P.M. from now on). You can also move an appointment by using the clipboard. If you use this technique to move a recurring appointment, only the single instance you move is changed.

Delete

Deleting Appointments

Deleting an appointment is quite simple. Tap it to select it, and then tap the Delete button or press SHIFT+BACKSPACE. A confirming dialog box appears because after you delete an appointment, it is gone for good. The next time you synchronize your Handheld PC with your desktop PC, the corresponding appointment will be deleted from Schedule+ on the desktop PC.

If you delete a recurring appointment, a different dialog box appears because you can either delete just this instance of the appointment (the weekly staff meeting is canceled today but will meet next week as usual) or all instances of the appointment (you aren't having any more weekly staff meetings).

Creating Events

You'll learn about Agenda view later in this chapter.

Events are activities that you want to track but that occur at no specific time during the day. For example, if I am on a business trip, I create an event for the days I am away. That way I know not to book new appointments on those days. Recurring events are especially useful for remembering birthdays and anniversaries. Events are displayed in Day view and in Agenda view. If there is more than one event on a given day, only one of them is displayed in Day view. It appears in a box just above the appointment area. To see the others, you must tap the down-arrow to the right of the box to open the list of events.

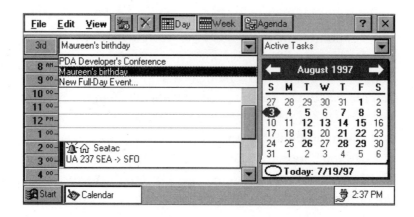

To create a new event, tap the New Full-Day Event item in the list. This displays the familiar Appointment dialog box with a slight difference.

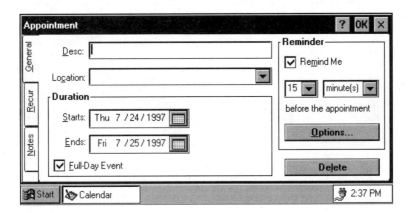

In the lower left corner, Full-Day Event has been selected, and there is no time specified for the appointment. The rest of the fields work as described for regular appointments, as do the Recur and Notes tabs.

If you clear the Full-Day Event check box, you turn the event into an ordinary appointment, where you can specify the starting and ending times. You can't modify or delete an event from Day view as you can with regular appointments. You can do that only from this dialog box.

 IP   I have created full-day events for all the various anniversaries and birthdays I need to remember. I set reminders for them one or two weeks in advance so that I have time to buy the card or gift.

Week View

Tapping the Week button on the Calendar command bar switches the display to Week view, which displays a week at a glance. It is simply five or seven Day views displayed at one time, so each day in Week view works like the single day displayed in Day view. The 5-day Week View command on the View menu controls how many days are displayed in Week view—five or seven.

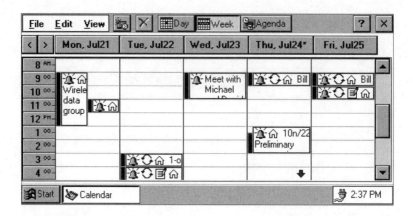

You can create new appointments and delete or modify existing appointments in Week view. You can move an appointment simply by dragging it to the new time. Because Week view displays much less of each appointment than Day view does, it is not so good for seeing the details of each day's schedule but it is great for seeing your entire week at a glance. You can quickly jump to Day view for any day displayed in Week view simply by tapping the day's date. To jump to the previous week or the next week, tap the < button or the > button, just below the File menu.

The * on Thursday, July 24 in the previous illustration indicates that an event is scheduled on this day, since there is just no room to display the event anywhere else in this view. You can also see that if you have overlapping appointments, as seen here on Thursday, not much of each appointment is displayed.

Agenda View

You'll learn about the Tasks program in the next section of this chapter.

To switch to Agenda view, tap the Agenda button on the Calendar command bar. Agenda view links your daily schedule with your active tasks. It displays a summary of the day's appointments and events and the tasks that are active on that day.

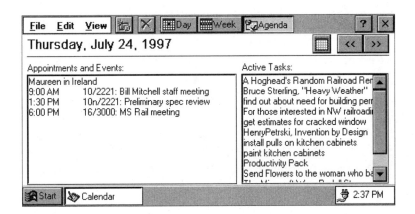

If you need to see quickly what's going on and what you need to do today, this is the view to use. To jump to Day view or Week view, tap the appropriate button on the command bar. To jump to the Tasks program, tap its button on the taskbar if it's there. If it is not on the taskbar, tap the Calendar's taskbar button (this minimizes the Calendar and displays the desktop), and then double-tap the shortcut to Tasks.

If you display the current day in Agenda view, your next appointment appears highlighted by default. If there are no more appointments today, or if you view a day other than today, no appointment is highlighted. You cannot manipulate either the appointments or the tasks displayed in this view; you can only look at them.

Date Picker

In Agenda view, there are three buttons at the upper right of the screen. Tapping the Date Picker button displays a date picker from which you can jump to any other date.

Previous Day and Next Day

The right two buttons take you to the previous day or the next day.

Tasks

Tasks is the program that really helps you get organized. Here is where you record all the things you need to do. Tasks helps you organize these items so that you can always work on the most important ones first. At last you can harness the power of modern electronics to nag you, any time of the day or night. Additionally, if you synchronize your Handheld PC with your desktop PC, you can have both machines harass you to get those things done! With the Tasks program, you can generate and view a list of tasks, set priorities for them, sort the tasks by various criteria, and have Windows CE remind you when it's time to work on them.

To start Tasks, go to the desktop and double-tap the Tasks shortcut. Tasks opens in the main view, which will be blank if you have no tasks entered yet.

Creating Tasks

New Task

To create a new task, tap the New Task button. The Task dialog box appears.

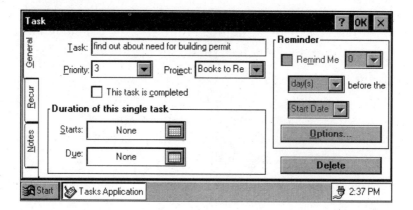

Here you can fully specify the task. The Task dialog box is very similar to the Calendar's Appointment dialog box, described earlier in this chapter. You enter the description of the task in the Task field and the priority in the Priority field. You can set the priority of tasks from 1 to 9 and A to Z, with 1 being the highest priority, A lower than 9, and Z the lowest. The purpose of the Priority field is to allow you to sort your tasks by priority in the main view. That way you can work on your highest priority tasks first. You, of course, decide what meaning a priority of 1, 2, or A has.

If you are like most people and have a lot of tasks to do, you can create different projects and assign the tasks to them. This way, you can group tasks together. For example, perhaps you are preparing a presentation. You might have tasks to remind you to do some research, set up some meetings, work on the presentation, have it reviewed, and then deliver it. All these tasks might be grouped in a project called "prepare presentation." Assigning tasks to projects lets you display all the related tasks of a project together. If you want to create a new project for the task you're creating, just tap the Project field and start typing.

> **TIP**   I keep my personal projects as well as my work projects on my Handheld PC. I have personal projects titled "house projects," "yard work," "automobile," "vacation," "books to read," "gifts to buy," and so on. If I'm sitting somewhere and I suddenly remember something I need to do, or if someone mentions a good book to read, I grab my Handheld PC and enter a new task. After a Saturday spent doing chores and errands, I really enjoy marking those tasks completed!

If you want the task to have a starting date and a due date, enter those dates in the Starts and Due fields. The due date must be on or after the starting date. If you choose to set the task's duration, you can choose whether you want to be reminded about the task. You can set the reminder for some number of minutes, hours, days, or weeks before the task's starting or due date. Tapping the Options button displays exactly the same notification options available for alarms in the World Clock, which were discussed in the "Setting Alarms" section of Chapter 3.

When you mark a task completed by selecting the This Task Is Completed check box, the duration information is replaced by the date on which the task was completed. If you later clear the check box to mark the task not completed after all, you can enter new duration information.

The Task dialog box has three tabs. So far I've been describing the General tab. The Notes tab is just like the Notes tab in the Appointment dialog box, described in "Creating Appointment Notes" earlier in this chapter. You can type information about the task here, or you can paste text from the clipboard. The remaining tab is the Recur tab, which will be covered in "Creating Recurring Tasks," later in this chapter.

When you are done entering information about the task, tap the OK button. Tasks returns to the main view.

✒ **TIP** Often you'll have information from another program that relates to the task you are creating. The Notes tab is the perfect place to store this information, and the Windows CE clipboard is the easiest way to get it there.

Viewing, Sorting, and Editing Tasks

When you have some tasks entered, the main view of Tasks looks something like this:

Status	Tasks △	Priority	Starts	Due	Project
☐	A Hoghead's Random...	4	None	None	Books to ...
☐	Bruce Strerling, "Hea...	4	None	None	Books to ...
☐	Decide on RHI excha...	3	09/30/1997	08/31/1997	Leisure
☐	find out about need fo...	3	None	None	House
☐	For those interested in...	3	None	None	Books to ...
☐	get estimates for crac...	3	None	None	House
☐🔔	install pulls on kitchen...	3	08/01/1997	08/01/1997	House
☐🔔	paint kitchen	3	08/01/1997	08/01/1997	House

File Edit [All Tasks ▼] ? ✕

Start Tasks Application 2:37 PM

In the Calendar's Agenda view and in the tasks box in Day view, which is above the date picker, only active tasks are displayed.

You can sort the list of tasks by any of the columns by tapping the column title. This way you can quickly view all the tasks of a specific project, all your high-priority tasks, and so on. Centered on the command bar at the top of the screen is a box that lets you select which tasks are displayed. You can display all tasks, all active tasks, all completed tasks, or all the tasks in any one project. An active task is a task with no starting date or due date or a task for which the starting date has been reached or passed.

Active tasks are always calculated relative to today's date. Unfortunately, in the Tasks program you cannot display which tasks will be active on some future date (to see what you need to be working on next week, for example). To do that, display all tasks and then sort by starting date, or use Agenda view of the Calendar to view the active tasks for a specific date.

Show Edit Panel

In the main view, you can tap the Show Edit Panel button to turn on Edit view. You tap the button again to turn Edit view off. Edit view gives you more information about the currently selected task in the list.

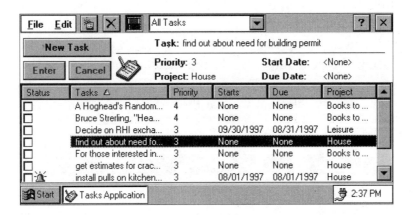

To open the Task dialog box for an existing task, double-tap the task.

Edit view also allows you to edit a task while viewing other tasks in the list. Edit view is for quick entry of the most common properties of a task, so you cannot edit every task property here. Instead, use the Task dialog box where you have access to all the properties of the task.

From within Edit view, you can easily create a new one-time task (but not a recurring task). To do this, tap the New Task button. The cursor is placed in the Task field, and you can immediately start typing a description of the new task. You can press the TAB key to move quickly from field to field. You can create a new project by typing its name in the Project field; if you press the TAB key without typing anything, the task is created without being assigned to a project. When you have filled in the fields you want, press the ENTER key to record the new task.

Creating Recurring Tasks

When you have a task that repeats regularly, it makes sense to set it up as a recurring task. You can create recurring tasks that repeat on a daily, weekly, monthly, or yearly basis. The number of times the task is to repeat can be specified as a range of dates or as a specific number of times. If you want to be reminded of each occurrence of the task, you can specify that as well.

New Task

Recurring tasks are a little tricky, so let's walk through setting one up. Suppose you need to produce a weekly progress report every Friday. Tap the New Task button in the main view, and then fill in the task information. In this example, for Task, enter *write progress report*, and leave the other fields as is. At this point, you have created a one-time task. To turn it into a recurring task, tap the Recur tab. Tap the Weekly button, as this task will repeat once a week, and then tap the Fri check box to set the task to recur every Friday. Tapping Friday does not clear any other days that were already selected, so clear them if needed. At this point, the screen should look like this:

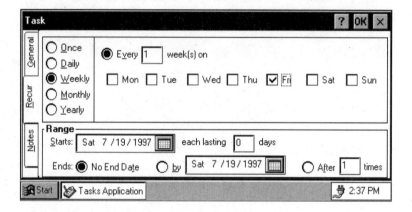

The Recur tab in Tasks is very similar to that in the Calendar. In fact, the settings for daily, weekly, monthly, or yearly recurrence are exactly the same as in the Calendar. The only thing different here is the Range section. Here you set the range of dates within which the task is to be repeated. By default, the starting date is set to the starting date you entered on the General tab, or if you did not enter a starting date there, it is set to today's date. In the previous illustration, today's date is July 19, which is a Saturday. Since the task starts on a Friday, it will begin on the following Friday, July 25. If you're setting up a task that does not start until some time in the future, set that starting date here. Otherwise, you can just leave the date as is.

As for the end of this recurring task, you have three choices. First, you can specify no ending date (your work is never done). Second, you can specify a particular ending date. For example, you might choose this if you are setting up a task to work every week on an upcoming presentation; you would set the ending date to be the date of the presentation. The third choice is to specify the number of times the task repeats. For this example, don't set an ending date, as you need to prepare that progress report for the foreseeable future. Now tap the General tab to verify the reminder settings.

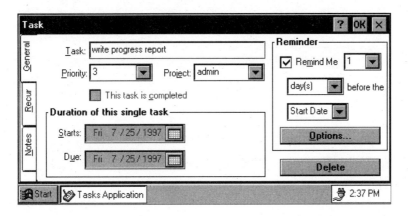

If you look at the Reminder area at the right side of the screen, you will see that you will be reminded 0 days before the start of the task, which means that this reminder will be delivered at 8:00 A.M. on the day of the task. So each Friday morning, your Handheld PC will alert you to work on your progress report. If you prefer to be notified the day before—Thursday in this example—set the reminder to occur one day before the starting date of the task.

Pretty simple, right? Unfortunately, there are some "gotchas." In this example, each Friday when you complete your progress report, you must mark this task completed. (To mark a task completed, select the This Task Is Completed check box in the Task dialog box or select the Status check box to the left of the task description in the main view.) Only then will the reminder for the following week's occurrence of the task be activated. If you don't mark the task completed, you will not be notified again. When you mark the task completed, it is displayed as a new, separate task, so you'll see two tasks in the main view: the just completed task and the next occurrence of the task.

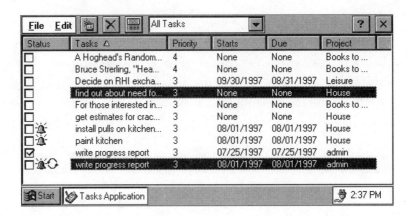

Status	Tasks △	Priority	Starts	Due	Project
☐	A Hoghead's Random...	4	None	None	Books to ...
☐	Bruce Strerling, "Hea...	4	None	None	Books to ...
☐	Decide on RHI excha...	3	09/30/1997	08/31/1997	Leisure
☐	find out about need fo...	3	None	None	House
☐	For those interested in...	3	None	None	Books to ...
☐	get estimates for crac...	3	None	None	House
☐	install pulls on kitchen...	3	08/01/1997	08/01/1997	House
☐	paint kitchen	3	08/01/1997	08/01/1997	House
☑	write progress report	3	07/25/1997	07/25/1997	admin
☐	write progress report	3	08/01/1997	08/01/1997	admin

There are other difficulties with recurring tasks if you synchronize your Handheld PC with Schedule+ or Outlook on your desktop PC, but I'll defer that bad news until Chapter 6.

Deleting Tasks

Delete

You delete a task the same way you delete an appointment in the Calendar. In the main view or in Edit view, you select the task, and then you press SHIFT+BACKSPACE or tap the Delete button. When you are in the Task dialog box, you can tap the Delete button in the lower right corner to delete the task. To delete all completed tasks, tap the Edit menu and then tap the Delete Completed Tasks command. Whichever way you do it, a dialog box appears to confirm your action because once you delete a task, it is gone, both on the Handheld PC and on your desktop PC when you next synchronize them. If you delete a recurring task, you will be prompted as to whether you want to delete a single instance of it or all instances.

Using Microsoft Pocket Excel and Microsoft Pocket Word

Pocket Excel and Pocket Word are built into Windows CE. They are designed to provide you with the spreadsheet and word processor features that are most useful when you're away from your desktop PC. In this chapter I assume that you have used Microsoft Excel (and Microsoft Word) on your desktop PC or are at least familiar with basic spreadsheet and word processor concepts.

Pocket Excel

Think of Pocket Excel as the essence of Microsoft Excel. It provides you with the key features of Excel so that you can have access to workbooks while you're on the go. Yes, there are some features you will miss; I miss the charting capabilities in particular. The developers who created Pocket Excel had to make some difficult choices: if they included all of Excel in Windows CE, your Handheld PC would no longer fit in your pocket. The Windows CE development team derived Pocket Excel's features by studying data about Excel's most commonly used features and commands. All of Excel's features were evaluated in terms of their usage frequency and their expected usefulness on a handheld device.

Early users of Pocket Excel reported that it is really useful to be able to download workbooks to their Handheld PCs for reference during meetings. These workbooks might be departmental budgets, schedules, sales reports, inventory lists, or employee salary numbers. The early users didn't always modify the workbooks using their Handheld PCs, but just having the information for reference purposes proved to be extremely valuable.

Pocket Excel uses a different file format than Excel does. This is because Pocket Excel does not include all the features of Excel, and the designers of Windows CE did not want to waste storage space on large workbook files full of data you could not use. So when you move files between your desktop PC and your Handheld PC via H/PC Explorer, a data conversion must take place. Because Pocket Excel is a subset of Excel, when you convert a file from Excel workbook format (.xls) to Pocket Excel format (.pxl) some data can be lost. This conversion process is covered in detail in Chapter 6.

N **OTE** Excel 97 uses a new file format but retains the same filename extension—.xls. H/PC Explorer version 1.0 cannot convert this new format. However, version 1.1 of H/PC Explorer can convert Excel 97 workbooks. If your Handheld PC came with version 1.0, you can get version 1.1 for free from the Internet. It is available from the Windows CE Web site (http://www. microsoft. com/windowsce). See Chapter 6 for more information about H/PC Explorer and converting files.

How do you print your Pocket Excel workbooks? You don't—at least not directly. Since Windows CE does not support printing, the only way to print a workbook is to transfer it back to your desktop PC, where it is automatically converted to Excel workbook format. Then you can use Excel to apply any additional formatting you might want and to print the workbook. This process isn't elegant, but it gets the job done, and it's not really that clumsy once you've done it a couple of times.

Pocket Excel does not support templates, but you can work around this as well. On your H/PC, create a workbook that contains all the formatting you want. For example, you might set the font, number formats, and column widths. Don't put any data in the workbook; leave it blank. Then save this file, perhaps giving it a name like Expense Report Template. Now when you want to create a workbook that has this format, open up the "template" and immediately save it with a new name.

You start Pocket Excel by double-tapping its icon on the Windows CE desktop. Pocket Excel opens, displaying a new, blank workbook. Your screen will look like this:

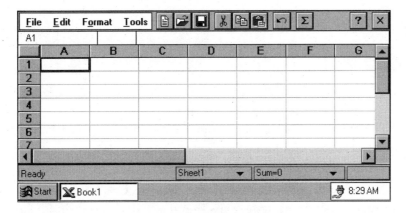

Pocket Excel comes with several sample workbooks. The easiest way to become familiar with the program is to open up one of the sample workbooks and use it to explore. Tap the Open command on the File menu to display the Open dialog box. Select the Amortize workbook, and tap the OK button.

If you tap cell B4 and then tap the cell's value at the top of the screen (which opens the cell for editing), your screen should look like the figure on the next page.

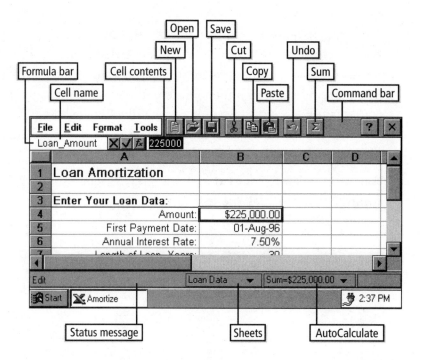

The command bar at the top of the screen contains 10 buttons. Starting from the left, the first three buttons are New, Open, and Save. Not surprisingly, these buttons create a new workbook, bring up the Open dialog box, and save the current workbook. The next three buttons are the familiar Cut, Copy, and Paste buttons that move data between Pocket Excel and the clipboard. The next button is Undo. It lets you take back the last change you made to the workbook. To its right is the AutoSum button, which automatically sums a range of cells. The rightmost two buttons are the usual two, Help and Close. They work the same here as they do in all the other programs in Windows CE.

Navigating Workbooks

Because Windows CE does not have overlapping windows as Windows 95 does, Pocket Excel handles multiple workbooks differently than Excel does. When you open a second workbook in Pocket Excel, you essentially open another instance of the Pocket Excel program, complete with a second button on the taskbar. This makes switching between the two workbooks very easy: just tap the appropriate taskbar button. There is no intrinsic limit to the number of workbooks you can have open; you can open as many as will fit into memory.

On a Handheld PC keyboard, ALT+UP ARROW and ALT+DOWN ARROW are the equivalent of PGUP and PGDN.

To move around in a worksheet, just tap the cell you want to go to. To select a range of cells, touch the stylus to one cell in the range and then slide the stylus across the screen to highlight the other cells you want. When you use Excel on your desktop PC, you might be used to pressing the PGUP and PGDN keys to scroll quickly through a large worksheet. In Pocket Excel this does not work as well for two reasons. First, because a Handheld PC screen is so much smaller than a desktop PC screen, each scroll does not move you as far through the worksheet. Second, Pocket Excel does not repaint the screen as fast. In fact, it is much slower. This is partly because the LCD display of your Handheld PC does not update as fast as the display of your desktop PC and partly because the Handheld PC's processor is slower.

The keyboard shortcut for the Go To command is CTRL+G.

Because of this, you will probably want to jump to a specific cell instead of scrolling. One method is to use the Go To command on the Tools menu. This pops up a dialog box into which you can type a cell reference or name, and Pocket Excel will immediately jump there. The other method is to tap the cell name area at the left of the formula bar and then type the cell reference or name to which you want to go. Because you can go to a name, you might want to use names in your workbooks more frequently than usual just to facilitate navigation.

To move to another worksheet in the workbook, tap the sheets area on the status bar. It displays the name of the current sheet until you tap it, at which point a pop-up list of all the sheets appears.

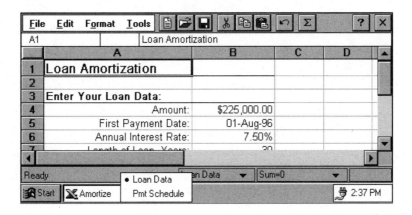

Tap the name of the sheet you want to make the current sheet.

Entering Data into a Workbook

Another way to get data into a workbook is to use the Fill command on the Edit menu. This is described in "Menu Commands," later in this chapter.

Two kinds of data can be placed in a cell: constant values and formulas. A constant value is simply text or numbers. A formula, on the other hand, is a sequence of values, cell references, names, functions, and operators—or some combination of these—that is evaluated to produce a value. When you enter a value into a cell, Pocket Excel applies different default formatting depending on what you type. If your entry is recognized as a date, time, currency value, or percentage, the appropriate formatting is applied. You can alter the formatting for the cell as you wish, and of course, there are other formats you can apply to cells. The formats available for constant values and the particulars of entering formulas are discussed in more detail in the next few sections.

A major difference between Pocket Excel and Excel on your desktop PC is that the latter features in-cell editing. That is, when you start typing a value into a cell, it is displayed directly in the cell. The same is true when you edit an existing value. In contrast, Pocket Excel displays new values as you enter them in the Formula Bar (the editing area above the grid). Only when you complete the entry is the value displayed in the cell. The same is true when you edit a cell. Select the cell to edit, and then tap the Formula Bar editing area or press CTRL+E. Edit the cell contents, and when you are finished, press the ENTER key or tap the ENTER button to accept the new value, or press the ESC key or tap the CANCEL button to cancel.

Text

A text value can be up to 255 characters long. By default, it is aligned to the left of the cell. Sometimes you might want a number to be treated as text. If you just enter it normally, it will be treated as a number, subject to the formatting defaults for numbers. If you prefix the number with a single quote ('), it will be treated as text.

Numbers

A numeric value can be entered as a decimal number or in scientific notation (for example, *1.23e5*). By default, it is aligned to the right of the cell. Numeric values are stored with 14 digits of precision internally, regardless of how many digits are displayed in the cell. If you enter a number that includes a space or a comma (for example, 123,456) the number will be treated as text; if you follow a number with spaces they are ignored. By default, a negative number is displayed with a leading minus sign, although you can enter a negative number either prefixed by a minus sign or enclosed in parentheses.

Dates and times

A cell can display a date, a time, or both. Actually, the cell always contains a date and a time, but you can choose whether to display both. Open the Format menu, and tap the Cells command. In the Format Cells dialog box, select either the Date category or the Time category. Then choose how you want the contents of the cell to be displayed by tapping the appropriate format in the Type box. Both the Date category and the Time category offer a format that displays the date and the time.

Regardless of how you choose to display a date in a cell, you can enter the date in any of the formats in which Pocket Excel can display dates. For example, you can separate the month, day, and year from each other with slashes (/) or hyphens (-). You can specify the month by using a number, by using the three-letter abbreviation, or by fully spelling it out. Pocket Excel supports dates from 1900 through 2078.

The range of dates supported by Pocket Excel is different from that supported by the Calendar and Tasks programs.

To enter a time, use any of the formats in which Pocket Excel can display time. You can enter *3:00 PM* or *15:00,* for example. If you enter a time without the trailing *AM* or *PM*, Pocket Excel treats the time as on a 24-hour clock. You can enter a date and a time in the same cell by separating them with a space.

 OTE   In comparison to Excel, there are some minor inconsistencies in the way Pocket Excel formats dates and times when you enter them into a cell not specifically formatted to display date and times. Always format cells that will contain dates or times to display them the way you want, and you won't have problems.

Currency

If you enter a number prefixed by the currency symbol ($), the cell is formatted to display currency values. The default number of digits displayed after the decimal point is 2, and the maximum that can be displayed is 15. If you enter more digits after the decimal point than the cell is formatted to display, the number displayed is rounded appropriately. By default, a negative currency value is displayed enclosed in parentheses, although you can enter a negative currency value either prefixed by a minus sign or enclosed in parentheses. Like numbers, currency values are right-aligned in the cells, although a space is added after positive numbers so that they will line up with negative numbers that are enclosed in parentheses.

Percentages

If you enter a number followed by the percent sign (%), the cell is formatted to display a percentage. If you want to enter the value as a decimal number (such as .05 instead of 5%), you must manually format the cell to display a percentage, either before or after you enter the value.

Formulas

I don't cover all the rules for formulas in this book. If you need more information, refer to one of the many books available about Excel.

Formulas in Pocket Excel work just like those in Excel. Formulas begin with an equal sign, a plus sign, or a minus sign. (The equal sign is the Excel standard; the other two are supported for compatibility with other spreadsheets.) You can use any of the following elements in a formula: values, operators, cell references, Pocket Excel functions, and names. Values are just numbers or text, and names will be covered in "Tools menu commands," later in this chapter.

Operators   There are three types of operators.

- Arithmetic operators (+, -, /, *, %, ^) perform basic mathematical operations on numeric values.

- Comparative operators (=, >, <, >=, <=, <>) compare two values and produce the logical value of TRUE or FALSE.

- The text operator (&) joins two or more text values into a single combined text value.

Cell references   There are also three types of cell references.

- Relative references (A5, B3) are always relative to the cell containing the formula. For example, say that cell H12 contains a formula with a reference to G9, which is three cells up and one cell to the left of H12. If the formula is copied to F20, the reference in the copy of the formula changes to E17, which is three cells up and one cell to the left of F20.

- Absolute references ($A$5, $B$3) are fixed and always refer to the same cell even if the cell containing the reference is copied.

- Mixed references are a combination of the two ($A5, B$3).

References to other sheets in the same workbook are always absolute, although references to a cell or cells in another sheet can be relative. Cross-sheet references are made up of the sheet name, an exclamation point, and the cell reference in that sheet (Sheet2!A5). If the sheet name contains spaces, enclose it in single quotation marks ('July Sales'!$A$3). Unlike Excel, Pocket Excel does not support references to other workbooks.

The range operator (:) and the union operator (,) assist in creating references to multiple cells. You use the range operator to refer to a contiguous range of cells (Sheet1:Sheet3!A1:B3), and you use the union operator to refer to noncontiguous cells (Sheet1!A1,Sheet3!A1,B1:B3).

You can enter a reference in a formula by typing it or by selecting the cell or range directly in the worksheet. You can make a selection in a formula only when it is appropriate to do so. As you make the selection (by sliding the stylus or using the arrow keys) it is outlined with a dotted border, and the reference to the cell or range appears in the formula. You can directly select only cells that are in the same worksheet as the formula.

Functions   The built-in functions in Pocket Excel perform standard worksheet calculations. The values on which a function performs calculations are called arguments. The value that the function returns can be displayed in the cell or can be used as an argument to another function in the same formula.

All functions begin with the function name followed by an open parenthesis, and they end with a close parenthesis. The arguments go inside the parentheses—for example, SUM(A1:A10). You must include both parentheses, with no spaces before or after them. Arguments can be numbers, text, logical values, arrays, error values, or references. The arguments you designate must produce a valid value as called for by the function. Arguments can also be formulas, and the formulas can contain other functions. When an argument to a function is itself a function, it is said to be nested. You can create very complex formulas in Pocket Excel. Depending on the functions used, you can nest them to around 30 levels. If the formula is too long, or if you nest functions too deeply, an error message indicating that the formula is too complex is displayed.

NOTE   You can use 3-D references—which include a cell or range of cells on more than one worksheet, such as Sheet2:Sheet4!A1:E3—with only certain functions (AND, AVERAGE, COUNT, COUNTA, MAX, MIN, PRODUCT, STDEV, STDEVP, SUM, VAR, and VARP).

Functions are described in more detail in "Tools menu commands," later in this chapter. All the Pocket Excel functions are summarized in the online Help for Pocket Excel.

Menu Commands

In this section I'll discuss the Pocket Excel commands available on each of the menus. Most of the commands have keyboard shortcuts as well. All the commands are also in Excel. In Pocket Excel, they might be subsets of the commands available in Excel, or they might have been relocated to a different menu for space or usability considerations.

File menu

The Open command (which has the keyboard shortcut CTRL+O) brings up the Open dialog box so that you can open a workbook. The New command (CTRL+N) opens a new, blank workbook, and the Save command (CTRL+S) saves the current workbook to storage memory. If you have just created a new workbook, made some changes, and then tapped Save, this command will work as if you had tapped Save As, because you have not yet given your new workbook a name. The Save As command opens a dialog box that lets you save the current workbook with a name you specify. You can also browse through your files and folders and create a new folder in which to save your new workbook.

If you have more than one workbook open in Pocket Excel, you can cycle through them by pressing CTRL+< or CTRL+>.

Toward the bottom of the File menu, Pocket Excel displays the names of the last three workbooks you opened, because the workbook you are most likely to open next is the last one you worked on. Tap a workbook name to open it. Finally, Close closes the current workbook. If you have made changes since you last saved the workbook, you will be prompted as to whether you want to abandon those changes before closing the workbook.

When you close the last open workbook, Pocket Excel closes as well. Unlike Excel, Pocket Excel cannot be open without an open workbook.

Edit menu

Pocket Excel provides the standard workbook editing features found in Excel. You can cut, copy, paste, and clear one or more cells, columns, or rows. Also, you can undo, redo, and repeat specific actions, and find and replace text in a worksheet. You can also cut, copy, and paste text to and from the cell name area and the cell value area on the formula bar. As always, the Cut, Copy, and Paste commands store the information being moved on the clipboard, which means it is accessible to other programs. Because of this it is very simple to do some calculations in Pocket Excel, copy them to the clipboard, and then go to Pocket Word and paste the results into a report.

Paste Special   When you paste a cell or range of cells in Pocket Excel, you paste all the cells' attributes, including formulas, values, formats, and borders. Sometimes this is not what you want—you might not want the borders, for example. In this case, use Paste Special instead of Paste.

In the Paste Special dialog box, you can control what is pasted. The All option gives you the same result as the regular Paste command. Formulas pastes only the formulas from the source, with relative references updated for the new location. Values pastes just the displayed values, not any formulas behind them. Formats pastes only the cell formats, not their contents. All Except Borders does what you'd expect: it pastes the cell formulas, values, and formats but not their borders.

Clear   The Clear command lets you clear one or more cells, rows, or columns.

*Pressing SHIFT +
BACKSPACE is the
same as selecting
Clear Contents.*

You can clear either the formats or the contents, or by default, both.

Fill   The Fill command lets you fill a range of cells with a copy of the contents of the first cell in the range or with a series of values.

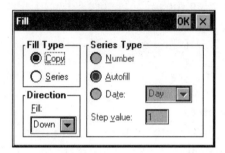

To fill a range of cells, select the range and then tap the Fill command. If you want to copy the contents of the first cell to the other cells within the range, leave Fill Type set to Copy, choose the direction of the fill, and then tap the OK button. To fill more than one column or row, you'll need to do this twice; once filling up or down and the second time filling left or right.

If you want to create a series, set Fill Type to Series, choose the direction of the fill, and then choose the type of series you want. A Number series starts with the number in the first or last cell (depending on the direction you chose) and fills the range with numbers incremented by the specified step value. The starting cell must have a number in it for this type of fill to work. For an Autofill series, the starting cell can contain a day of the week, a month of the year, or any text followed by a number, as in *Chapter 1*. There is no step value, as Pocket Excel can figure out what the rest of the entries should be based on what's in the initial cell. A Date series starts with the date in the starting cell of the range, and you can choose to have the day, month, or year of that date incremented by the specified step value.

The keyboard shortcut for the Find/Replace command is CTRL+F.

Find and Replace The Find/Replace command lets you search for text on the current sheet, and if you want to, replace it with other text.

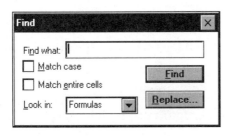

The keyboard shortcut for the Find Next command is CTRL+4.

In the dialog box, simply type the text you want to find. You can choose whether case is important, whether the entire cell must exactly match the text you're searching for, and whether to look in formulas or in the displayed values of cells. Then tap the Find button to begin the search. Pocket Excel conducts the search by rows, starting from the active cell. If you want to continue the search after finding the first occurrence, tap the Find Next command on the Edit menu.

If you want to replace some text with other text, use the Replace dialog box.

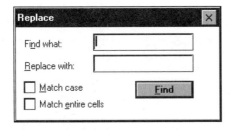

You can open it by tapping the Replace button in the Find dialog box, or you can open it directly by pressing CTRL+H. Text can be replaced only in formulas, so there is no Look In option in this dialog box. After the first occurrence of the text is found, a smaller dialog box appears that gives you three options. You can continue the search without replacing the found text, you can replace the found text with the specified text, or you can replace all occurrences of the text in the worksheet. You can, of course, abandon further searching by pressing the ESC key or tapping the Close button.

Format menu

The Format menu commands give you control over the shape and appearance of a worksheet.

The keyboard shortcut for the Format Cells command is CTRL+1.

Cells   The most frequently used command on the Format menu is the Cells command. Before tapping the command select the cell or cells you want to format. Pocket Excel performs best if you select a specific range of cells instead of an entire row, column, or sheet.

The Format Cells dialog box has four tabs, which allow you to specify how numbers are displayed, how values are aligned in the cells, in what font the values are displayed, and how the cell borders should be drawn.

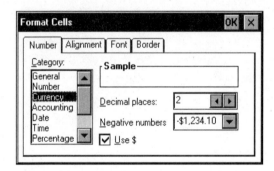

The Number tab has 10 categories of number formats. For each category you can specify different options; take some time to try each of them so that you know what is possible. The Sample field shows the results of the options you select so that you can preview them before making your final choice.

The Alignment tab controls how values are aligned within the cells, both horizontally and vertically.

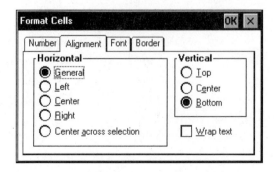

You won't notice changes in the vertical alignment unless you increase the height of the row. A nice feature is the capability to center text across several cells, which is useful for titles and column headings. You can also specify whether text that is too long to be displayed in full in a cell should be wrapped to multiple lines within the cell. You won't be able to see this change unless you increase the row height sufficiently.

It is easy to down-load additional fonts from your desktop PC to your Handheld PC; that is covered in Chapter 6.

The use of the Font tab is pretty self-evident. You can select from the available fonts, sizes, and styles, and you can preview the results of your selection in the Sample area before confirming it with the OK button.

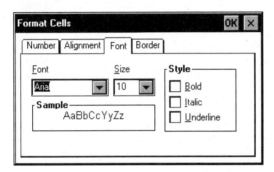

Finally, the Border tab lets you specify that a black border completely outline each cell in the selection or just be placed on one side of each cell.

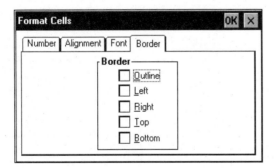

For example, this is the way to have a horizontal line drawn at the bottom of a column of numbers, separating them from the total below. Simply place a border on the bottom of the last cell in the column. By selecting different cells and specifying the appropriate border, you can easily emphasize different areas of your worksheet.

Row Height and Column Width   The Row Height and Column Width commands let you specify the height of the selected rows or the width of the selected columns. You can also hide the rows or columns.

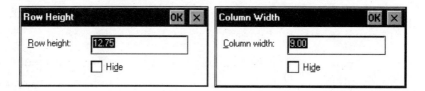

Insert   The Insert command lets you insert one or more new cells, rows, or columns into the worksheet.

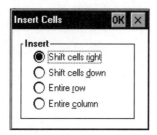

If you want to insert cells (but not an entire row or column), select the cells where you want new ones to be inserted, and then tap the Insert command. In the Insert Cells dialog box that appears, choose whether to shift the displaced cells down or to the right, and then tap the OK button.

TIP   Don't forget Undo on the Edit menu (or its keyboard shortcut, CTRL+Z). If you insert some cells, rows, or columns and the operation does not turn out the way you wanted, just undo it. Of course, Undo also applies to any operation you perform on your workbook. And don't forget Redo, which undoes what Undo did.

If you want to insert a row or column (or multiple rows or columns), you have two options. The easiest method is to select the rows or columns where you want new ones to be inserted, and then tap the Insert command. The new rows or columns are automatically inserted above or to the left of the selection. You can also use the Insert Cells dialog box to insert a single row or column, which will be inserted above or to the left of the selected cells.

Any references within shifted cells, rows, or columns are updated to point to the same place they pointed to before the insertion.

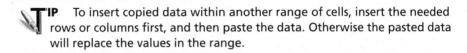

TIP To insert copied data within another range of cells, insert the needed rows or columns first, and then paste the data. Otherwise the pasted data will replace the values in the range.

Delete   The Delete command works much the same way as the Insert command.

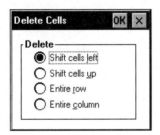

In the Delete Cells dialog box, you choose which cells are to move into the space formed by the deleted cells. Either the cells to the right of the deleted cells move to the left, or the cells below the deleted cells move up. Or you can specify that the cells you have selected represent an entire row or column to be deleted.

If you select rows or columns, they are automatically deleted when you tap the Delete command.

Tools menu

The Tools menu contains the Go To, Insert Function, Define Name, and Modify Sheets commands. The Go To command was described in the "Navigating Workbooks" section, earlier in this chapter.

Insert Function   Because it would be difficult to remember all the functions in Pocket Excel, the Insert Function command is provided to help you quickly enter the function you need.

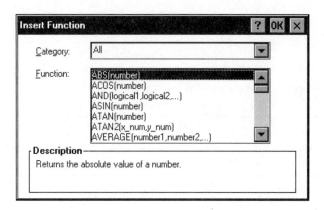

Insert Function

You can open the Insert Function dialog box by tapping Insert Function on the Tools menu or by tapping the Insert Function button on the formula bar when you are editing a cell. The Category box lets you choose to view just the functions from one category or all the functions. You can then scroll through the function list and pick the one you want. When you have selected a function, tap the OK button or press the ENTER key. The function is placed into the editing area of the formula bar, where you can replace the prototype arguments with real ones.

If you press the ? button, Help for the currently selected function appears. This is useful if you are not sure what the arguments to the function are. In Help, you can scroll to view information about any of the functions, in case the one you started with proves not to be the one you need.

Define Name   The Define Name command allows you to apply a name to a cell or range of cells. You can use this name in formulas or with the Go To command when navigating through the worksheet.

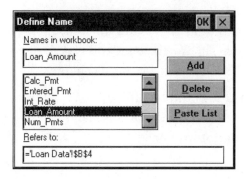

You can apply names to 3-D cell ranges as well. For example, the name Annual_Revenue could be defined as =Sheet1:Sheet4!C5, where C5 contains the quarterly revenue on Sheet1 through Sheet4. You can use names that refer to 3-D ranges with only certain functions (AND, AVERAGE, COUNT, COUNTA, MAX, MIN, PRODUCT, STDEV, STDEVP, SUM, VAR, and VARP).

A name cannot contain any spaces, and it can be no longer than 255 characters. The first character of the name must be a letter or an underline (_). Don't create names that look like cell references (A5 or R1C2, for example). You can use capitalization when creating a name, to make it more readable. When you reference the name later you don't have to match this capitalization; that is, a formula containing *total* will match the name *Total.*

The Add button adds a newly defined name to the list of names, and the Delete button removes the selected name. The Paste List button causes a list of the names and the contents of the cells to which they refer to be copied into the worksheet.

Calc_Pmt	='Loan Data'!$B$10	
Entered_Pmt	='Pmt Schedule'!$D$4	
Int_Rate	='Loan Data'!$B$6	
Loan_Amount	='Loan Data'!$B$4	
Num_Pmts	='Loan Data'!$B$8	

The list is pasted starting at the current cell and overwriting any data in cells that get underfoot.

By default, the names you create can be accessed from any sheet in the workbook. If you want a name to be local to a specific sheet, when you define the name, prefix it with the sheet name (*Sheet3!GrandTotal,* for example). If you are on the specific sheet, you need enter only the name (*GrandTotal*); you don't need to include the sheet name. However, if you want to reference one of these local names from another sheet, you must enter the sheet name as well (*Sheet3!GrandTotal*).

Modify Sheets   The Modify Sheets command allows you to manipulate the worksheets that make up your workbook.

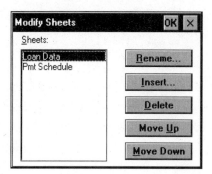

The names of the sheets currently in the workbook are displayed in the Modify Sheets dialog box. You can use the buttons to rename a sheet, insert a new sheet into the workbook, delete a sheet from the workbook, or change the order of the sheets by moving a selected sheet up (toward the front) or down (toward the back).

AutoSum and AutoCalculate

You will no doubt use the AutoSum and AutoCalculate features of Pocket Excel regularly. A study of Excel users has revealed that the SUM function is the most frequently used of all the worksheet functions. To make summing a range of numbers as convenient as possible, the Pocket Excel designers placed the AutoSum button on the command bar. Simply select a cell adjacent to the column or row you want to sum, and press the button. Pocket Excel tries to be smart about which cells should be summed, but if it does not guess correctly you can easily fix the range selection by sliding the stylus across the correct range of cells, starting with the cell that you want to contain the total.

When a range of cells is selected, the AutoCalculate feature displays the sum of those cells in the status bar. To use this feature, just look at the AutoCalculate area in the status bar; you don't have to type a function or formula. If you tap the AutoCalculate area, you can choose to have a calculation other than Sum applied to the selected range. The available calculations are Average, Count, Count Nums, Max, Min, and Sum. By default, Sum is the selected calculation. When you choose one of the other calculations, that remains the selection until you choose another.

> **UN**   Go to cell AA1000 and type *credits*. When you press the ENTER key, the names of the people who developed Pocket Excel are displayed. When you are done looking at the names, press ENTER to dismiss the dialog box.

Pocket Word

If you are familiar with WordPad, the modest word processor that comes with Windows 95, you can think of Pocket Word as WordPad plus outlining. If you have used WordPad, Word, or really any word processor for Windows, you'll be able to start using Pocket Word without any difficulty at all. You might want to simply skim this chapter for an overview of the features of Pocket Word and for any tips that might prove useful to you.

Pocket Word and your Handheld PC are not what you should use to write that 1000-page novel you've been meaning to get to. Instead, Pocket Word is designed to let you take notes, compose a memo, outline a paper, or get started writing a report, no matter where you are. Then when you return to your desk, you can easily transfer the documents to your desktop computer and complete them using Word.

The Windows CE designers envision three typical usage scenarios for Pocket Word:

- Creating and editing short, simple documents that reside primarily on your Handheld PC. These might be notes taken at meetings, ideas that you want to jot down, shopping lists, and so on. You would tend not to use these files on your desktop computer, except perhaps to print them.

- Beginning to write documents such as a trip reports, memos, or presentations while you are away from your desk. Then you would transfer the documents to your desktop computer to continue work on them, print them, or send them to colleagues.

- Downloading documents from your desktop computer for reference or review while you are away from your desk. Reference information such as contracts or schedules that you might need in a meeting can be more discreetly viewed on an Handheld PC than on a laptop computer. You probably would not modify these documents at all on your Handheld PC.

What the designers do not expect you to do is major editing of long or heavily formatted documents created on a desktop PC. The Handheld PC keyboard is just too small to spend much time typing on, so they expect this kind of serious document processing will continue to take place on your desktop or laptop computer.

Pocket Word does not support templates, but you can work around this. Create a document that contains all the formatting you want. Don't put any words in the document; leave it blank. Then save the file, perhaps giving it a name like Business Letter Template. Now when you want to create a document that has this format, open up the "template" and immediately save it with a new name.

Pocket Word can use files in two formats: Pocket Word Documents (.pwd) and Plain Text Documents (.txt). Files in Pocket Word format are automatically converted to and from Microsoft Word format (.doc) when you move them between your Handheld PC and your desktop computer by using H/PC Explorer. You'll learn how to do this in Chapter 6. Files in Plain Text format are processed directly by Pocket Word; no conversion is needed.

OTE Word 97 uses a new file format but retains the same filename extension—.doc. H/PC Explorer version 1.0 cannot convert this new format. However, version 1.1 of H/PC Explorer can convert Word 97 documents. You can get version 1.1 for free from the Windows CE Web site (http://www.microsoft.com/windowsce). See Chapter 6 for more information about H/PC Explorer and converting files.

When you start Pocket Word, it opens a new document.

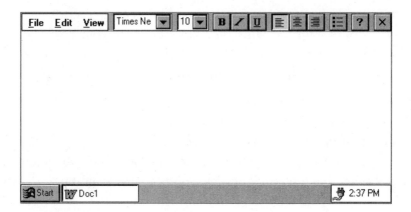

The keyboard shortcut for the Open command is CTRL+O.

If you're going to create a new document, just start typing, and then give the document a name when you save it. If you want to open an existing document, tap the Open command on the File menu. The Open dialog box appears.

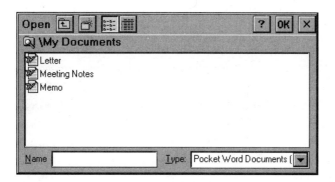

Up One Level

Here you can browse through the files and folders on your Handheld PC. Double-tap a folder in the dialog box to open it, or tap the Up One Level button to move "up" from a subfolder to the folder that contains that subfolder. The Type box in the lower right corner lets you choose to display just Pocket Word documents, just plain text documents, or all the files in the folder. Unfortunately, there is no way to display just the files that Pocket Word can handle—.pwd and .txt. (Typing *.* in the Name box displays all the files in the folder, only some of which Pocket Word can open.) When you find the file you want to open, double-tap it, or tap it and then tap the OK button.

You might have noticed that all of this works just as it does in Pocket Excel. The two programs were designed to handle files in the same way. In fact, their File menus are identical. Just as in Pocket Excel, the New command (CTRL+N) creates a new, empty document. The Open command, which was just described, opens an existing document. The Save command (CTRL+S) saves changes to the current document. The Save As command saves the current document with a new name. The Close command closes the current document, first prompting you to save unsaved changes if there are any. Toward the bottom of the File menu, the names of the last three documents you have opened are displayed. If you have more than one document open in Pocket Word, you can cycle through them by pressing CTRL+< or CTRL+>. And just like in Pocket Excel, when you close the last document, Pocket Word closes.

Command Bar

At the top of the screen is Pocket Word's command bar.

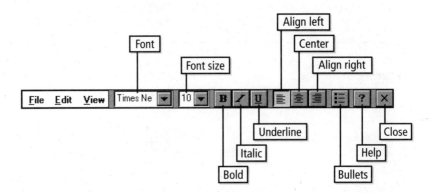

In Chapter 6 you'll learn how to download additional fonts to your Handheld PC from your desktop computer.

The buttons give you access to all Pocket Word's formatting capabilities; there is no Format menu. At the left are the font and font size boxes. You can use these to select which font you want to use and how large you want it to be. The next three buttons allow you to make text bold, italic, or underlined. You can select any combination of these formats. To the right of these buttons are the alignment buttons. You can use them to make the text left-aligned (the default), centered, or right-aligned. The next button lets you create bulleted lists. And of course, the rightmost two buttons are Help and Close.

Entering and Manipulating Text

Pocket Word works just like any other word processor. Enter your text, and use the arrow keys or the stylus to move around your document. To select text, slide the stylus across the characters, words, or paragraphs you want, to highlight them. The following table lists some methods for making selections.

To Select	Do This
One or more characters of text	Slide the stylus over the characters
A picture	Tap the picture
A word	Double-tap the word
A paragraph	Triple-tap anywhere within the paragraph
The entire document	Tap Select All on the Edit menu, or press CTRL+A

After you have selected a picture, some text, or the entire document you can do something with that selection. If you've selected text, you can tap one of the command bar buttons to alter its appearance. To alter the text alignment of a paragraph, just tap anywhere in the paragraph and tap the appropriate command bar button. The following table lists some other possibilities.

To	Do This
Copy a selection	Tap Copy on the Edit menu (or press CTRL+C), tap where you want the selection to go, and then tap Paste on the Edit menu (or press CTRL+V)
Remove a selection and place it on the clipboard	Tap Cut on the Edit menu (or press CTRL+X)
Delete a selection	Press the DELETE or BACKSPACE key
Move a selection	Tap Cut on the Edit menu (or press CTRL+X), tap where you want the selection to go, and then tap Paste on the Edit menu (or press CTRL+V)

Whenever you start a new paragraph (by pressing the ENTER key) that paragraph inherits the formatting characteristics of the previous paragraph. For example, if you want to create a bulleted list, press ENTER to create the first paragraph of the bulleted list, and then tap the Bullets button to format it. Now just enter your text, pressing ENTER between paragraphs in the list. Each new paragraph you create will have the bulleted list format. Press the ENTER key once more after the last paragraph in the list. Tap the Bullets button again, and this new paragraph returns to normal formatting.

If you make a mistake, tap the Undo command on the Edit menu or press CTRL+Z. Only the last change you made to the document can be undone. If you change your mind and want to undo the undo, tap the Redo item on the Edit menu (located where Undo was) or press CTRL+Z again.

Finding and Replacing Text

The Find command and the Replace command on the Edit menu let you quickly search for text in your document and replace it with other text if you want. Unlike Word, Pocket Word always searches the entire document for the specified text, beginning from the location of the insertion point.

The keyboard shortcut for the Find command is CTRL+F.

Searching for text is quite simple. On the Edit menu tap the Find command. The Find dialog box appears.

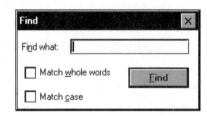

The keyboard shortcut for the Find Next command is CTRL+4.

Enter the text you want to find, and choose whether you want to search for only whole words (searching for *the* will not find *theme*) and whether you want to search for a word whose case matches that of the word you enter (searching for *the* will not find *The*). Tap the Find button or press the ENTER key, and the search begins. If the text is found, it is selected, and the search ends. If not, a message is displayed, and the Find dialog box remains on screen so that you can modify your search. Of course, you can dismiss the dialog box by tapping the Close button or by pressing the ESC key. You can easily repeat the search to locate the next instance of the specified text by tapping the Find Next command on the Edit menu.

The keyboard shortcut for the Replace command is CTRL+H.

Replacing text is simple as well. Tap the Replace command on the Edit menu. This displays the Replace dialog box, which is the same as the Find dialog box plus an additional field.

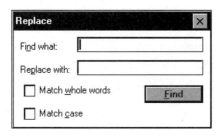

Here you enter the text you want to replace the found text. All the other fields are as described for the Find dialog box. After you have filled in the text you want to search for and the text you want to replace it with, tap the Find button or press the ENTER key. If the text is not found, a message is displayed, and you can try again or dismiss the dialog box. If the text is found, it is highlighted, and this dialog box is displayed:

Now you have four choices. You can tap the Find button to continue the search, leaving this found text unchanged. You can tap the Replace button to replace the found text with the new text you entered in the Replace dialog box. If you do this, Pocket Word highlights the next occurrence of the found text. You can tap the Replace All button to replace all occurrences of the specified text, in the entire document, with the new text. Finally, you can tap the Close button at any time to dismiss the dialog box and abandon the search.

Formatting Your Document

I can already hear you asking, "What happened to justified text? And numbered lists? And paragraph indenting? And…"

Well, Pocket Word is not Word. Your Handheld PC is the place to capture your ideas, take notes, or refine your thoughts. It is not the place to polish the formatting of a 50-page document. So think content, not format, and you'll find Pocket Word a useful tool. Thus there is no Format menu in Pocket Word.

There is also no horizontal ruler in Pocket Word, so you can't set margins or tabs. The tabs are fixed at half-inch intervals. However, if you set custom tabs in a Word document on your desktop computer, those settings are preserved when you transfer the document to your Handheld PC by using H/PC Explorer.

You can play a similar trick with paragraph indentations. Set the paragraph indentations the way you want in a Word document on your desktop computer, and then transfer that document to your Handheld PC. Now you can copy the paragraph that has the desired formatting and paste it into your Pocket Word document. When you select the text of the paragraph and replace it by typing new text, the formatting is retained. This is a little clumsy, but it gets the job done.

Pocket Word does not support automatic spacing between paragraphs, nor any page layout formatting. See Chapter 6 for information about which formatting information is retained when you move between Pocket Word and Word on your desktop PC.

It is very easy to download fonts from your desktop computer to your Handheld PC; this is covered in Chapter 6.

Windows CE comes with several fonts built in. These include Arial, Courier New, MS Sans Serif, and Times New Roman. These fonts were chosen because they are the fonts in Windows 95 that are used most frequently. If you transfer a document to your Handheld PC, and if that document contains a font that is not on your Handheld PC, Pocket Word uses the font closest in size and style to display the document. Any new text you enter is displayed in this substitute font. When you transfer the document back to your desktop computer by using H/PC Explorer, the original font is used to display both the original text and the new text.

The keyboard shortcut for the Select All command is CTRL+A.

The default font for a new Pocket Word document is 10-point Times New Roman. To choose a new default font for a document, select the first blank paragraph in the document by tapping the Select All command on the Edit menu. Then select a font name and size from the appropriate boxes on the toolbar. This font and size will now be the default for the document.

Downloading documents to your Handheld PC is covered in Chapter 6.

Although Pocket Word is fairly limited in terms of the formatting it supports, there are some easy ways you can work around these limitations to get the results you are after. If you put symbols and formats into a Word document and then download that document to your Handheld PC, you can copy them to new Pocket Word documents. For example, you could copy the copyright and trademark symbols and a certain paragraph indentation. You might want to create a special document containing paragraph formatting or symbols you often use and download it to your Handheld PC just for this purpose. If the symbols you want to use this way are in a specific font (such as Symbol or Wingdings), you must have that font on your H/PC for this to work.

The formatting for a paragraph is contained in its paragraph mark, which is an invisible character just after the last character of the paragraph. To start a new paragraph with the same formatting as an existing paragraph, select and copy the paragraph mark to the clipboard. Then paste the paragraph mark where you want to start the new paragraph, and begin typing. You can use this method to copy paragraph formatting within a Pocket Word document or from one Pocket Word document to another. The easiest way to select a paragraph mark is to position the insertion point at the end of the paragraph and press SHIFT+RIGHT ARROW.

Outline View

I use Outline view all the time for taking notes in meetings and for starting memos and reports. Then I upload the outlines to my desktop PC, where I use Word to flesh them out. Outline view is also useful if you have downloaded a large document to your Handheld PC and you need to use just a specific section of it. You can display the document in Outline view and then open up just the section you want to read. If you have used Outline view in Word, you're ready to go: Pocket Word works just the same.

To switch to Outline view, tap Outline on the View menu. Your screen will look something like this:

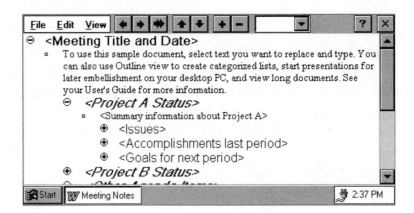

To return to Normal view, tap Normal on the View menu. The indentations and symbols used in Outline view are not part of your document and do not affect the way it looks back in Normal view. You can use Outline view with an existing document or when creating a new document.

In the previous illustration, "Meeting Title and Date" and "Project A Status" are headings that have their content expanded; hence they begin with a minus symbol. If you double-tap that symbol, the heading will "collapse" and all of its contents will be hidden. The headings "Issues," "Accomplishments last period," and "Goals for next period" are all collapsed headings. You double-tap the plus symbol to expand their content. The other lines of the outline are paragraphs in the body content style. The paragraph immediately under the top header is an example of this.

In Outline view the command bar changes, and a set of buttons different from those in Normal view appears. The File, Edit, and View menus are unchanged.

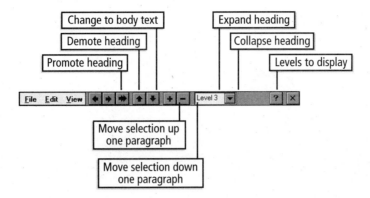

The buttons act on the current selection, or if no text is selected, they act on the paragraph containing the insertion point. The leftmost button promotes a heading one level. If the selected text is body text, it is promoted to a heading. The next button demotes a heading one level. You can repeatedly tap these two buttons to easily alter the level of any of the headings in your document. The third button changes a heading to body text. This is useful when you want to enlarge a heading with more text: you change it to body text, and then you can easily add additional paragraphs by just pressing the ENTER key.

The next two buttons move the current selection up or down one paragraph. With these buttons you can easily reorder your outline as needed. I find using these buttons quicker than using the Cut and Paste commands on the Edit menu (although Cut and Paste are still available).

The next two buttons control how much of your outline is displayed. You can expand a heading to view all its subheadings and body text by tapping the heading and then tapping the + button. You can collapse a heading so that all its subheadings and body text are hidden by tapping it and then tapping the - button. As mentioned previously, you can also expand or collapse a heading by double-tapping the minus or plus symbol to the left of the heading.

Finally, the box to the right of the Outline view buttons lets you control how many levels of the outline are displayed. If you are viewing a large document and want to see just the top level headings, tap the down-arrow to open the list and then tap Level 1 or Level 2. To return to viewing the entire document outline, tap All Levels at the top of the list.

 TIP   Because the formatting buttons on the command bar in Normal view are absent in Outline view, use the keyboard shortcuts to apply formatting: CTRL+B for bold, CTRL+I for italic, CTRL+U for underline, CTRL+SHIFT+< to decrease the font size, and CTRL+SHIFT+> to increase the font size.

PART

2

Communications

Connecting to
Your Desktop PC

If you don't have a desktop PC, or if you don't plan ever to move data between your Handheld PC and a desktop PC and you don't expect ever to install additional programs on your Handheld PC, you can ignore this entire chapter. But I would argue that you would be missing out on the main point of Microsoft Windows CE, which is to allow your Handheld PC to be a companion to your desktop PC. By "companion" I mean that your Handheld PC becomes, in effect, an extension of your desktop PC and that you can easily move data between the two machines. For example, one of the key goals of Windows CE and the Handheld PC is to provide convenient access to your critical data when you are away from your desk. For many people, their critical data is located on their desktop PC.

H/PC Explorer runs on Windows 95 or Windows NT version 4.0; Windows 3.x is not supported.

It is H/PC Explorer and its synchronization capabilities that distinguish the Handheld PC from most electronic organizers and PDAs (Personal Digital Assistants). After H/PC Explorer is installed, keeping the appointments, contacts, and tasks on your Handheld PC in sync with those on your desktop computer is a "no-brainer" operation. H/PC Explorer keeps track of what has changed on each device and copies the necessary data between the two devices during the synchronization process.

Your Handheld PC can be the synchronization partner of a single desktop PC. So if you have two PCs—say, one at your office and one at home—you need to choose one of them with which to synchronize your Handheld PC. Your Handheld PC can exchange files with the other desktop machine as a "guest" partner.

H/PC Explorer manages several kinds of data transfer between your Handheld PC and your desktop PC:

- Synchronization of the appointments, contacts, and tasks on your Handheld PC with those in either Microsoft Schedule+ or Microsoft Outlook on your desktop PC. Schedule+ is part of the Microsoft Exchange electronic mail system; a copy of it is shipped with every Handheld PC. Outlook is part of Microsoft Office 97.

- Drag-and-drop file transfer and conversion of files between your Handheld PC and your desktop PC. This is how you move Microsoft Word and Microsoft Excel documents to and from your Handheld PC.

- Back up of the contents of your Handheld PC to a file on your desktop PC. This includes all changed files, the Calendar, Contacts, Inbox, and Tasks databases, Registry entries, and programs installed on your Handheld PC. If you ever lose or break your Handheld PC, you can restore the backed-up data from your desktop PC to a replacement Handheld PC and establish the new H/PC as the synchronization partner.

Versions of H/PC Explorer

The first wave of Handheld PCs shipped with version 1 of H/PC Explorer. In April 1997, version 1.1 was released. It added support for Microsoft Windows NT version 4.0 and synchronization support for Microsoft Outlook. It is version 1.1 that I am describing in this chapter. If you don't have that version, be sure to download it from the Windows CE Web site (http://www.microsoft.com/windowsce).

■ Installation of new programs on your Handheld PC. Although H/PC Explorer does not directly manage the installation process, you must install H/PC Explorer before you can install additional programs on your Handheld PC.

■ Transfer of e-mail messages between the Microsoft Exchange Inbox on your desktop PC and the Inbox on your Handheld PC. This is an optional feature of H/PC Explorer. It allows you to download messages from your Exchange Inbox to your Handheld PC, read them, reply to them, and compose new messages while away from your desk. When you return to your desk, you can transfer all the mail in your Handheld PC's Outbox to Exchange, where it is sent to its destination. This means that even if you don't have a modem for your Handheld PC, you can still work on your e-mail while away from your desk. I'll cover the Inbox Transfer feature, along with the rest of the Inbox, in Chapter 8.

Synchronization applies only to the programs in Windows CE that share data with Schedule+ or Outlook on your desktop computer: the Calendar, Contacts, and Tasks programs. Synchronization of these programs means that the same information is maintained on both your Handheld PC and your desktop PC. It's important to realize the implications of this: if you

What If You Don't Use Schedule+ or Outlook?

Perhaps you use a different Personal Information Manager (PIM) on your desktop PC—say, Lotus Organizer or Ecco. Although H/PC Explorer cannot perform synchronization between the Calendar, Contacts, and Tasks programs on your Handheld PC and your desktop PC PIM, other programs can do this. Desktop To Go, from DataViz, and IntelliSync, from Puma Technology, both provide synchronization solutions that support a variety of PIMs. Both of these programs are described in Appendix B. Even if you install one of these programs, you will want to use H/PC Explorer to transfer files and to back up data on your Handheld PC.

> ### Schedule+ Contacts List vs. Exchange Address Book
>
> One point of common confusion is the Contacts list in Schedule+ and the Personal Address Book in Exchange. The Contacts list is used to keep track of names, postal mailing addresses, and phone numbers, and the Personal Address Book is used to maintain your personal list of e-mail addresses. Unfortunately, the two are not connected, and Microsoft provides no way to move data between them. H/PC Explorer synchronizes the Windows CE Contacts data with the Schedule+ Contacts list, not with the Exchange Personal Address Book. This problem is cleared up in Outlook, as its Contacts list combines these two functions, and H/PC Explorer synchronizes with it. If you use Outlook, when you want to remember someone's e-mail address, create a new contact for that person. This way it will be synchronized to your Handheld PC. If you create a new Address Book entry in Outlook, it will not.

add a new contact on your Handheld PC, when you next synchronize it with your desktop PC, the new contact is copied there and appears in your Schedule+ or Outlook Contacts list. Likewise, if you delete an appointment on your H/PC when you next synchronize, that appointment is deleted from your desktop PC as well. The same is true in the reverse direction. Word and Excel files, files from other programs, and e-mail messages are not automatically synchronized between your Handheld PC and your desktop PC. You can, however, easily copy them back and forth, as will be seen in this chapter.

Before you can experience how easy it is to synchronize your data, you have to endure the process of...

Setting Up H/PC Explorer

Actually, it's not that bad. But I suggest sitting down with a cup of coffee to keep you company while you go through the process. To connect your Handheld PC to your desktop PC, you need a free serial port on your desktop PC. Look at the back of your machine; they are usually labeled.

Refer to the documentation for your computer if you have trouble locating one. Most every PC has one serial port, and some have two or even more.

The two devices most likely to be plugged into a serial port are a mouse or an external modem. If you have only one serial port and it is already in use by the mouse, you must either purchase a type of mouse that does not use a serial port or you must install a serial port expansion card to create a second serial port. If an external modem is connected to your only serial port, you can either install a serial port expansion card or you can manually plug and unplug the modem and the Handheld PC connector and switch back and forth between them. You can purchase a switch box and some cables to make this a little easier. If you install a new serial port, make sure it is working properly before installing H/PC Explorer, perhaps by connecting an external modem to it or by using it to transfer files to another desktop PC via a serial cable.

After you have located a serial port and, if necessary, freed it up, put the Windows CE CD-ROM in your desktop PC. The H/PC Explorer welcome screen should appear.

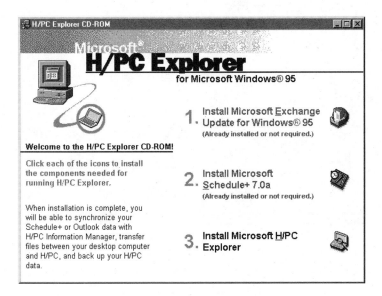

If this screen does not appear, click the Start button, click Run, and then type *d:setup*, where *d* is the letter of the CD-ROM drive that contains the H/PC Explorer CD-ROM.

TIP   If you don't have a CD-ROM drive, you can copy the H/PC Explorer installation files to floppy disks and install H/PC Explorer from them. You'll need to use a computer that does have a CD-ROM drive, of course. Instructions for doing this are in the Readme.txt file on the H/PC Explorer CD-ROM.

Follow the instructions on the welcome screen. As the screen states, there are three steps to installing H/PC Explorer. Depending on which programs you already have installed on your desktop PC, you might not need to install the Exchange update or Schedule+. For example, if you have Outlook already installed, Schedule+ will not be added to your PC. The installation program will determine just what is needed and will install the appropriate programs for your machine.

During the installation of H/PC Explorer, you can select which components you want to install.

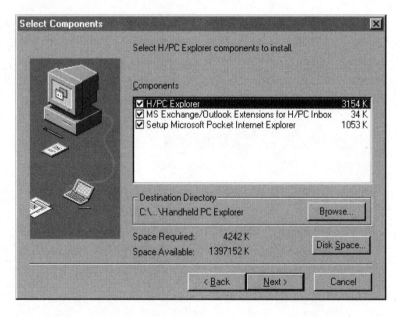

You must install H/PC Explorer because it is required if you want to connect your Handheld PC to your desktop PC. The second check box lets you choose whether to install the Exchange and Outlook extensions for the H/PC Inbox. If you use Exchange or Outlook to send and receive e-mail, you will definitely find this extension useful, since it allows you to easily move e-mail messages back and forth between your Handheld PC and your desktop PC. If you don't use Exchange or Outlook for e-mail, clear this check box. The third check box sets up Microsoft Pocket Internet Explorer. If you think you might connect to the Internet from your Handheld PC, select this option. You can always uninstall Pocket Internet Explorer later if you find you don't use it. If your Handheld PC has Pocket Internet Explorer already installed in ROM, you don't need to install it again.

During the installation of H/PC Explorer, the Windows 95 or Windows NT communications components it will be using are configured. If you are going to run into problems installing H/PC Explorer, this is probably when it will happen. H/PC Explorer uses the Dial-Up Networking and Direct Cable Connection facilities of Windows 95 to connect to the Handheld PC. If you have not used these features of Windows 95 before, they might not have been installed or they might not have been properly configured when they were installed. To complete the installation and configuration of the Windows 95 networking features, you might need your original Windows 95 CD-ROM or floppy disks.

TIP Be sure to select the option to place a shortcut to H/PC Explorer in your StartUp folder. You will almost always want to have H/PC Explorer running, and this ensures it is started each time you turn on your computer.

After H/PC Explorer has been installed, it starts automatically. You will then be asked to select the serial port to be used for communications between your desktop PC and your Handheld PC. You can choose any serial port on your PC as long as nothing is plugged into it, no internal device (such as a modem) is using it, and it is installed and enabled in Windows 95.

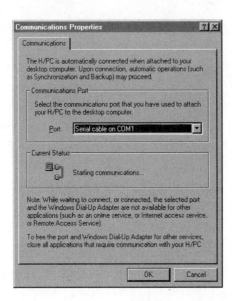

If all goes well, when the configuration is completed, H/PC Explorer is running on your desktop, waiting for you to connect your Handheld PC. Be sure you actually plug the cable from your Handheld PC into the same port you select in the dialog box. (Don't laugh—this baffled me one morning.)

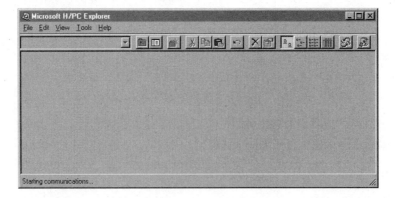

If you have a mainstream PC and have successfully used a modem or a serial cable to do communications before, you will most likely have no problem getting your Handheld PC to connect to your desktop PC. During the testing of H/PC Explorer, the Windows CE team found that most users had no problems. But a few did. These tended to occur on PCs in which the serial ports had never been used or were not working correctly. If all does not go well with the configuration, or if nothing happens when you connect your Handheld PC, you have a communications problem. See the "Troubleshooting" section, a little later in this chapter, for help.

Connecting to Your Desktop PC

Before you connect your Handheld PC to your desktop PC for the first time, there are two things you should do. First, be sure both machines are set to the same time zone. On your desktop PC, double-click the time in the status area (or open the Date/Time Control Panel program), and then select the Time Zone tab in the Date/Time Properties dialog box. On your Handheld PC, double-tap the time in the status area, tap the Time Zones tab, and make sure that the home city you specified is located in the same time zone specified on your desktop PC. This ensures that when appointments are copied to your Handheld PC during synchronization they are set at the correct time. Your appointment schedule will be very confusing if the time zone settings aren't the same.

Second, you might want to personalize the default Notification Options in the Calendar and Tasks programs on your Handheld PC. This way, the defaults you want will apply to all the appointments and tasks that are downloaded to your Handheld PC at the first synchronization, as well as to any future ones you create. For example, I set the Sound Notification default to Alarm2 because I find that to be the most irritating (and therefore the most effective) sound. To change the defaults in the Calendar and Tasks programs, tap the Reminder Defaults command on the Edit menu and then tap the Options button.

Now you are ready to connect the two machines. This is usually quite simple. For most people it will work the first time; for some there will be a little fiddling initially, but once you get it to work it tends to keep on working.

1. Start H/PC Explorer if it isn't already running.

2. Plug one end of the connection cable in to your desktop PC.

3. Turn on your Handheld PC, and plug the other end of the cable in to your Handheld PC. If your Handheld PC came with a docking cradle, connect it to your desktop PC with the cable, and then place the Handheld PC in the cradle.

You should see the following message appear on your desktop PC, and a similar one on your Handheld PC.

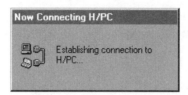

If you do, smile, because you've made it past the point where most of the communications problems lie. If you don't, see the "Troubleshooting" section later in this chapter.

After the two machines have connected, the Setup New Partner Wizard walks you through the steps needed to establish your Handheld PC as the synchronization partner of your desktop PC. Don't worry—you need to do this only once.

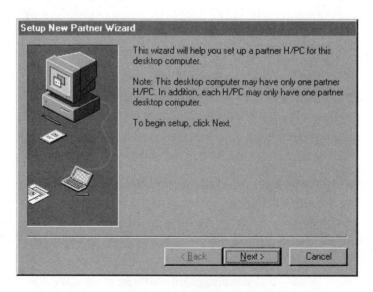

The wizard asks whether you want to synchronize your Handheld PC with your desktop PIM—either Schedule+ or Outlook—now. If you want

H/PC Explorer to automatically synchronize your Handheld PC with your desktop PC whenever you connect the two, choose to perform the synchronization now. This sets automatic synchronization as the default.

Likewise, you can choose to have H/PC Explorer back up the contents of your Handheld PC now or to leave that for later. The backup can take several minutes to perform, during which time you cannot use your Handheld PC. You can choose to have a backup performed automatically each time you connect your Handheld PC to your desktop PC. See "Backing Up Your Handheld PC," later in this chapter.

After you complete the wizard, H/PC Explorer displays the contents of the Windows CE desktop from your Handheld PC.

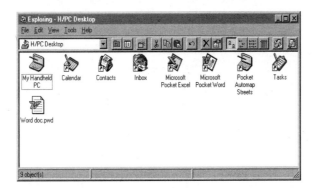

You'll find most of the buttons on H/PC Explorer's toolbar the same as those on Windows Explorer's toolbar. The second and third from the left and the two on the right are unique to H/PC Explorer, though. Let's take these four buttons in turn. The Show/Hide Folder List button switches H/PC Explorer between a two-pane view with the folder hierarchy on the left and a one-pane view with no folder hierarchy displayed. The folder hierarchy can make it easier to navigate to a particular folder on your Handheld PC. The New Folder button simply creates a new folder in the currently displayed folder. The Synchronize Now button causes immediate synchronization of contacts, appointments, and tasks between the Handheld PC and Schedule+ or Outlook on the desktop PC. Tap this button if you have made some changes in Schedule+ or Outlook that you want reflected on your Handheld PC. Finally, the Back Up Now button causes H/PC Explorer to back up the contents of your Handheld PC to your desktop PC.

Troubleshooting

There are three sources of help for troubleshooting communications problems. First, you can consult the "Fine-tuning and Troubleshooting" chapter of the *Handheld PC User's Guide* that came with your Handheld PC. Second, the H/PC Explorer Help system features an extensive Communications Troubleshooter that can assist you. Although this can be somewhat tedious to plow through, I have found it to be effective in solving communications problems. Third, you can call the product support number supplied by the manufacturer of your Handheld PC.

To use the Communications Troubleshooter, open the Help menu in H/PC Explorer on your desktop PC, click H/PC Explorer Help Topics, double-click Troubleshooting, double-click Communications Problems, and then double-click Communications Troubleshooter.

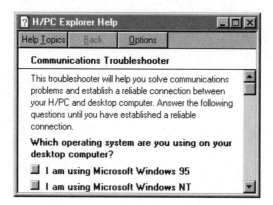

The wizard will walk you through a rather long series of steps to resolve your problem, as it uses a somewhat brute force approach. Be patient. It might take 15 or 20 minutes to go through all the steps, but in most cases they will be able to help you resolve the problem. Go through all the steps, even if you have completed them before.

Although I can't look over your shoulder to help you figure out why communications aren't working, I can offer some general advice based on the problems we most often saw during the early testing of H/PC Explorer.

■ Verify that the serial port you are using on your desktop PC is working. Can you open HyperTerminal, specifying the port in question? If HyperTerminal cannot open the port, there is a problem with the port's configuraton. If HyperTerminal can open the port, this verifies that Windows at least recognizes the port. To start HyperTerminal on your desktop PC, click the Start menu, point to Programs, point to Accessories, and click HyperTerminal. HyperTerminal will prompt you to create a new connection. Set the Connect Using field to the serial port you are trying to use with H/PC Explorer.

- Can you send and receive data using the port? If you connect two desktop PCs via a null modem serial cable and run HyperTerminal on both, you should be able to type words on one and see them displayed on the other. This verifies that the port is physically working.

- When you connect your Handheld PC to your desktop PC, does the Handheld PC attempt to connect to the desktop PC? A message is displayed while five attempts are made. This verifies that the cable is properly connected to the two machines.

- Start the Windows Direct Cable Connect program on your desktop PC by clicking the Start menu, pointing to Programs, pointing to Accessories, and clicking Cable Connect. Specify your desktop PC as the host, and then connect your Handheld PC to your desktop PC. The two machines should be able to successfully establish a connection (although nothing will happen over it). This verifies that the Direct Cable Connection networking, which H/PC Explorer uses, has been properly set up.

- Check that both your desktop PC and your Handheld PC are communicating at the same speed. The next section will walk you through this procedure.

Connecting at a Faster Speed

The default connection speed over the serial cable is 19,200 baud, which is a little less than 2000 characters per second. This speed was chosen because it is the fastest speed at which many older desktop PCs can communicate. If you have a newer desktop PC—say, with a Pentium processor—it probably can support communications over the serial cable at faster speeds. Using a faster connection speed can cut down significantly the time it takes to synchronize.

To reset your connection speed, follow the steps in the next section, "On your Handheld PC," and then follow the steps in either "On your PC running Windows 95" or "On your PC running Windows NT version 4.0." You might need to follow these procedures more than once to determine the fastest speed at which the two machines can reliably connect. Even if your desktop PC supports a speed faster than 57,600 baud, it is likely that the best performance will be achieved at 57,600 baud. Setting the speed faster than 57,600 baud might actually slow down rather than speed up overall data transfer speed. You should experiment with different speeds to determine the optimal setting for your two machines. The easiest way to do this is to time how long it takes to transfer a file from your desktop PC to your Handheld PC.

 ARNING   Changing these settings can halt communications with your Handheld PC or make them unreliable. If you experience problems, undo these changes or consult the H/PC Explorer Communications Troubleshooter.

On your Handheld PC
First you need to create a new remote networking connection on your Handheld PC.

1. Disconnect the serial cable from your Handheld PC.

2. Tap Start, tap Programs, and then double-tap Communications. Double-tap Remote Networking, and then double-tap Make New Connection.

3. Enter a name in the Type A Name For The Connection field. For example, you might enter *Desktop @ 57,600*. Then tap Next.

4. Tap Configure, select the desired speed in the Baud Rate list, and then tap OK. I recommend using 57,600.

5. Tap Finish.

Now you need to open the Control Panel and indicate that the new connection you just created should be used when connecting to your desktop PC.

1. Tap the Start menu, and then tap Settings to open the Control Panel. In the Control Panel, double-tap the Communications icon.

2. Tap the PC Connection tab, and then tap Change.

3. To open the list of connections, tap the down-arrow to the right of the Connect To Desktop Computer Using box. Then select the connection you created above.

4. Tap OK, and then tap OK again to close the Communications program.

On your PC running Windows 95

Follow these steps if you are using Windows 95 on your desktop computer. You will set the communications port you use to communicate with your Handheld PC to the new speed.

1. Click the Start button, point to Settings, and click Control Panel to open the Control Panel. Then double-click the System icon.

2. On the Device Manager tab, double-click Modem, and then select the port to which you connect the cable from your Handheld PC. Typically this is COM1, which is listed as Serial Cable On COM1. Be sure you select the correct port. If you are unsure which communications port to select, start H/PC Explorer and click the Communications command on the File menu. This displays the port being used.

3. Click Properties, and then click the Modem tab. In the Maximum Speed list, select the same speed you specified on your Handheld PC.

4. Close all programs on your desktop PC, and restart Windows 95. This is required; be sure to do it.

5. After Windows 95 restarts, open H/PC Explorer and reconnect the Handheld PC cable.

At this point, your two machines should successfully connect at the new, higher speed.

On your PC running Windows NT version 4.0

Follow these steps if you are using Windows NT version 4.0 on your desktop computer. You will set the communications port you use to communicate with your Handheld PC to the new speed.

1. Click the Start button, point to Settings, and click Control Panel to open the Control Panel. Then double-click the Modems icon.

2. Select the modem and port that you use to connect the cable from your Handheld PC to your desktop PC. The modem will be listed as Dial-Up Networking Serial Cable Between 2 PCs. Typically this is listed as COM1 in the Attached To column. If you are unsure which communications port to select, start H/PC Explorer and click the Communications command on the File menu. This displays the port being used.

3. Click the Properties button below the list.

4. In the Maximum Speed section, select the same rate you specified on your Handheld PC from the list. Click OK. Click Close in the Modems Properties dialog box.

5. Open H/PC Explorer, and reconnect the Handheld PC cable.

At this point, your two machines should successfully connect at the new, higher speed.

Connecting as a Guest

Perhaps you're in a colleague's office and you would like to print a copy of a document that is on your Handheld PC. If your colleague has H/PC Explorer installed on his or her desktop PC, this is a simple task. Just start H/PC Explorer on the desktop PC, and connect your Handheld PC. You will see the following dialog box displayed:

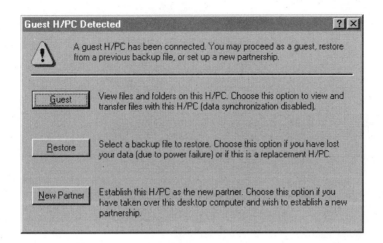

Click Guest, and H/PC Explorer establishes a connection to your Handheld PC over which you can transfer files and install programs. In fact, you can do everything but synchronize your appointments, contacts, and tasks. To print a file that is on your Handheld PC, use H/PC Explorer to locate it on the Handheld PC, and then drag it to the desktop of the desktop PC. Then you can open and print it.

Synchronizing Your Appointments, Contacts, and Tasks

Synchronize Now

To start H/PC Explorer every time you turn on your computer, put a shortcut to H/PC Explorer in the StartUp folder of your desktop PC.

To synchronize your appointments, contacts, and tasks, start H/PC Explorer on your desktop PC and then connect your Handheld PC to your desktop PC. If you synchronized the two machines when you completed the Setup New Partner Wizard, synchronization now proceeds automatically. If you didn't, click the Synchronize Now button to start the synchronization process.

Although I like automatic synchronization, you might not. Some people find it frustrating when programs start running automatically, seemingly of their own accord. I suggest you try it for a while in the automatic mode described here and then switch to manual mode if you find it annoying. You'll learn how to switch to manual mode in the "Customizing Synchronization Settings" section, later in this chapter.

If you synchronize on a regular basis, it normally takes only a couple of minutes for the synchronization process to be completed. During synchronization, the following animated message box entertains you on your desktop PC.

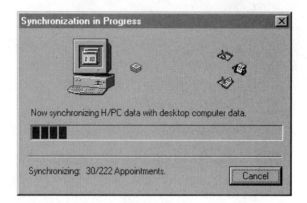

If you leave your Handheld PC connected to your desktop PC and continue to work in Schedule+ or Outlook on the desktop PC after synchronization is completed, any changes you make will not be synchronized automatically with your Handheld PC until you next connect the two machines. If you want to synchronize the two machines again without disconnecting and then reconnecting them, click the Synchronize Now button.

Unfortunately, Contacts, Calendar, and Tasks programs in Windows CE are not perfect companions to Schedule+ or Outlook on your desktop PC. Things to watch out for are

■ Notes cannot be as big on your Handheld PC as they can on your desktop PC. Notes in Contacts, Calendar, or Tasks can be no larger than 4095 characters. The limit in Schedule+ or Outlook is much larger. If you create a large note on your desktop PC, you will receive a message during syncrhonization warning of data truncation.

- Recurring tasks work differently on your Handheld PC than they do in Schedule+. But all is well as long as you work with recurring tasks only from the Handheld PC side: create them, edit them, mark them complete, and delete them from your Handheld PC. As long as you only view them in Schedule+, you'll be OK.

- Recurring tasks on your Handheld PC work better with Outlook. You can create, edit, and delete them and mark them complete from either your Handheld PC or from Outlook on your desktop PC. The only "gotchas" are that multiday recurring tasks are not always synchronized properly and that sometimes duplicates are created. This is pretty rare, however.

Resolving Synchronization Conflicts

It is possible to create appointments and tasks on your Handheld PC or your desktop PC that won't properly synchronize. Most people will probably never run into this problem, but if you do, you'll see a message like this during synchronization:

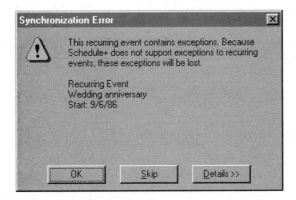

Your choices here are simple: You can click the Skip button to forgo synchronization of this item and have it remain out-of-sync between your desktop PC and your Handheld PC. You can click the OK button to synchronize the item and lose some of your data. Click the Details button to learn what you will lose.

The notion of conflicts and the process of resolving them is the same here as in the Windows 95 Briefcase. If you have used that, all this should seem very familiar.

A conflict occurs when an item (an appointment, a contact, or a task) has been modified on both the Handheld PC and the desktop PC since the last synchronization. For example, if you changed the time of an appointment on your Handheld PC and changed the location on your desktop PC, you created a conflict.

 TIP   If you don't want to worry about conflicts, here is a way to avoid them. Turn on automatic synchronization. Always connect your Handheld PC to your desktop PC when you are working on your desktop PC. While they are connected, work only on your desktop PC. Manually synchronize the two machines before you disconnect them.

It is not a conflict if you created a new appointment on your Handheld PC scheduling a meeting with Mary at 1 P.M. on Tuesday when you already had a dentist appointment scheduled at that time on your desktop PC. Although that is indeed a conflict for you, as far as your calendar is concerned you've merely scheduled two appointments for the same time. When you synchronize your Handheld PC with your desktop PC, the overlapping appointments will be clearly visible.

The synchronization process is not capable of automatically merging the changes that created the conflicts, so you must choose which one "wins." In the next section, "Customizing Synchronization Settings," you'll learn how to specify the default method for resolving conflicts. You can choose to have all changes made on the desktop PC automatically override those made on the Handheld PC, or you can choose to have all changes made on the Handheld PC automatically override those made on the desktop PC. Both these settings allow synchronization to proceed in a completely hands-off manner. Consider, however, that not being prompted to resolve conflicts is potentially dangerous, as you might lose data (by having it replaced during conflict resolution) without realizing it.

You can also choose to be prompted to resolve each conflict manually. This lets you treat each conflict on a case by case basis. If you select this option, the following dialog box appears when a conflict is found:

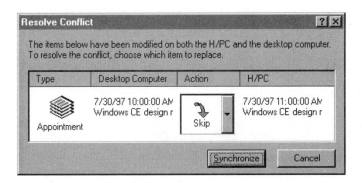

The dialog box displays which type of item is in conflict—an appointment, a contact, or a task. It summarizes the item as it exists on the desktop PC and on the Handheld PC. In this illustration, an appointment is in conflict. On the Handheld PC, the meeting is scheduled for an hour later than on the desktop PC. Since only you know which machine has the correct information, you must resolve the conflict.

Between the two summaries is the Action column. You can click the down-arrow to open a list of possible actions.

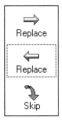

The top choice, with the right-pointing arrow, causes the item on the desktop PC to replace that on the Handheld PC. The next choice, with the left-pointing arrow, is the opposite; it causes the item on the Handheld PC to replace that on the desktop PC. The third choice skips this conflict; the item remains different on each of the PCs, and you will not be asked again to resolve this conflict until you next synchronize the two machines.

If you click the Cancel button in the Resolve Conflict dialog box, it is the same as if you had clicked Skip for every conflict in the list. The next time you synchronize, you'll be asked about the conflicts again.

Customizing Synchronization Settings

You control the settings for the synchronization process by using the Synchronization Manager.

To start it, click Synchronization Manager on the Tools menu of H/PC Explorer. Normally you need to customize your settings only once.

General tab

The General tab allows you to select whether you want to synchronize certain items and to specify how synchronization conflicts should be resolved. Select the first check box if you want your Handheld PC's time to be set the same as that on your desktop PC. If you tend to keep your desktop PC clock set correctly, this ensures your Handheld PC's time is always accurate.

Select the second check box if you want to synchronize the appointments, contacts, and tasks on your Handheld PC with those in Schedule+ or Outlook on your desktop PC. If you don't use Schedule+ or Outlook on your desktop PC, be sure to clear this check box so that H/PC Explorer won't try to activate Schedule+ or Outlook every time you connect your Handheld PC to your desktop PC. If you clear this check box, the remainder of the options in the dialog box are disabled.

If you choose to synchronize your two machines, I recommend you select Automatically Synchronize Upon Connecting. This causes synchronization to occur as soon as you connect your Handheld PC to your desktop PC, and thus you don't have to think further about it.

The Status area informs you of the synchronization state of the two machines. If synchronization is not up to date, you can click the Synchronize Now button to initiate synchronization.

In the Conflict Resolution area, you set the default values for conflict resolution. I strongly suggest that you click the Prompt Me option so that you will be prompted to resolve conflicts. This way you won't inadvertently overwrite an appointment, a contact, or a task and lose the changes you made earlier. After you have become used to synchronizing your data, you might consider choosing not to be prompted. When you select the Prompt Me option, the field below is enabled, and you can choose which of three possible actions you want to be the default.

If you select the Don't Prompt Me option, conflicts are resolved automatically according to the rule you specify, and synchronization always proceeds to completion without bothering you. If you choose this option, it's a good idea to follow these rules to avoid creating conflicts:

■   Always synchronize your Handheld PC with your desktop PC as soon as you connect them. An easy way to ensure this happens is to turn on automatic synchronization.

■   Use your desktop PC only when the two machines are connected, and use your Handheld PC only when they are not. Or never modify the same item on both machines.

■   Always synchronize the two computers just before you disconnect them. You can do this by clicking the Synchronize Now command on the Tools menu in H/PC Explorer.

When you select the Don't Prompt Me option, the field below is enabled and you can choose which computer overrides the other if there is a conflict. Pick the machine on which you tend to enter most of your appointments, just in case you forget to follow the above rules.

If you've given an assistant the access permissions necessary to make changes to your appointments in Schedule+ or Outlook, the opportunity for conflicts is greater. In this case, I don't recommend the use of automatic conflict resolution.

Databases tab

The Databases tab of the Synchronization Manager allows you to control in detail how the Appointments, Contacts, and Tasks databases are synchronized with Schedule+ or Outlook.

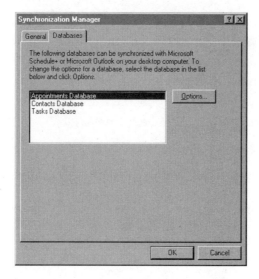

This tab is active only when your two machines are connected. To view the synchronization settings for a particular database, select the database in the list and click the Options button.

Synchronize Now

If you know many people, meet with them all the time, and have lots of things to do, these databases can become quite large. The synchronization settings you select affect the sizes of the databases, which affect the performance of your Handheld PC. To display the size of each of your databases, use H/PC Explorer to open the Databases folder (located in My Handheld PC). In general, databases smaller than 64 KB give you very good performance, while databases larger than that increase the startup time for the Calendar, Contacts, and Tasks programs on your Handheld PC. If any of your databases is too large, you can adjust its synchronization settings, click the Synchronize Now button to resynchronize your machines, and recheck the size of the database. For best performance, keep what you need on your Handheld PC, but no more than that.

Appointments   The Appointment Synchronization Options dialog box lets you choose whether to synchronize all your Schedule+ or Outlook appointments, or only some of them.

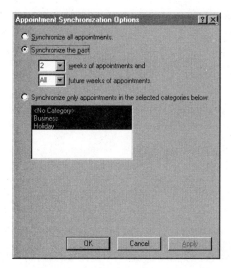

I have my machine set to synchronize only the past two weeks of appointments but all my future appointments. On my Handheld PC, this results in an Appointments database that is about 19 KB, which is not very large. I recommend that you keep the Appointments database smaller than 64 KB, if possible. In general, this keeps the Calendar's performance nice and peppy.

You can also choose with which Schedule+ or Outlook data file you will synchronize. I strongly recommend you leave this setting alone. By default, it is set to the same file used by Schedule+ or Outlook.

Contacts   The Contact Synchronization Options dialog box lets you choose which Schedule+ or Outlook contacts you want to have synchronized with your Handheld PC.

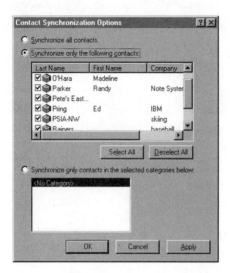

You can choose all your contacts or only some of them. To facilitate selecting the contacts you want synchronized, you can sort the list of contacts by clicking the column heading of the field you'd like to sort by. You can also Shift-click or Ctrl-click to highlight several contacts at once, and then you can press the spacebar to turn their selection off or on.

The guiding principle for selecting contacts to synchronize is the same as for selecting appointments. Synchronize the contacts you need on your Handheld PC, but realize that the more contacts you have, the slower the Contacts program starts. When you have a great many contacts—say, more than 1000—the Contacts program takes much longer to start. If you have more than 3000, startup time can take as long as 50 seconds or so. Also, changing the sort order of the columns takes much more time if you have thousands of contacts. After you have started the Contacts program, however, scrolling through the list or opening a particular card is quick, regardless of the number of contacts in the database. If you must have many contacts stored on your Handheld PC, just leave the Contacts program open all the time; minimize it by tapping its button on the taskbar instead of closing it.

Tasks The Task Synchronization Options dialog box lets you control how Schedule+ or Outlook tasks are synchronized.

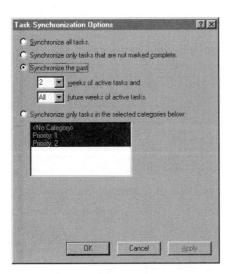

You can choose to synchronize all tasks, all but completed tasks, only active tasks within a specified range of time, or only tasks that belong to specified projects.

If you don't have hundreds of tasks, just select Synchronize All Tasks. I have about 150 tasks, and the Tasks database on my Handheld PC is smaller than 5 KB. I suggest you try to keep the Tasks database smaller than 64 KB to maintain good performance.

If you have many tasks, or if you are far more organized than I, you might want to control which tasks are synchronized. A simple way to limit the number of tasks on your Handheld PC is to select Synchronize Only Tasks That Are Not Marked Complete. This way, when you complete a task and presumably don't need to worry about it any more, it is removed from your Handheld PC when you synchronize. The task remains in Schedule+ or Outlook on your desktop PC, however, in case you want to review any of your completed tasks.

You can also choose to synchronize only those active tasks that are within a range of weeks relative to the current date. I have found this less useful because if I do not complete a task on time, it eventually disappears from my Handheld PC.

If you have organized your tasks into projects—which is a good idea, by the way—you might have some projects that can be worked on only while you are at your desktop PC. If you don't need to reference those tasks when you're away from your desk, you might want to save space on your Handheld PC by not synchronizing them.

Optimizing Synchronization with Schedule+ or Outlook

Here are some ways you can improve the efficiency of the partnership between your Handheld PC and Schedule+ or Outlook on your desktop PC:

- If your desktop PC is connected to a Schedule+ server, open Schedule+, click the Options command on the Tools menu, and then click the Synchronize tab. Clear the Synchronize Every 15 Minutes check box, and ensure that Always Synchronize Upon Exit is selected. Here, synchronization refers to keeping the copy of your schedule on your desktop PC in sync with the copy on the Schedule+ server. Setting the options as described here ensures that synchronization with your Handheld PC will not be interrupted. Your schedule will be synchronized with the server only just before Schedule+ is closed.

- In Schedule+, on the General tab of the Options dialog box, set the Prompt To Archive Data field to no more than three months. This way you will be prompted to archive your old appointments, which you should do. Having fewer appointments in your Schedule+ database speeds up synchronization.

    In Outlook, on the AutoArchive tab of the Options dialog box, set the AutoArchive field to no more than 3 months. This will automatically clean out old appointments and tasks from the Outlook database and will speed up synchronization.

- In Schedule+ or Outlook, keep in mind that marking a task completed does not delete it. Delete completed tasks regularly— say, on the first of every month. This, too, speeds up synchronization.

■ If you want the Calendar to operate faster, consider reducing the number of appointments you store on your Handheld PC. The previous section of this chapter lists instructions for doing this. For example, you might choose to synchronize only the past week and the next eight weeks of appointments.

■ Don't store large amounts of data on the Notes tab of an appointment, contact, or task. Instead, create a document in Pocket Word, and refer to that document by name in the note. (Keep in mind that the document is not synchronized along with the appointment, contact, or task.) If you create an appointment in Schedule+ or Outlook by accepting a meeting request, the text of the meeting request is placed on the Notes tab. So if someone invites you to a meeting and places 20 pages of text in the invitation, you might want to delete the text from the appointment in Schedule+ or Outlook before you synchronize.

■ Group related people on a single address card. For example, use only one card for all the members of a family living at the same address. You might store the individual family names on the Notes tab, for example.

Moving Files to and from Your Handheld PC

To start Windows Explorer, click Start, point to Programs, and click Windows Explorer. Or use the right mouse button to click the Start button, and then click Explore.

Many programs on the Handheld PC use different file formats than their counterparts on the desktop PC. For example, Pocket Word uses a different file format than Word does. Therefore, when you copy most files from your desktop PC to your Handheld PC, the files must be converted to a format your Handheld PC can work with. H/PC Explorer version 1.1 includes converters for Word files, Excel files, and font files. When you install H/PC Explorer, the font file converter is all set up for you. If you have Word and Excel installed on your desktop PC, the Word and Excel file converters are also set up. If you have Microsoft Works 4.0 or Word on your desktop PC, you might have additional text file converters set up. For example, if you have installed Works 4.0 and its converters, you can convert between Works documents and Pocket Word documents.

Downloading vs. Uploading

For some reason, lost in the antiquities of computer lore, moving data from a big computer to a smaller computer is called downloading, and moving data in the opposite direction is called uploading. So moving data from your desktop PC to your Handheld PC is downloading, and moving data from your Handheld PC to your desktop PC is uploading.

Installing other programs on your Handheld PC might install additional converters. For example, word processors from other companies might install converters that enable direct conversion of their documents, and installing Paint from the Microsoft Windows CE Web site installs a bitmap file converter. (The Paint program can be found in the Power Toys package.) Additional converters are available from the Windows CE Web site (http://www.microsoft.com/windowsce). You can see which converters are installed on your desktop PC by clicking the File Conversion command on the Tools menu of H/PC Explorer.

If you have a converter for a particular file type installed, H/PC Explorer converts the file automatically when you copy the file to your Handheld PC. The easiest way to copy files to your Handheld PC is to follow these steps:

1. Start H/PC Explorer, if it isn't already running, and connect your Handheld PC to your desktop PC.

2. In H/PC Explorer on your desktop PC, open the folder on your Handheld PC where you want the file to be placed. I recommend the My Documents folder.

See "Files That Don't Need Conversion," later in this chapter, for information about which types of files have the same format on both desktop PCs and Handheld PCs.

3. Start Windows Explorer on your desktop PC, and open the folder containing the file you want to copy to your Handheld PC. Position the Windows Explorer window on your screen so that you can also see at least part of the H/PC Explorer window.

4. Select the file in the Windows Explorer window, and drag it to the H/PC Explorer window.

When you release the mouse button, dropping the file on the H/PC Explorer window, the file is converted and copied to your Handheld PC. A dialog box on your desktop PC keeps you updated about the status of the copying and conversion operation.

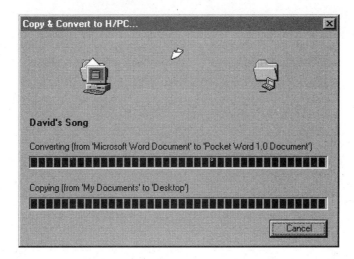

An alternate way to copy files to your Handheld PC is to use the keyboard shortcuts for Copy and Paste (CTRL+C and CTRL+V). For example, you can use CTRL+C to copy a file in Windows Explorer, and then you can switch to H/PC Explorer and press CTRL+V to paste it. The file is then converted and downloaded to your Handheld PC.

Downloading Word and Excel Files

As mentioned in Chapter 5, Pocket Word and Pocket Excel do not contain all the features of Word and Excel, and thus, some Word and Excel documents might contain attributes that can't be displayed on your Handheld PC. If you copy such a document to your Handheld PC, you'll see a message like this displayed on your desktop PC while the document is being converted:

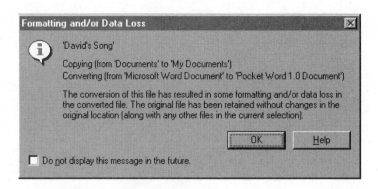

The message warns you that some items in the document will not be converted. There's not much you can do about this, except perhaps to avoid using Word and Excel features that are not available on your Handheld PC in documents that you want to transfer between the two machines. However, this situation is not as bad as you might think. Many document attributes are retained when the document is converted for use on the Handheld PC; they simply are not displayed. They reappear correctly when the document is converted back for use on your desktop PC.

The best thing to do is to transfer some documents to your Handheld PC, edit them using Pocket Word, and then save the modified documents using new names. Transfer these modified documents back to your desktop PC, and open them using Word. Compare each modified document to its original to see which formatting information did not make the round trip successfully.

Converting Word files to Pocket Word

H/PC Explorer can convert Word 6/Word 95 and Word 97 (.doc) files and Rich Text Format (.rtf) files to Pocket Word (.pwd) files. If you have a document stored in the format of an earlier version of Word, open it in Word 95 or Word 97 and save it as a Word document. This will cause it to be converted to Word 95 or Word 97 format. You can use the same process to convert word processor files in other formats—such as WordPerfect files—to Word 95 or Word 97 format.

If you use any of the really fancy features of Word, those document attributes are not going to make the trip down to your Handheld PC. The following table explains what happens to them during conversion. In some cases, you might not want to replace your original Word document with the one uploaded from your Handheld PC. You shouldn't have any problems with ordinary documents such as letters, memos, and reports, however.

Attributes	What Happens During Conversion
Colors	Retained and displayed on your Handheld PC in the closest color available—light gray, dark gray, black, or white.
Fonts	Retained and displayed in the closest available font. The following fonts are built into Windows CE and are always available: Arial 8, 9, 10, 12, 16, 20; Comic Sans MS 10; Courier New 8, 10; MS Sans Serif 8, 10; Symbol 10, 12; Terminal 5; Times New Roman 8, 10 ,12, 14, 18, 22; and Wingdings 10. If you download the fonts used in the file, Pocket Word uses those fonts instead.
Formatting	Tabs, alignment, bullets, indentation, and simple numbered lists are retained and correctly displayed. Built-in heading styles are retained and correctly displayed. Column styles are retained, but multiple columns are not displayed. Horizontal, vertical, and text wrap attributes are retained; they are correctly displayed except for vertical text, which is displayed horizontally. Spacing between paragraphs is lost.
OLE object pictures (metafiles)	Pictures are converted to 4-color bitmaps for display by Pocket Word, and they are converted back to 16-color bitmaps when the document is copied back to the desktop PC. If the picture is stored in the document, it is converted and displayed. If the picture is linked to but not stored in the document (it is stored in a separate file), it is not converted or displayed.
Tables of contents and indexes	The text of a table of contents is retained during the conversion, but text set at right-aligned tab stops might wrap to the next line when displayed in Pocket Word. The text of an index is retained.

(continued)

(continued from page 163)

Attributes	What Happens During Conversion
Tables	Retained and displayed as tab-delimited text. (A tab is inserted between the text that was in each cell in the Word table.) If any text wraps within a cell, or if a cell contains tabs or multiple paragraphs, you get a pretty unreadable table in Pocket Word. Simple tables are displayed just fine.
Other elements	The text and document attributes of headers and footers, footnotes, revision marks, and annotations are removed during the conversion from Word to Pocket Word format and are lost. OLE object data, page setup information, sections, borders, shading, and custom style sheets are also lost.

Converting Excel files to Pocket Excel

H/PC Explorer can convert Excel 5/Excel 95 and Excel 97 (.xls) files to Pocket Excel (.pxl) files. If you have a workbook stored in the format of an earlier version of Excel, open it in Excel 95 or Excel 97 and save it as an Excel workbook. This will cause it to be converted to Excel 95 or Excel 97 format. You can use the same process to convert spreadsheet files in other formats—such as Lotus 1-2-3 or Quattro Pro files—to Excel 95 or Excel 97 format.

During the conversion to Pocket Excel format, most of the data in your workbook is retained; it will appear in Pocket Excel just as it does in Excel on your desktop computer. The following table explains what happens to certain data and file attributes during conversion. Some of them are modified or even removed because Pocket Excel does not support all the features of Excel. In some cases, you might not want to replace your original Excel document with the one uploaded from your Handheld PC.

Attributes	What Happens During Conversion
Chart objects, drawing objects, pictures, text boxes, and controls	Removed.
Chart sheets, dialog sheets, Excel version 4 macro sheets, and Visual Basic for Applications modules	Removed and replaced with a blank sheet.
Fonts	Retained and displayed in the closest available font. The following fonts are built into Windows CE and are always available: Arial 8, 9, 10, 12, 16, 20; Comic Sans MS 10; Courier New 8, 10; MS Sans Serif 8, 10; Symbol 10, 12; Terminal 5; Times New Roman 8, 10 ,12, 14, 18, 22; and Wingdings 10. If you download the fonts used in the file, Pocket Excel uses those fonts instead.
Formats	Horizontal text and wrapped text alignment are retained and correctly displayed. Vertical text is retained but is displayed as horizontal text. Custom number formats are changed to match the closest format supported by Pocket Excel. Borders are retained but are displayed as single lines. Colors and patterns are removed.
Formulas	Supported functions and formulas are retained and are displayed correctly. Unsupported functions are removed and are replaced by their returned value. Formulas containing external links or intersection range references are converted to values. Formulas entered as arrays or containing array arguments are converted to values.
Names	Names that reference worksheets within other workbooks, arrays, array formulas, or intersection ranges are removed from the name list. Names removed from the list are left in formulas and functions, causing those formulas to resolve as #NAME? All hidden names are unhidden.
PivotTable dynamic views data	Converted to values.
Protection	You must remove password protection before converting a workbook. Document protection is disabled but not removed upon conversion.

Downloading Fonts

You can't upload fonts from your Handheld PC to your desktop PC.

To conserve space, Windows CE includes only a few fonts. If you want to use other fonts in the documents on your Handheld PC, you can download them from your desktop PC. In general, TrueType fonts (.ttf) work the best on your Handheld PC, but bitmap fonts (.fon) can be converted as well. Fonts take up quite a bit of space, typically 8 to 15 KB per font per size, so don't go crazy and download them all; you'll have no room left for anything else!

N **OTE**   Remember that if a document contains a font that isn't on your Handheld PC, you don't have to download the font to be able to view the document. Windows CE displays the document in the closest available font and remembers the original font for when the document is uploaded back to your desktop PC.

The process of downloading fonts is quite simple.

1. On your desktop PC, start H/PC Explorer if it isn't already running, and then connect your Handheld PC to your desktop PC.

2. In H/PC Explorer, open the Windows folder on your Handheld PC. Then open the Fonts folder.

3. On your desktop PC, start Windows Explorer, and open the Windows folder and then the Fonts folder.

4. Drag the fonts you want to download from the Windows Explorer window to the H/PC Explorer window.

   A dialog box opens, listing the sizes available for that font on your desktop PC. Along with each size, the amount of storage space it will take up on your Handheld PC is displayed.

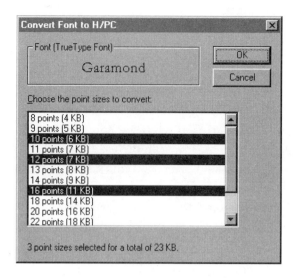

5. Select the font sizes you want to download, and click OK.

    After you have downloaded the fonts, they are available for use
    in Pocket Word, Pocket Excel, or any other program that can use
    additional fonts.

If you later decide you don't need a particular font you have downloaded,
just go to the Windows\Fonts folder on your Handheld PC and delete the
font file. The built-in system fonts are not displayed in this folder, as they
cannot be deleted.

Files That Don't Need Conversion

Some files on your desktop PC can be downloaded to your Handheld PC
without conversion. The good news is that if you upload them back to
your desktop PC (or to another desktop PC), they are intact; no data has
been lost.

- HTML (.htm) files can be opened and displayed in Pocket Internet Explorer.

- Some sound (.wav) files can be played on your Handheld PC. The sound files must be in 11-KHz, 8-bit monophonic format. The default sounds in Windows 95 are in this format. If you have a sound in 16-bit stereo format, such as a sound from Microsoft Plus! for Windows 95, or if you have a sound in another format, you must convert it before downloading it. Sounds in other formats can be downloaded to your Handheld PC, but they cannot be played. Many sound cards come with utility programs that can convert sounds from one format to another. You can use the Control Panel Volume & Sounds program to set downloaded sounds to be played for specific events.

- Text files (.txt and other file types) can be opened and displayed in Pocket Word.

Backing Up Your Handheld PC

You can use H/PC Explorer to back up all the data on your Handheld PC to a file on your desktop PC. The entire contents of the storage memory of the Handheld PC are backed up. This includes all your appointments, contacts, tasks, and e-mail; all documents and folders; any programs you have installed and any data they have created; and all data and preferences stored in the Windows CE Registry.

NOTE   Files or other data stored on PC memory cards are not backed up, nor are any databases created by installed programs.

Should some disaster befall your Handheld PC, forcing you to replace it, you can restore your backed-up data to the new device, and all will be just as it was when the backup was made. You cannot restore selected files or databases from the backup; it's an all or nothing operation. Also, the replacement Handheld PC must be the same model as the original, and it should have the same amount of memory.

To back up your Handheld PC, connect the two machines and then click the Backup/Restore command on the H/PC Explorer Tools menu. The Backup/Restore Properties dialog box appears.

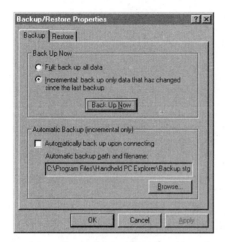

You can choose whether to back up all the data on your Handheld PC (perform a full backup) or to back up only the data that has changed since the last backup (perform an incremental backup). You also can specify whether an automatic incremental backup is to be performed each time you connect your Handheld PC to your desktop PC. Depending upon how much data has changed on your Handheld PC, the incremental backup can take several minutes. Thus you might find the automatic backup inconvenient. Try it and see. If you choose to specify the location of the backup file, don't specify the temporary folder (typically, C:\Windows\ Temp). Files in that folder are periodically erased, and you wouldn't want to lose your backup file.

When you start the backup procedure, you might be prompted to synchronize your Handheld PC with your desktop PC. Do it so that you'll be saving up-to-date information in the backup. Be sure to resolve all conflicts during the synchronization process.

Restoring Data

Should you want to restore the backed-up data to your Handheld PC, simply connect the Handheld PC to your desktop PC and click the Restore button in the Guest H/PC Detected dialog box.

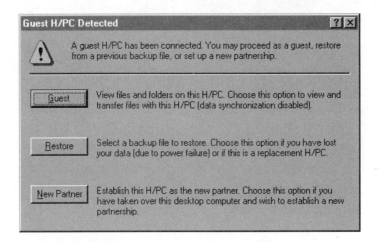

Because the Restore operation will completely erase and replace any data currently on the Handheld PC, you are prompted before the Restore operation proceeds.

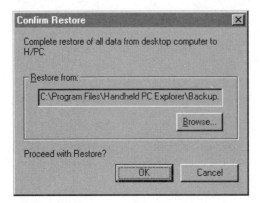

During the Restore process, which might take several minutes, do not use your Handheld PC. After the data transfer is completed, you must disconnect the two machines and reset your Handheld PC. When you next synchronize your Handheld PC with your desktop PC, you will be prompted to choose whether you want to combine the appointments, contacts, and tasks on the two machines or to overwrite these items on your Handheld PC with those from your desktop PC.

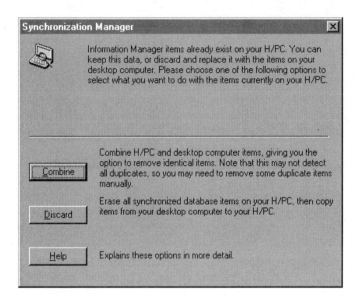

This step is necessary because H/PC Explorer does not know which items on your Handheld PC match which on your desktop PC. If the data in Schedule+ or Outlook on your desktop PC is up to date, choose Discard. This does not destroy any documents, files, or e-mail restored to your Handheld PC. It affects only appointments, contacts, and tasks.

You need to choose Combine only if there are appointments in the backup file (now restored to your Handheld PC) that are not in Schedule+ or Outlook on your desktop PC. This would happen only if you had created or modified an item on your Handheld PC and backed up the Handheld PC but had not synchronized with your desktop PC. The Combine process examines every appointment, contact, and task on your Handheld PC and attempts to match it to the equivalent item on your desktop PC. As you might guess, this process takes several minutes. When the Combine process has finished, a list of all the duplicate items is displayed.

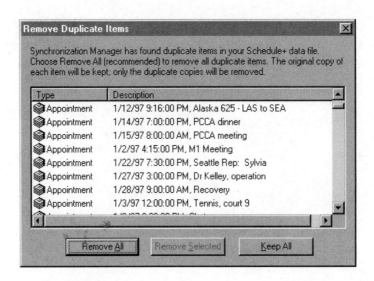

Normally there is no reason to keep the duplicates, so just click the Remove All button.

After you restart your Handheld PC, you will need to recalibrate its touch screen, as the restored calibration data will be inaccurate. Press CTRL+ALT+= to display the calibration screen.

Installing Programs on Your Handheld PC

Installing programs on your Handheld PC is very similar to installing programs on your desktop PC. Since the installation process uses the same communication mechanism as does H/PC Explorer, it's a good idea to connect your Handheld PC to your desktop computer before you begin the installation. Also, having H/PC Explorer running during the installation process is a good idea because that way you are sure the connection between the two devices is functioning properly.

Check the documentation that came with the program you are installing for instructions about how to run the Setup program. When you insert some CD-ROMs, the Setup program runs automatically.

To install a program, put the floppy disk or CD-ROM for the program in your desktop computer. Then run the Setup program on the disk or CD-ROM, which walks you through the installation process. For example, here is the initial screen that appears when you run the Setup program for the Microsoft Entertainment Pack for Windows CE:

The installation process has two parts. First the program files are copied from the floppy disk or CD-ROM to the hard disk of your desktop computer. Depending on the program you are installing, you might be offered choices as to which components you install and in which folder you install them. Then the files are copied to your Handheld PC, and the appropriate settings are made in the Windows CE Registry.

 OTE Be sure to start H/PC Explorer and connect your Handheld PC to the desktop PC, as either the synchronization partner or as a guest. This ensures that the Setup program installs the files appropriate for the type of processor in your Handheld PC.

Removing programs from your Handheld PC was described in Chapter 4, in the "Remove Programs" section.

Connecting to Other Computers and the Internet

In Chapter 8, you'll learn how to use the Inbox program, which lets you send and receive e-mail on your Handheld PC.

Windows CE includes comprehensive communications capabilities. Its communications programs enable you to send and receive e-mail, explore the World Wide Web, perform online transactions with a bank, connect to the computer network at your office, and much more. This chapter covers the Terminal, Remote Networking, and Pocket Internet Explorer programs. Terminal allows you to connect to a UNIX system, a mainframe computer, or another system that expects your Handheld PC to act as if it is a terminal. Remote Networking lets you establish a connection between your Handheld PC and a network server. You need to set up such a network connection before you can use e-mail or connect to the Internet. Pocket Internet Explorer allows you to explore the Internet.

To connect to another computer, you need a modem and an account on the computer to which you are going to connect. This account might be with a local Internet Service Provider, your company's corporate network, or some other organization.

Using a Modem with Your Handheld PC

A modem is a device that translates data from digital format to sounds that can be transmitted over an ordinary telephone line. If you listen in on a phone line being used by computers, you hear loud static. Some Handheld PCs, such as the Hitachi, LG Electronics, and Philips Electronics devices, have built-in modems. (The Philips Electronics Handheld PC features a modem implemented in software.) To communicate using most other Handheld PCs, you must use a PC Card modem or connect an external modem to your Handheld PC's serial port. Since an external modem is plugged into an electrical outlet, it doesn't drain the batteries of your device the way many PC Card modems do.

NOTE   The programs that come with Windows CE are pretty much designed for wired communications—that is, communicating through a modem over telephone lines. However, you can purchase programs that allow H/PCs to communicate wirelessly. Some wireless communications programs are described in Chapter 8.

Not all PC Card modems are compatible with Windows CE. For more information, consult the manufacturer of your Handheld PC, or check the hardware compatibility list on the Windows CE Web site (http://www.microsoft.com/windowsce/hpc/partners).

PC Card Modems Drain Batteries

Most PC Card modems, especially older models, were designed for laptop computers. Many of them will drain the pair of AA batteries in your Handheld PC in a matter of minutes. The 28.8K modems seem to be worse, in general, than the 14.4K modems. I recommend that you obtain an AC adapter for your Handheld PC and use it whenever you're using a PC Card modem. As mentioned previously, some Handheld PCs have built-in modems that don't have this problem. See Appendix A for details about various models of Handheld PCs.

Using the Terminal Program

The Terminal program provides TTY or VT-100 terminal emulation. This means that you can connect to computers that require your H/PC to act like a teletypewriter (TTY) or a terminal that uses VT-100 character codes. You might need to use Terminal to connect to some electronic bulletin board systems, e-mail systems, or other computers—particularly UNIX-based systems and mainframes.

Terminal provides a subset of the capabilities of the HyperTerminal program in Windows 95. If you have used HyperTerminal or most any other terminal emulator, a feature you will probably miss in Terminal is the ability to download files. The Terminal program in Windows CE does not support file uploading or downloading.

Setting Up a Terminal Connection

A remote computer is any computer not in the same place you are.

Make a New Connection

Before you can connect to a remote computer, you must set up a connection for it. If you are using a PC Card modem, insert the card into your Handheld PC. Then tap the Start button, tap Programs, double-tap the Communications folder, and double-tap the Terminal icon. The Terminal program starts and displays the Make A New Connection icon. Double-tap the icon to display the Session Properties dialog box.

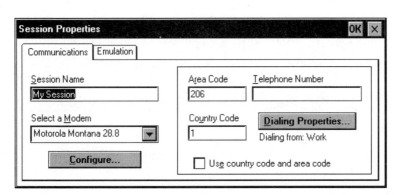

On the Communications tab of this dialog box, in the Session Name field, type a descriptive name for the connection. The name of the system you are calling is probably a good one to use. For example, I use Terminal to connect to my bank and perform simple transactions. I named the connection for my bank "Credit Union." In the Telephone Number field, type the phone number of the system you are calling. By default, the area code is the one you entered as your home area code when you completed the Welcome Wizard. You can type a new area code if necessary.

For more information about the Communications program, see Chapter 3.

Below the Dialing Properties button, the name of the current dialing location is displayed. You can change the dialing location or create a new location by tapping the Dialing Properties button. Tapping this button opens the Communications Properties dialog box, which is also accessible from the Communications program in the Control Panel.

The modem you have inserted in the PC Card slot (or the built-in modem, if your Handheld PC is so equipped) is displayed in the Select A Modem field. If the proper modem is not displayed, tap the down-arrow to the right of the field and select the correct modem from the list. To use an external modem connected to the Handheld PC's serial port, choose Hayes Compatible On COM1. If you are using a PC Card modem and the modem name isn't in the list, make sure the PC Card is fully inserted into the slot in your Handheld PC. If, after this, the modem name is still not displayed, Windows CE is not recognizing the modem and you will have to try another modem.

In most cases you will not need to configure the modem. If the remote computer is picky about line speed, parity, or other connection parameters, tap the Configure button to open the Device Properties dialog box.

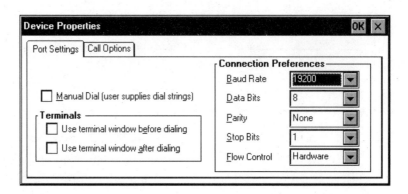

On the Port Setting tab, in the Connection Preferences section, set the parameters to whatever the remote computer requires. For example, a bulletin board system might specify a connection of 9600, 8, None, 1, Hardware. That is shorthand for 9600 baud rate, 8 data bits, no parity, 1 stop bit, and hardware flow control.

The other options on this tab are needed only in special cases. The Manual Dial check box lets you control the dialing process: select it if you want to specify the exact modem commands used to dial the remote computer. The two Terminals check boxes let you control whether the Terminal program appears on screen before or after the remote computer is dialed. You might want it to appear after dialing if you need to enter special commands to gain access to the remote computer (a second password to gain access to a communications subsystem before you log onto the remote computer, for example).

The Call Options tab lets you control how the phone call to the remote computer is placed.

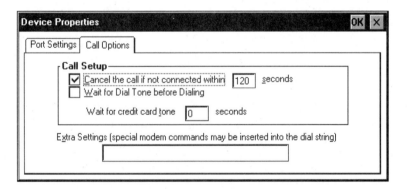

You can specify that the call be canceled if a connection is not established within a certain amount of time. (Two minutes is the default.) You can also specify that Windows CE should wait for a dial tone before dialing the call or that it should wait a specified time for a credit card tone (the "bong" sound). If your modem requires special commands to set it up, enter those commands in the field provided. The commands are sent to the modem before the call is dialed. When you're done setting options in the Device Properties dialog box, tap the OK button to accept the settings and close the dialog box. The Session Properties dialog box is still open.

You probably won't need to change anything on the Emulation tab of this dialog box.

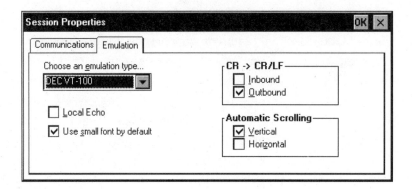

The default emulated terminal is a Digital Equipment Corporation VT-100, which is supported by virtually all systems that you connect to by telephone. The other emulated terminal is a generic TTY (teletypewriter). Select the Local Echo check box if the remote computer doesn't display, or *echo*, what you type on your H/PC screen and if you want your H/PC to echo what you type. Normally you will want the Use Small Font By Default check box to be selected. The small font allows the complete display of a 24-by-80-character terminal screen.

The check boxes in the CR -> CR/LF section allow you to specify whether a carriage return in data sent to or from your Handheld PC is translated into a carriage return and a linefeed. Normally you do this for outbound data only. Check with the administrator of the system to which you are trying to connect to determine whether you need to change either of these settings. The check boxes in the Automatic Scrolling section let you specify whether the data on screen is automatically scrolled when the cursor moves to the edge of the screen. This applies only when you use the large font and a full screen of text cannot be displayed without scrolling.

Credit Union

When you have completed setting the session properties, tap the OK button to record them and close the Session Properties dialog box. The Terminal program will attempt to dial the remote computer, as described in the next section. After you disconnect from the remote computer. The connection you created is displayed as an icon. As an example, the icon for my Credit Union connection is shown next to this paragraph.

Connecting to a Remote Computer

After you have set up the connection, you can use it. The first thing you need to do is plug your modem into the phone jack of an analog telephone line. An analog line is the kind that you have at home. Many offices and some hotels have digital phone systems instead of analog ones. Don't plug your modem into a digital phone jack: it could damage the modem. Some digital telephones have analog jacks that you can use.

Next, start the Terminal program, if it isn't already running, and double-tap the connection icon for the computer you want to call. Terminal dials the computer, and you'll see a dialog box similar to this:

The dialog box displays the telephone number being dialed. It's a good idea to double check this. For example, is a 9 being dialed if it's needed to reach an outside line? If the number is wrong, tap Cancel, and then hold down the ALT key and tap the icon for the computer you're calling. Tap the Properties command on the shortcut menu that appears. The Session Properties dialog box opens, and you can correct the phone number or you can tap the Dialing Properties button to change the dialing location (you can change it from Home to Work, for example).

After the remote computer answers the phone, the Terminal program displays any data sent from that computer. A sample is shown here:

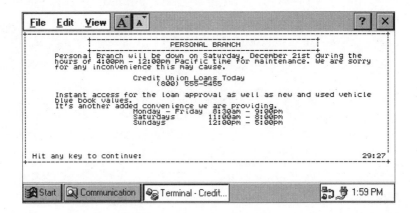

Other than the standard Help and Close buttons, there are only two buttons on the Terminal program's command bar. These let you switch between the small font and the large font. The small font has the advantage of displaying an entire 24-by-80-character terminal screen, but it is harder to read. The large font is easier to read, but the Terminal window must be scrolled to view all the information. The previous illustration shows a sample session displayed in the small font. Here is the same session displayed in the large font:

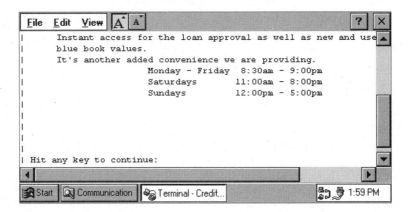

If you are using a fast modem and are trying to display a lot of data, the Terminal program will have trouble keeping up. I have found that it works somewhat better with the small font.

The menus in the Terminal program don't include any other special functionality. The File menu has a Save As command that lets you save the connection under a new name, in case you want to make a copy of it and then perhaps later modify the copy. The Edit menu has the usual Select All and Copy commands. The only way you can save information displayed in a Terminal session is to copy it to the clipboard and then paste it in another program such as Pocket Word.

When you close the Terminal program, either by tapping the Close command on the File menu or by tapping the Close button, Terminal disconnects your Handheld PC from the other computer, hanging up the phone.

Connecting to Computer Networks

The Remote Networking program allows you to connect to a remote network server so that you can use the network. You need to establish this type of connection to use the Inbox or Pocket Internet Explorer. You might also use Remote Networking to connect to the network at your office.

Setting Up a Remote Network Connection

Before you can call a remote network, you need to set up a connection for it. Unfortunately, setting up a network connection is still more complicated than it should be. This problem is not specific to Windows CE; in my opinion, the process is too complicated regardless of the computer you are using.

The instructions for setting up a network connection are different for each situation: creating an Internet connection might require different settings than creating a connection to your corporate network. Ask your Internet Service Provider (ISP) or network administrator for the specific settings you'll need to set up the connection. For example, when I wanted to start using the Internet, I contacted a local ISP and signed up. They gave me an account and sent me a page of information with the information in the table on the following page.

Field	Value
Telephone number	206-555-5455
IP address	set to dummy address (1.1.1.1)
Host name	leave blank
Domain name	Pravonia.com
Login startup command	leave blank
Domain name server (DNS) address	123.123.123.1
Secondary DNS address	234.234.234.1
POP mail account name	same as your login name
POP mail account password	same as your password
SMTP Mail gateway	mail.pravonia.com
POP3 Mail server	mail.pravonia.com
World Wide Web server	www.pravonia.com

 OTE   You might have noticed that the previous table specifies a POP3 Mail server and an SMTP Mail gateway. The Windows CE Inbox supports only the POP3 and SMTP protocols. If the service you want to use does not support these protocols, you can't use the Inbox with that service. E-mail programs that will work in your situation might be available from other software vendors. See Appendix B for details about the programs available for Windows CE.

With the settings information in hand, you can begin setting up the connection. If you're using a PC Card modem, insert it into your Handheld PC. Then tap the Start button, tap Programs, double-tap the Communications folder, and double-tap the Remote Networking shortcut. This opens the Remote Networking folder, where icons that establish network connections are stored. Double-tap the Make A New Connection icon. A wizard starts, which will walk you through the necessary steps.

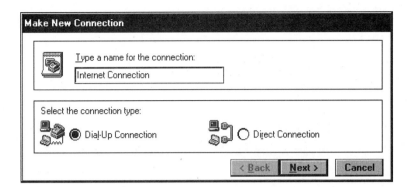

Type a name for the network connection. I chose *Internet Connection* for this example. Tap the Dial-Up Connection option, as this connection will be made using a modem instead of a cable. Then tap Next to continue setting up the connection.

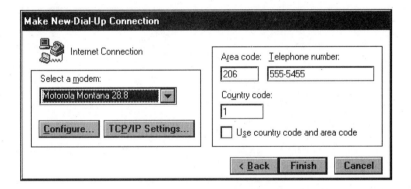

On this screen, you specify the details of the network connection. Tap the down-arrow to the right of the Select A Modem field, and in the list that appears, choose the modem you will use. The list includes any built-in modem and any modem plugged into the PC Card slot of your Handheld PC. If you're using a PC Card modem, be sure to insert the modem before trying to set up the network connection. To use an external modem connected to the Handheld PC's serial port, choose Hayes Compatible On

COM1. If the modem you are using is not in the list, it is not being recognized by Windows CE. If you're using a PC Card modem, be sure it is completely plugged into the card slot.

Type the area code and phone number of the remote computer in the appropriate fields. If the number is not local, be sure to select the Use Country Code And Area Code check box.

Next tap the Configure button to set up the modem. The Device Properties dialog box appears.

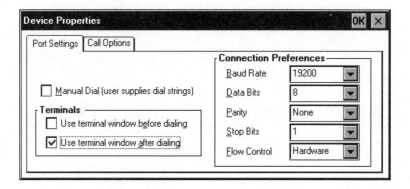

Set the baud rate to the highest number supported by your modem and the system you are dialing. You will need to select the Use Terminal Window After Dialing check box only if you need to manually log onto the network. This isn't necessary in most cases, but if Windows CE is unable to automatically log you onto the network, return to this dialog box and select this check box. The Call Options tab is the same as that for the Terminal program. See the "Setting Up a Terminal Connection" section, earlier in this chapter, for information about it.

You probably won't need to fiddle with any of the other settings in this dialog box. Tap OK when you are finished, and the Make New Dial-Up Connection screen reappears. Tap the TCP/IP Settings button, and you'll see the following dialog box:

TCP/IP Settings [OK] [X]

☑ Server-assigned IP address

IP address: [0 . 0 . 0 . 0]

☐ Log on to network

☐ Use software compression

☐ Use IP header compression

☐ Server-assigned name server addresses

Primary DNS: [123.123.123. 1]

Secondary DNS: [234.234.234. 1]

Primary WINS: [0 . 0 . 0 . 0]

Secondary WINS: [0 . 0 . 0 . 0]

To fill in this dialog box, refer to the information supplied by the administrator of the network to which you are connecting. In the case of my
Internet Service Provider, I filled in the dialog box as shown here. I
checked the Server-Assigned IP Address check box because almost all
networks assign remote computers an IP address; you will rarely need to
specify one here. The Log On To Network check box doesn't do anything,
so feel free to check it or not, depending on your mood.

Even if the network administrator says the network supports compression,
I strongly recommend that you clear the two compression check boxes
initially. Later, after you have successfully connected to the network, you
can return to this dialog box, select these check boxes one at a time, and
see whether you can still establish the connection. If it works, leave them
selected, as the compression will speed data transmission.

Some network servers, such as Microsoft remote access servers, assign all
needed addresses; if yours does, select the Server-Assigned Name Server
Addresses check box. In the example here, I did not select that box but
instead entered the addresses supplied by my Internet Service Provider.

Internet
Connection

When you're done specifying the settings, tap OK to accept them and
close the dialog box. Then tap Finish to complete the creation of the
network connection. A new icon that represents the connection is displayed. It will be similar to the icon shown next to this paragraph.

IP   You can create a shortcut to a network connection in any folder on your Handheld PC or on the Windows CE desktop. I have shortcuts on my desktop to the two networks I frequently access. Instructions for creating a shortcut are in Chapter 3.

Connecting to a Remote Network

For information about connecting to an analog phone line, see "Connecting to a Remote Computer," earlier in this chapter.

Now you can attempt to connect to the remote network. I say "attempt" because it often does not work the first time. But take heart—once you get it working it is quite reliable. Connect the modem to an analog phone line, and double-tap the connection icon for the network. The Connect To dialog box appears.

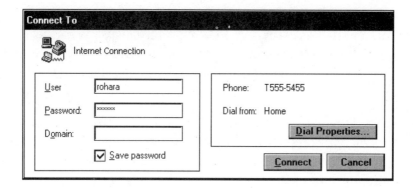

Type your user ID and password in the appropriate fields. These might be case sensitive. If you are logging onto a Windows NT domain network, type the domain name in the Domain field. If you don't want to have to type your password each time you connect to the network, select the Save Password check box. Keep in mind, however, that if you do this anyone who picks up your machine can gain access to this network using your user ID (unless, of course, you've protected your entire H/PC with a power-on password, as was described in Chapter 3).

For information about creating a dialing location, see the "Communications" section of Chapter 3.

On the right side of the dialog box, the telephone number about to be dialed (including any prefix numbers) is displayed. Just below it is the dialing location (Home, in the previous illustration). If you have changed locations since you last connected to this network, tap the Dial Properties button. The Communications Properties dialog box opens, and you can change the dialing location or create a new location.

After you have verified that the dialing location is correct, tap Connect to dial the telephone. You'll hear the phone being dialed, and a dialog box similar to this will inform you of your progress:

When the remote network server's modem answers the call, you'll hear the two modems whistle and screech at each other for a few seconds. Then Windows CE will attempt to log onto the network. If this is successful, a message similar to this appears:

At this point you can tap the Hide button, and the message box disappears. When you want to end the connection, you can recall the message box by double-tapping the Remote Networking icon in the status area of the taskbar. Then tap the Disconnect button in the message box.

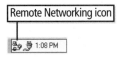

If Windows CE is unable to log onto the network, double-check to be sure that you correctly entered your user ID and password. If it still does not work, you can try to connect by manually logging on. To do this, hold down the ALT key and tap the connection icon for the network in the Remote Networking folder. Tap Properties on the shortcut menu to display the Dial-Up Connection screen, which has fields you filled out when you set up the connection. Tap the Configure button, and then select the Use Terminal Window After Dialing check box on the Port Settings tab of the Device Properties dialog box. Tap the OK button to return to the Dial-Up Connection screen, and then tap its OK button to return to the Remote Networking folder.

Now double-tap the connection icon for the network to reattempt the connection. After the modems have recognized each other, a Terminal window will appear that looks something like this.

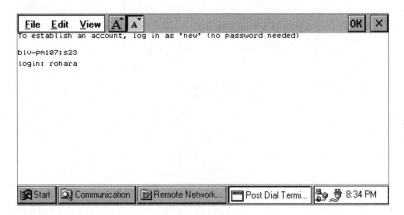

Enter your user ID at the prompt, and press ENTER. (If you don't see some kind of prompt, try pressing ENTER.) You will be prompted to enter a password. Enter it (it won't appear on screen), and press ENTER. When your logon is successful, the screen will look something like this:

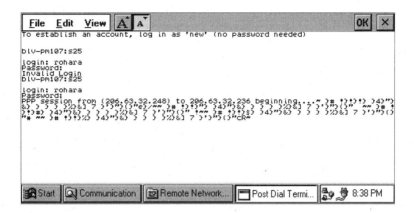

I had to log on twice because I mistyped my password the first time. The gibberish characters are the start of your remote session. Tap the OK button to continue. If your attempt to manually log on fails, contact the system administrator to verify that the settings you entered when setting up the connection are correct. If they seem correct, you might try connecting from your desktop PC. If you can connect from there, you should be able to connect from your Handheld PC.

After you have established a connection to a remote network, there are two built-in programs you can run: the Inbox and Pocket Internet Explorer. (To run the Inbox, the network you connect to must have a POP3 server; to run Pocket Internet Explorer, the network must have a Web server.) Pocket Internet Explorer is covered next, and the Inbox is covered in Chapter 8. Of course, you can install other programs that make use of a remote network connection, such as Telnet or an Internet news reader.

Exploring the Internet

Pocket Internet Explorer gives you access to the Internet from your Handheld PC. Now, you are probably not going to want to cruise the World Wide Web on the small, gray Handheld PC screen, but when you need information from the Internet, Pocket Internet Explorer lets you quickly and easily get it.

NOTE   If you haven't ever explored the World Wide Web, I suggest you try it first from your desktop PC. There are lots of books available on this subject. In this book, I'll concentrate on explaining the features of Pocket Internet Explorer and how using it is different from using a Web browser on your desktop PC.

Microsoft
Pocket
Internet
Explorer

Pocket Internet Explorer is not installed by default on all Handheld PCs, so you might need to install it from your desktop PC. To do this, connect your Handheld PC to your desktop PC, click the Start button on your desktop PC, select Programs, select Handheld PC Explorer, and then select Setup Microsoft Pocket Internet Explorer. When Pocket Internet Explorer is installed, the Microsoft Pocket Internet Explorer shortcut icon appears on the Windows CE desktop.

Connecting to the Internet

If your corporate network provides Internet access, you can double-tap the connection you set up to dial that network. You'll need to set up a proxy server, as described in "Pocket Internet Explorer Options," later in this chapter.

Before you can use Pocket Internet Explorer, you need to connect to the Internet. Open the Remote Networking folder, and double-tap the connection icon you set up to dial your Internet Service Provider. When the connection has been established, you are ready to start Pocket Internet Explorer.

NOTE   If you'd like Pocket Internet Explorer to establish the connection to the Internet for you, you can use its AutoDial feature. This way you don't have to bother opening the Remote Networking folder. AutoDial will also automatically disconnect you from the Internet if your Handheld PC is idle for a period of time you specify. To set up AutoDial, see "Pocket Internet Explorer Options," later in this chapter.

Download the Latest Version

Because the Internet is constantly growing and evolving, so must browsers such as Pocket Internet Explorer. The latest version of Pocket Internet Explorer is always available from the Windows CE Web site (http://www.microsoft.com/windowsce). I've described version 1.1 here, because it is the current version at the time this book is being written. Download a newer version if it is available.

To start Pocket Internet Explorer, double-click the Microsoft Pocket Internet Explorer shortcut icon on your desktop. The default startup page appears.

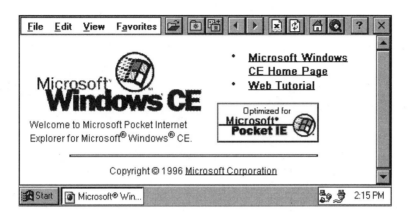

Changing the default startup page is covered in "Pocket Internet Explorer Options," later in this chapter.

There are two links at the top of this page, one to the Windows CE home page, and one to a World Wide Web tutorial at the Microsoft Web site. These links are underlined. Tap either link to move to the corresponding Web page.

You will notice some differences in exploring the Internet from your Handheld PC versus your desktop PC. First of all, since Handheld PCs don't have color screens, links to other Web pages cannot be highlighted with color. (Links are typically blue on your desktop PC.) On the Handheld PC, links that would be highlighted with color are underlined. Second, when you're browsing the Web from your desktop PC, you can locate links that aren't highlighted because the mouse pointer changes shape when you move it over a link. When you're using Pocket Internet Explorer, there is no pointer on screen, so you won't be able to tell where unmarked links are. On most Web pages this is not a problem, as links are well marked. On others, you'll just have to try tapping here and there.

NOTE Like Microsoft Internet Explorer on your desktop PC, Pocket Internet Explorer works with your e-mail program when you tap a link that invites you to send e-mail. Pocket Internet Explorer starts the Inbox and creates a pre-addressed message for you to complete and send. Of course, you need to have an e-mail account—through your Internet Service Provider, your corporate network, or some other source—to be able to send the message. See Chapter 8 for more information about using the Inbox.

Using Pocket Internet Explorer

The most commonly used functions of Pocket Internet Explorer are available through buttons on the command bar, and additional functions are available from the menus.

Command bar buttons

The command bar buttons look like this:

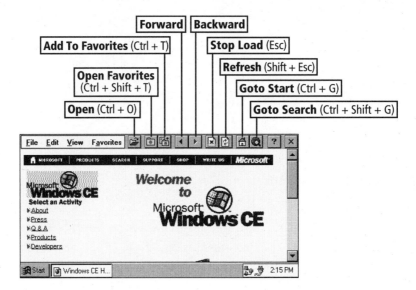

The Open button, at the left, opens a Web page or another document, folder, or computer on the Internet. When you tap this button, the following dialog box appears:

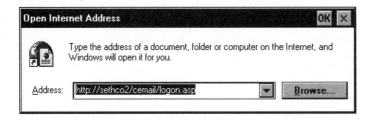

In the Address box, type the address of the Web page or Internet resource you want to open, and press ENTER. You can also use this dialog box to

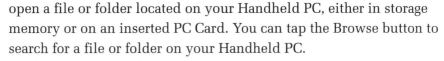

Secure mode means that Pocket Internet Explorer is communicating with the server by using Internet security protocols. These protocols allow you to safely enter private information, such as a credit card number, knowing that it is sent to the server in encrypted form.

open a file or folder located on your Handheld PC, either in storage memory or on an inserted PC Card. You can tap the Browse button to search for a file or folder on your Handheld PC.

Tapping the down-arrow to the right of the Address field displays a list of addresses you have recently visited. Each address you enter during a Pocket Internet Explorer session is added to this list. A quick way to go back to an address you visited earlier in your session is to tap the Open button, open this list, tap the address, and tap OK. In the list, World Wide Web pages might have the prefix *http//:,* pages that you open in secure mode have the prefix *https//:,* files on the Internet that you can download have the prefix *ftp//:,* and files on your Handheld PC have the prefix *file://.*

While Pocket Internet Explorer is searching for and loading a requested Web page or other Internet resource, the animated icon shown in the margin appears in the upper right corner of the screen, just below the command bar.

The Add To Favorites button adds the address of the currently displayed Web page to the Favorites folder so that you can easily open your favorite pages. When you tap the Add To Favorites button, a dialog box appears that lets you give the page any name you wish. To open the page later in the same Pocket Internet Explorer session or in another session, tap the Open Favorites button and then tap the name of the page. To remove a page from your list of favorites, use Windows CE Explorer to open the Favorites subfolder of the Windows folder. Then you can delete any or all of your favorites.

The Backward and Forward buttons let you navigate through the pages you have visited in the current session. Backward opens the page you visited prior to the current page, and Forward opens the page you visited after the current page. If either of these buttons is disabled, it means there is not a previous or a next page to visit.

Sometimes it takes Pocket Internet Explorer a long time to find and load a Web page. If Pocket Internet Explorer is searching for or loading a page and you want to stop the process, tap the Stop Load button. If you are displaying a page and if you want to reload it from the Web, tap the Refresh button. You might want to do this for a page displaying stock market quotations, for example, to make sure you are seeing the latest information.

See "Pocket Internet Explorer Options," later in this chapter, for information about how to change the startup page or the search page.

The Goto Start button opens your startup page. By default, this is the Default.htm file in the Windows folder on your Handheld PC. The Goto Search button opens the default search page, from which you can use various services to search the Internet. The default search page is http://www.msn.com/access/allinone.htm.

Menu commands

The keyboard shortcut for the New Window command is CTRL+N.

A couple of the commands on the File menu are especially useful. The first of these is New Window. It starts a second copy of Pocket Internet Explorer and opens the same Web page that's open in the first copy. If you find yourself referring back and forth between two pages, use this command to open a second copy of Pocket Internet Explorer, and then open the other page you want to view. Now you can move between the two pages by tapping their buttons on the taskbar.

The second especially useful command is Desktop Shortcut. If you want to quickly jump to a particular page, you can place a shortcut to it on your Windows CE desktop. Then, when you double-tap the shortcut, Pocket Internet Explorer starts, connects to the Internet, and displays the page. (Of course, you must connect your modem to a telephone line before you double-tap the shortcut.)

The remaining commands on the File menu are more generic. The Open command works the same way as the Open button, which was described earlier. The Save As command saves the current page as an Internet Document on your Handheld PC. You can then use Pocket Internet Explorer to open and display the saved page even when you are not connected to the Internet. The Properties command opens the Properties dialog box.

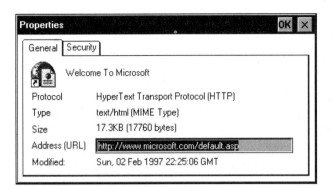

More information about Internet security is located in the Help file on the H/PC. Open Help and then tap Other Help. Scroll down until you find Overview: Security On The Internet.

The General tab of this dialog box gives overall information about the current page. The Security tab displays any security certificates the page contains.

The remaining two File menu commands are About and Close. About displays copyright and version information for Pocket Internet Explorer, and Close exits the program.

The keyboard shortcut for the Select All command is CTRL+A.

The Edit menu contains the usual Cut, Copy, and Paste commands, which move text between Pocket Internet Explorer and the Clipboard. Select All selects all the text on the current page.

Most of the commands on the View menu are also available as command bar buttons and were described earlier. These commands are Start Page (CTRL+G), Search Page (CTRL+SHIFT+G), Stop (ESC) and Refresh (SHIFT+ESC). The History command displays a list of the pages you have visited during the current session. You can tap a page in the list and then tap OK to jump to that page. The Options command is described in the next section, "Pocket Internet Explorer Options."

The commands on the Favorites menu are the same as their command button counterparts, which were described earlier. They are Add To Favorites (CTRL+T) and Open Favorites Folder (CTRL+SHIFT+T).

Pocket Internet Explorer Options

The Options command on the View menu opens the Options dialog box, which you can use to tailor Pocket Internet Explorer to your needs. I suggest that you leave most of the options set to their default values initially, except any you must change to connect to the Internet. As you gain experience with Pocket Internet Explorer, you can change the other options to customize the way the program works. The Options dialog box has five tabs. I'll describe them in order. When you have finished setting the options, tap the OK button to save the new settings from all tabs. If you want to abandon the changes you have made, tap the Close button instead.

Appearance

The Appearance tab controls how Pocket Internet Explorer displays Web pages.

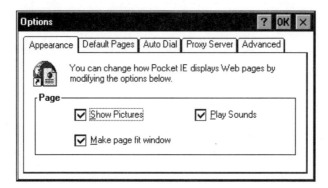

It has three options, which can be set independently of each other. By default, all the options are selected. Clear the Show Pictures check box if you do not want Web page graphics to be displayed. For example, here is the Microsoft home page displayed with its graphics:

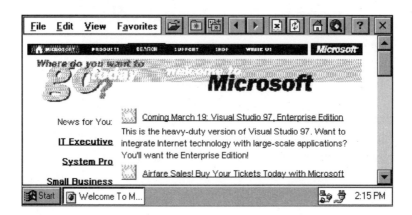

Displayed without its graphics, it looks like this:

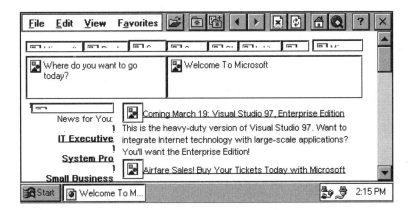

Because graphics take longer to load than text, you can greatly speed up your access to Web pages by clearing the Show Pictures check box.

Because Hewlett-Packard H/PCs have a wider screen than other H/PCs, Pocket Internet Explorer doesn't shrink Web pages as much to display them on the HP machines.

By default, Pocket Internet Explorer shrinks Web pages so that you don't have to scroll from side to side to view them. However this makes the text of some Web pages too small to read. If you clear the Make Page Fit Window check box, Pocket Internet Explorer shows the Web pages at their usual size. With this option cleared and the graphics displayed, the Microsoft home page looks like this:

Clearing the Make Page Fit Window check box works best if you have also cleared the Show Pictures check box. If graphics are displayed on a page, you will have to scroll from side to side to see the full width of the page. If graphics are not displayed, the text on the page is arranged so that you can see it's entire width without scrolling.

Finally, some Web pages play sounds when you open them, and these pages take extra time to load. You can clear the Play Sounds check box if you want to skip the sounds and save some time.

Default Pages

Goto Start

The Default Pages tab lets you change your startup page or your search page. The startup page is opened when you start Pocket Internet Explorer and when you tap the Goto Start button. The search page is opened when you tap the Goto Search button.

Goto Search

To change the startup page or the search page, first open the new page that you want to use. Then open the Options dialog box and switch to the Default Pages tab.

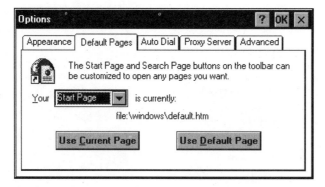

Tap the down-arrow, and select either Start Page or Search Page, depending on which one you want to change. Then tap the Use Current Page button. The address of the current page appears in the dialog box. If you want to use the built-in default again, tap the Use Default Page button.

Auto Dial

The Auto Dial tab allows you to enable the AutoDial feature.

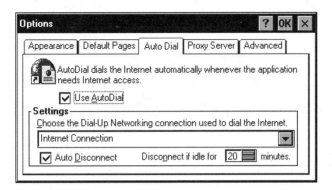

You'll probably want to do this because it makes connecting to the Internet as easy as it gets. Make sure the Use AutoDial check box is selected. Then tap the down-arrow in the Settings section, and select the network connection you use to connect to the Internet.

Pocket Internet Explorer automatically disconnects your network connection if it has been inactive for a specified time—20 minutes by default. This can save you telephone and connect-time charges. You can change the amount of time Pocket Internet Explorer waits before connecting, or you can disable this feature by clearing the Auto Disconnect check box.

After AutoDial is enabled, whenever you try to open an Internet address you are prompted to connect to the network if you are not already connected.

 OTE Disconnect your Handheld PC from your desktop PC before attempting to connect to an Internet address. If a remote networking connection is already active, Pocket Internet Explorer tries to access the Internet address via that connection. The connection between your Handheld PC and your desktop PC is considered a remote networking connection, and in this situation, Pocket Internet Explorer cannot find the Internet address.

Proxy Server

Your system administrator can tell you whether you need to use a proxy server to connect to the Internet using your account. You might need to if you are connecting via your corporate network or another RAS (Remote Access Service) account. If you are connecting through an Internet Service Provider, a proxy server usually isn't necessary.

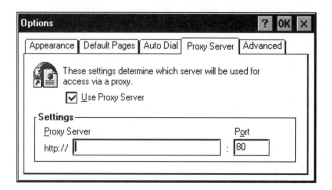

If you need to use a proxy server, select the Use Proxy Server check box, and type the address of the proxy server in the Proxy Server field. For many systems, you don't need to indicate the address of the proxy server; it is accessed through the standard port 80.

Advanced

Before you change options on the Advanced tab, I recommend that you use Pocket Internet Explorer for a while to get familiar with it and to discover the ways you typically use it.

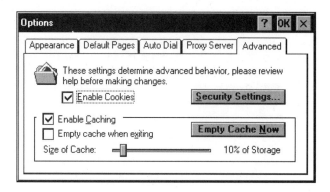

One of the features you can control from the Advanced tab is the Web page cache. When you display a Web page, it is downloaded to your Handheld PC and placed in the cache, which is a section of your storage memory. If you return to the page later during the same session, Pocket Internet Explorer loads the page from the cache, not from the Web. This greatly improves performance.

A neat thing about the cache is that pages stored there can be viewed when you are not connected to the Internet. So you can visit several pages and then refer to them later when you are nowhere near a telephone line. I've done this when visiting a city: before leaving on the trip, I display a page that lists restaurants in the city I'm going to visit, and I mark the page as a favorite. Then, when I am in the city, I open the page from my list of favorites, and the restaurant list is ready for referral.

By default, caching is enabled. You can clear the Enable Caching check box to disable it. You can also specify the maximum amount of storage memory to be used by the cache. The default is 10 percent of the total storage memory. Move the Size Of Cache slider left or right to change the value. If you want to store many pages for offline reference, you might want to temporarily increase the size of the cache. Later you can decrease it to reclaim the storage.

When the cache is full, the pages that have been there the longest without being referenced are discarded to make room for new pages. You can remove all pages from the cache by tapping the Empty Cache Now button. If you don't want to use the cache for offline reference, but merely to improve performance while you are connected to the Internet, select the Empty Cache When Exiting check box. This clears the cache whenever you close Pocket Internet Explorer.

You can also control how cookies are handled from the Advanced tab. In the context of the World Wide Web, cookies are not, unfortunately, edible. They are bits of information stored on your computer that customize certain Web pages you have visited. For example, if you visit the Microsoft Network home page, you can customize it to display information of your choosing. These preferences are stored on your computer in a file called a cookie. If you do not want this type of information stored on your Handheld PC, clear the Enable Cookies check box.

Finally, you can use the Security Settings button on the Advanced tab to control which security protocols are used by Pocket Internet Explorer when you are communicating over the Internet.

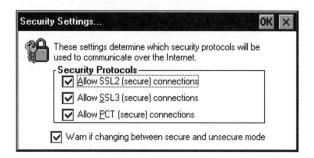

In most cases you will have no need to change these settings.

Using E-mail

The Inbox program in Windows CE lets you send and receive electronic mail (e-mail) on your Handheld PC. Although the Inbox is not as sophisticated as many e-mail programs available for desktop PCs, such as Microsoft Exchange or Lotus cc:Mail, it gives you a lot of functionality in an extremely compact package. If you use Microsoft Exchange on your desktop PC, you can use the H/PC Inbox Transfer feature to move mail between Exchange and the Inbox program on your Handheld PC. So even if you can't dial into your corporate e-mail system from a remote location, you can still use your Handheld PC to work with your e-mail.

If you are going to use only the H/PC Inbox Transfer feature to work with e-mail on your H/PC, you don't need to set up a mail service and you can skip the following section.

In this chapter, I assume that you have used e-mail on your desktop PC and that you understand basic e-mail concepts such as messages and folders. If not, I suggest you review the tutorial information that came with the e-mail program on your desktop PC.

Setting Up a Mail Service

To use e-mail, you must have an e-mail account with an Internet Service Provider, your company, or some other source, and you must have set up a Remote Networking connection to that account provider. This process is described in Chapter 7. The account provider will have one or more *mail servers,* computers that route messages to and from people who have an account with that provider. A program called a *mail service* transfers e-mail messages between the Inbox program on your Handheld PC and the mail server. Before you can use the Inbox, you need to set up your mail service. Don't worry; in comparison to setting up the Remote Networking connection, this is quite easy.

LAN stands for local area network. This type of network is used to connect the computers in one fairly localized area, such as the computers in one company.

A variety of mail services are available to work with different e-mail systems. The mail service built into Windows CE sends e-mail messages to mail servers by using SMTP (Simple Mail Transport Protocol) and receives messages by using POP3 (Post Office Protocol version 3). If your e-mail provider can use these protocols, you can use the built-in mail service. Most Internet Service Providers can use these protocols, as can many LAN-based e-mail systems, including those using Microsoft Exchange Server version 5.0.

If your e-mail system can't use the SMTP and POP3 protocols, you'll need to get and install another mail service for the Windows CE Inbox. Mail services that support a variety of e-mail systems and wireless communication devices are available. Some of them are described in the "Wireless Messaging" section at the end of this chapter; others are covered in Appendix B.

 OTE At the time this book is being written, The Microsoft Network cannot use the SMTP and POP3 mail protocols. The MSN staff are working on this problem though, so if you have an MSN account, check with them for updated information.

Network Security

When the mail service built into Windows CE connects to the mail server you have specified, it uses *basic authentication*, which means that the password you entered is transmitted as unencrypted text to the server. Some mail servers demand that the password be encrypted instead. Unfortunately, the Windows CE mail service cannot do this. If your mail server will not let you log on with basic authentication, you won't be able to access it using the built-in mail service. This problem might be corrected by the time you read this; check the Windows CE Web site for updated information.

I'll describe the other tabs of the Options dialog box in "Inbox Options," later in this chapter.

To begin setting up your mail service, double-tap the Inbox icon on the Windows CE desktop. The Inbox opens, displaying the Inbox folder. Tap the Compose menu, and then tap the Options command. The Options dialog box appears. Tap the Services tab.

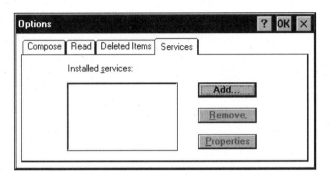

Because you have not yet set up any mail services, the list is empty. Tap the Add button, and a list of registered services appears. If you have not installed any services, the built-in mail service is the only service on your machine, and the list has a single entry, Internet Mail. Select the mail service you want to use, and tap the OK button. Now you need to provide a name for the service. If you are like most folks and will set up only a single service on your Handheld PC, the default name, Mail, is certainly sufficient. Tap the OK button after you have entered the name. The rest of the process depends on which service you're setting up. I'll describe how to finish setting up the built-in Internet Mail service. If you are setting up a different service, refer to the documentation for that service.

The Internet Mail service uses a three-step wizard to walk you through the setup procedure. Filling in the dialog box on the next page is the first step. The information on the left side of the dialog box is required. In the Connection field, select the Remote Networking connection you set up for your e-mail account. In the Mail Host field, type the network name of your mail server. Your e-mail account provider can give you this name, your user ID, and your password. In most cases, your user ID and password will be the same as those used for the Remote Networking connection.

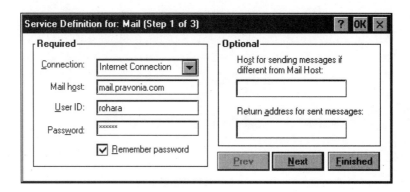

The information on the right side of the dialog box is optional. You don't need to fill in the Host For Sending Messages field unless a different mail server is responsible for sending messages, which is rare. Your e-mail account provider can tell you whether this is the case. In the Return Address For Sent Messages field, you can specify the address to which replies to your messages will be sent. If you have multiple e-mail accounts, you might want to take advantage of this. For example, I have a corporate e-mail account, which I use every day, and a personal e-mail account, which I use less often. When I set up the Windows CE Inbox for use with my personal e-mail account, I set the return address to my corporate e-mail account. Because that is the account I use on a daily basis, it's convenient to have replies to any of my messages delivered there. Think of it as putting your home return address on a letter you mail while visiting your mom.

When you have finished entering information in this dialog box, tap the Next button. Step 2 of the Setup Wizard appears:

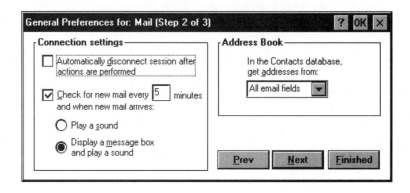

In this dialog box, you specify general settings for the Windows CE Inbox. If you select Automatically Disconnect Session After Actions Are Performed, the Inbox processes all pending actions when you connect to the mail server and then disconnects. This saves you time and connection charges. I suggest that you do not select this check box until you've become more familiar with using the Inbox.

> **NOTE** If you establish the network connection before starting the Inbox, the connection is not automatically disconnected. You must manually disconnect it when you are finished.

If you want to have the Inbox check for new mail every few minutes while you are connected, select Check For New Mail. If you select this option, you can specify the interval and what happens when new mail arrives. I suggest you don't use this feature. Whenever the Inbox performs the check for new mail, it locks you out of the program that you are currently working with. For example, you can't continue to scroll through another message while this is going on. Also, after the Inbox checks for new messages it does not always properly update the message list.

The Windows CE Inbox is linked to the Contacts program. When you address an e-mail message, you can enter the name of someone in your contacts list, and that person's e-mail address is retrieved and inserted. In the contacts list, you can specify up to three e-mail addresses for each person. On the right side of this dialog box, you can specify which fields in the Contacts program are to be searched for e-mail addresses. Normally you will want to search all e-mail fields. Some services, like the SkyTel Messenger service, use the Contacts Pager field instead of the e-mail fields.

Tap Next when you have finished with this dialog box. Step 3 of the Setup Wizard appears, as seen in the illustration on the next page.

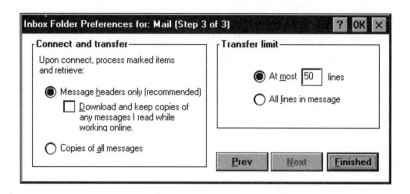

Here you specify how messages are to be copied from the mail server to your Handheld PC. Because the Handheld PC has limited storage capacity, you need to be careful how much data you transfer to it. Most people transfer only mail message headers when they connect to the mail server. The message *header* is the "envelope"—everything but the body of the message. This way you can scan the messages waiting for you and select which you want to read. To select this mode of operation, tap the Message Headers Only option. I also recommend that you select the Download And Keep check box. This way, when you open a mail message, a copy of it is downloaded to your Handheld PC so that you can read it again later when you are not connected to the mail server.

The other approach is to always download copies of all messages to your Handheld PC. If you want to read all your mail, and if you tend to get only a few messages at a time, this might work for you. Tap the Copies Of All Messages option to select this mode of operation. The advantage of this mode is that after the downloading is completed, you can disconnect and read your messages off line.

Regardless of which mode you choose, you can control how much of each message you want to download. (In Message Headers Only mode, this applies only when you have the Download And Keep check box selected.) You can specify that no more than the specified number of lines of each message be downloaded. This keeps you from filling up your Handheld PC with the copy of *War and Peace* someone forwarded to you. I suggest you initially leave this set at the default of 50 lines. You can change it later if that does not work well for you.

ARNING The Windows CE Inbox cannot work with files or other objects attached to e-mail messages. If you choose to download all lines in the messages you receive, any attachments are downloaded as well and then quietly thrown away. So if your colleague sends you a 3-MB spreadsheet, you'll waste quite a bit of time downloading it to your Handheld PC to no purpose.

When you are done with this dialog box, tap Finished, and you are indeed finished setting up the Internet Mail service. Tap OK to close the Options dialog box.

Working with Multiple Services

Most people set up only a single mail service on their Handheld PC. If you are one of the few people who has more than one e-mail account, you might set up a service for each account. You can set up the built-in Internet Mail service more than once, configuring it for different accounts under different names. Or, perhaps you access one account via the Internet and another via a wireless modem. Then you can set up the Internet Mail service for the Internet account and another mail service for the other account.

Connect

The key to working with multiple services is to realize that one of the services is the current service. This is the service that has the dot to the left of its name in the Service menu. You can switch among the services by tapping the name of the one you want to work with. The operations described in this chapter operate with respect to the current service. When you press the Connect button, you connect to the mail server by using the current service. When you compose a new message, the current service sends the message. Each time you use the Inbox, check that the current service is the one you want to use.

Sending and Receiving E-mail

Now, with the mail service set up, you are ready to send and receive e-mail. To start the Inbox, double-tap the Inbox icon on the Windows CE desktop. The Inbox opens, displaying the Inbox folder. Initially, of course, your Inbox folder won't have any messages in it.

OTE There is room for lots of confusion in this section, as the Windows CE e-mail program is named Inbox and the folder into which your newly delivered mail is placed is also named Inbox. I will try to keep things straight by always referring to the latter as the Inbox folder.

Tour of the Inbox

The main part of the Inbox window is divided into two sections. On the left, the folder list displays the folders for storing e-mail messages. On the right, the message list displays the contents of the currently selected folder. In the following illustration, the Inbox folder is selected, and its contents are displayed in the message list on the right.

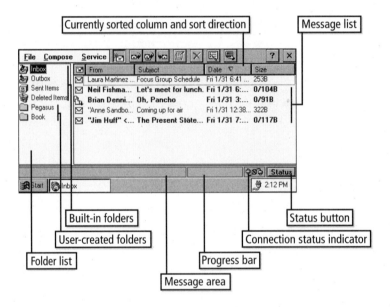

The Inbox, Outbox, Sent Items, and Deleted Items folders are built in and cannot be deleted.

Folder	Description
Inbox	All incoming messages are placed in the Inbox folder, regardless of which mail service delivered them. By default, the H/PC Inbox Transfer feature copies messages from Exchange on your desktop PC to this folder as well.

Folder	Description
Outbox	After you compose a message and tap the Send button, the message is moved to the Outbox folder. When you connect to the mail server, the message is sent and is removed from this folder.
Sent Items	Optionally, after a message is sent, a copy of the message is stored in the Sent Items folder.
Deleted Items	When you delete a message from a folder, it is moved to the Deleted Items folder. By default, this folder is emptied whenever you exit from the Inbox program.

You can create up to 21 additional folders in which to store messages. You cannot have folders within folders.

You can control the layout of the Inbox window to some degree. You can touch the divider between the folder list and the message list with the stylus and then slide it from side to side to give more room to one or the other. In the same way, you can adjust the width of any of the message list columns to allow more information to be displayed. You can sort the message list by any of the columns, in ascending or descending order. Tap the column header to sort by that column; tap it again to reverse the sort order.

Below the folder list and the message list is a status bar. It is divided into four areas.

Status Bar Area	Description
Message area	Displays informative and status messages.
Progress bar	Indicates progress during message downloading and uploading.
Connection status indicator	Shows whether you are connected to the mail server.
Status button	Tap this button to display a summary of the actions that will be taken when you next connect to the mail server and when you exit from the Inbox.

Here's an example of the Pending Actions dialog box that appears when you tap the Status button:

The next time the Inbox connects to the mail server, the messages currently in the Outbox folder will be sent, and two messages on the mail server will be copied to the Handheld PC. The next time the Inbox exits, four messages currently in the Deleted Items folder will be permanently deleted.

At the top of the Inbox window is the command bar. On the far right are the familiar Help and Close buttons, and as you would expect, they work the same here as they do in all the other programs in Windows CE. In the middle are eight buttons that provide quick access to the most frequently used Inbox commands.

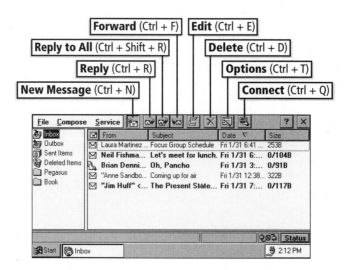

Button	Description
New Message	Creates a new message.
Reply	Creates a new message that is a reply to the selected message and is addressed to the originator of that message.
Reply To All	Creates a new message that is a reply to the selected message and is addressed to the originator and all the addressees of that message.
Forward	Creates a new message that contains as its body the body of the selected message.
Edit	Allows you to modify the selected message. This button is active only when the message is stored on the Handheld PC.
Delete	Moves the selected message or messages to the Deleted Items folder, by default, or deletes the message immediately if you have options set that way.
Options	Opens the Options dialog box. For more information about this dialog box, see "Inbox Options," later in this chapter.
Connect	Connects to the mail server if you are currently disconnected, or disconnects if you are currently connected.

At the left of the command bar are three menus: File, Compose, and Service. The commands on these menus will be discussed in the course of the rest of this chapter.

Connecting to the Mail Server

Connect

For more information about the Connect To dialog box, see "Connecting to a Remote Network" in Chapter 7.

When you are ready to get your e-mail, connect your modem to a telephone line, and tap the Connect button. A Connect To dialog box appears, containing information for the Remote Networking connection used by the current mail service. Here you can check the dialing location and the phone number that is about to be dialed. Tap the Connect button to connect to the mail server.

You'll hear the modem dial the phone number, and after the other machine answers the phone, the two modems will whistle at each other. A message on the screen will keep you posted of the progress.

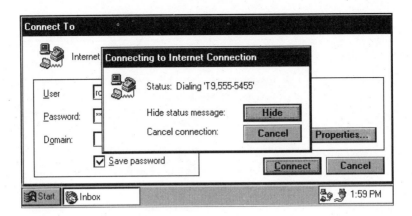

When the connection has been established, the Inbox appears. Now the Inbox program attempts to log onto the mail server. The progress of this attempt is displayed in the message area at the bottom of the screen.

N OTE   If the Inbox is unable to log onto the mail server, check the settings of the service you are using. In particular, ensure that your user ID and password are correctly spelled and that the mail server is correctly identified.

After the Inbox has logged onto the mail server, the contents of your Inbox folder on the server are copied to the Inbox folder on your Handheld PC. Your Handheld PC screen will look something like this:

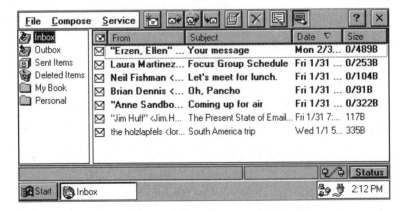

The connection status indicator shows that the Inbox is connected to the mail server. In the previous illustration, there are seven messages in my Inbox folder on the mail server. The first five are displayed in boldface, indicating that I have not yet read them. The last two are not bold, indicating that I have read the messages. The down-arrow in the Date column header indicates that the message list is sorted by date, from newest to oldest.

Take a look at the information in the Size column. The size of the first message is listed as 0/489B. This indicates that none of the message has been downloaded (0 bytes) and that the total size of the message on the mail server is 489 bytes. The two messages I have read have been downloaded in their entirety, so only a single number is displayed for the size of each.

By default, when you connect to a mail server by using the built-in Internet Mail service, the Inbox downloads only the message headers of new messages. This lets you choose whether you want to work with your mail while on line (still connected to the mail server by phone) or off line (you hang up the phone while working with your mail). There are advantages and disadvantages to either style of working. The nice thing is that you can easily switch between them as your needs of the moment dictate.

It is important to realize that the messages downloaded are copies of the messages residing on your mail server. Actually, they are *linked* copies. If you delete them from your Handheld PC, they are also deleted from the mail server. (You can delete just the copies of the messages on your Handheld PC by tapping the Clear All command on the Service menu.)

Working On Line

If you stay on line with the mail server, using the Inbox is similar to working with a LAN-based e-mail system. Double-tap a message and it opens. Compose a new message and it is transmitted as soon as you send it. You can save storage space on your Handheld PC by working on line and setting options not to download the messages you read. The advantage of this method is that no messages are taking up space on your Handheld PC; the disadvantage is that you can read messages only when you are connected to the mail server.

Working on line with the Inbox is different in some ways than using a LAN-based e-mail system, of course. When you double-tap a message to open it, by default, only the first 50 lines of the message are downloaded to your Handheld PC. You can adjust the number of lines that are down-loaded for all messages by using the Options dialog box, which is de-scribed in "Inbox Options," later in this chapter. If you want to override the default for a specific message, tap the message to select it, and then tap the Retrieve Full Text Copy command on the Service menu. If the message contains an attachment, the attachment is downloaded along with the message text and then thrown away because the Windows CE Inbox cannot work with message attachments.

By default, the Inbox periodically checks for new e-mail messages arriving on your mail server and adds them to the message list. You can set how often this happens, or you can turn it off if you prefer. See the "Inbox Options" section for more information. You can manually check for new messages by tapping the Refresh command on the Service menu.

Another potential disadvantage of working on line arises from the cost of connection charges. You might be billed for the cost of the telephone call, which can be quite expensive if it is long distance or over a cellular phone, and you might be billed for the time you are connected to your Internet Service Provider.

You can switch between working on line and working off line as your needs change. What works for many people is a combination of the two. While connected you might want to double-tap some messages to read (and download), and then later, after you disconnect, you can compose new messages and compose replies to downloaded messages.

Working Off Line
Working off line incurs fewer phone and connect-time charges, but it can be more inconvenient because you must reconnect to the mail server to send messages or to download messages you want to read. Also, any messages that you download consume storage space on your Handheld PC. On the other hand, because downloaded messages are stored locally, you can read them and compose replies when you are not connected to the mail server.

Connect

If you are connected to the mail server and want to work off line, tap the Connect button to disconnect and hang up the telephone. Now peruse the message list. You might be able to tell from just the sender and subject that you want to read a message. Or maybe there is a message you don't need to read at all and you want to delete it.

Message icon

Download icon

Double-tap messages you want to download from the mail server. The message icons change to the download icons, indicating that the messages will be downloaded the next time you connect to the mail server. To mark several messages at a time for downloading, select the messages and then tap the Retrieve A Copy command on the Service menu. By default, only the first 50 lines of each message will be downloaded. As mentioned previously, you can retrieve the entire text of a message by tapping the Retrieve Full Text Copy command on the Service menu.

Reply

Tapping the Reply button also marks a selected message for downloading, but you'll have to tap it again to compose the reply after you have connected to the mail server. While you are working off line, you can, of course, compose a new message or compose a reply to a message that has already been downloaded. The new message or the reply will be sent when you connect to the mail server.

In the following illustration, I have marked two messages for downloading by double-tapping them.

If you move or copy a message to another folder, that action also marks the message for downloading, and the move or copy action is executed after the message has been downloaded. To mark a message to be deleted, tap the message to select it, and then tap the Delete button. The message is moved to the Deleted Items folder. When you next connect to the mail server, the message will be deleted from your Handheld PC and from the mail server. If you change your mind before you connect to the mail server, open the Deleted Items folder and drag the message back to the Inbox folder. This cancels the request for deletion.

Connect

When you have finished working off line, tap the Connect button, and when the connection with the mail server is established, all the operations you marked are executed. Remember that you can tap the Status button to see a summary of what will happen when you connect.

In the following illustration, the two messages I had marked for downloading have indeed been downloaded.

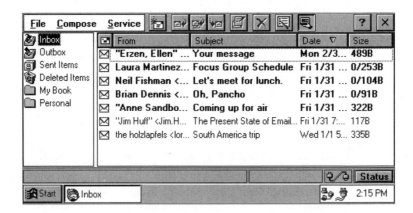

You can tell this because their size is no longer listed as zero. In this case, because the messages are short, both were completely downloaded.

Reading Messages

You can also open a message by tapping the Open command on the File menu.

To open a message and read it, double-tap it in the message list. If the message has been downloaded, it opens.

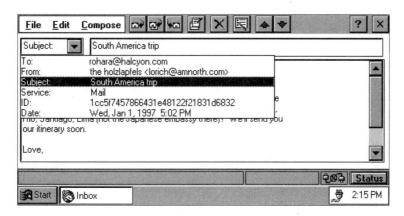

Options (Ctrl + T) **Previous** (Ctrl + <)
Edit (Ctrl + E) **Next** (Ctrl + >)

File Edit Compose

Subject: South America trip

Dear Bob,

We've told you that we are leaving soon for S. A. We were just wondering if you have heard from friends who have visited down there about any special things we shouldn't miss. Anything in Buenos Aires, Rio, Santiago, Lima (not the Japanese embassy there)? We'll send you our itinerary soon.

Love,

Status

Start Inbox 2:15 PM

If you open a message that contains multiple fonts, boldface text, or other enhancements, these enhancements won't appear on your Handheld PC.

You can also tap the Edit command on the Compose menu or press CTRL+E to edit the message.

When a message is open, the buttons on the command bar change. The New Message and Connect buttons disappear, and the Previous and Next buttons appear. To save memory, messages are opened read-only, so you can't make changes to them. If you want to change the text of a message, tap the Edit button. The Previous and Next buttons open and display the previous or next message in the message list. They let you move through your messages without taking the time to return to the message list display.

Below the command bar in an open message, the information in the message header is displayed. To save screen space, it is collapsed into a single line. Initially, the Subject field of the header is displayed. To display other fields of the header, tap the down-arrow. A list of all the header fields for that message appears.

File Edit Compose

Subject: South America trip

To: rohara@halcyon.com
From: the holzlapfels <lorich@amnorth.com>
Subject: South America trip
Service: Mail
ID: 1cc5f7457866431e48122f21831d6832
Date: Wed, Jan 1, 1997 5:02 PM
Rio, Santiago, Lima (not the Japanese embassy there)? We'll send you
our itinerary soon.

Love,

Status

Start Inbox 2:15 PM

You can simply read them here, or you can tap one to display it in the box. The following table describes the contents of each field.

Field	Description
To:	The address of the person to whom the message was sent. Multiple addresses are separated by semicolons (;).
From:	The originator of the message. Often there will be a "friendly name" displayed, followed by the actual address, which is enclosed in angle brackets.
Subject:	A brief description of the topic of the message. Some mail services don't support this, so it might be blank. And people don't always enter a subject when composing mail.
Service:	Which mail service delivered the message.
ID:	An internal identifier of the message. It can be used to detect duplicate messages.
Date:	The date and time the message was received at the mail server.

The header fields listed here are generated by the built-in mail service. Other mail services might not create all these fields, or they might create other fields.

To return to the message list, tap the Close button.

 UN   To see who wrote the Inbox program, edit a message, and change the Type field to *Who wrote this program?* Close the message, Save the change, and then open it again. A message displaying the authors' names appears. To restore the message, use the Edit button to reopen the original message and delete the entry from the Type field.

Composing New Messages

To compose a new message, tap the New Message button. A new, blank message appears:

Compose

IP   You can also tap the New Message command on the Compose menu or press CTRL+N to compose a new message.

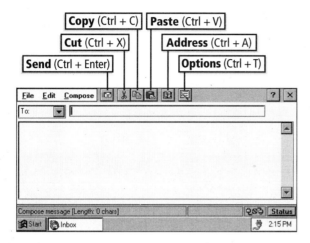

Again, the buttons on the command bar change. The following table describes the buttons that are displayed.

Button	Description
Send	Moves your message to the Outbox folder. All messages in the Outbox folder for the current mail service are sent the next time you connect to the mail server.
Cut, Copy, Paste	Cut, copy, and paste text to and from the clipboard.
Address	Helps you address your message by using information from the Contacts program.
Options	Opens the Options dialog box.

Just as when you read an e-mail message, the information in the header is collapsed into a single line, displayed below the command bar. Initially the To field is displayed because this is the only field of the header that must be completed to send the message.

Address

In the To field, you can type a complete e-mail address, or you can type part of the name of someone listed in your contacts list. If you type part of a name and tap the Address button, a Choose Address dialog box appears that contains all the names in your contacts list that include the text you typed and that have a value in at least one of the Email fields. If a contact has information in more than one of the Email fields, multiple addresses for that contact are listed. To choose one of the addresses, tap it and then tap the OK button.

You can control which fields from the contacts list are displayed in the Choose Address dialog box. See the "Inbox Options" section, later in this chapter, for more information.

If you tap the Address button without first typing part of a name in the To field, the Choose Address dialog box displays all your contacts that have e-mail addresses. You can scroll through the list and tap the one to whom you want to address the message.

To send your message to more than one person, type a semicolon (;) to separate each address from the next.

 OTE   The Inbox does not check to make sure the addresses you enter are correct; the addresses are checked by the mail server. When a message with an incorrect address is delivered to the mail server, you will receive a message informing you of this.

There are several other fields in the message header. You can access them by tapping the down-arrow, just as you did when reading a mail message.

Field	Description
Cc:	Cc stands for carbon copy. (You do remember carbon paper, don't you?) Enter the addresses of people who should receive a copy of the message.
Bcc:	Bcc stands for blind carbon copy. Enter the addresses of people who should receive a copy of the message but whose names should not be displayed to the recipients of the message.
Subject:	Enter a one-line summary of the message.
Type:	This field does not really do anything. It is part of a mechanism that allows registered programs to process specially formatted mail.
Replies:	These quick replies are used primarily by the SkyTel 2-Way Messenger mail service.
Service:	Specify the mail service that is to send this message. It is set by default to the current service. The only situation in which you would change this is if you have more than one service set up and if you want to compose a message to be sent by a mail service other than the current service.

When you are ready to enter the text of your message, press the TAB key to move the cursor to the next field. You can type the message text, or you can paste text from the clipboard.

Send

When you are done composing the message, tap the Send button to send it. This moves the message to the Outbox folder. If you are currently connected to the mail server, the message is uploaded to the mail server and sent. If you are not connected, the message remains in the Outbox folder, and it is sent the next time you connect to the mail server.

Replying To and Forwarding Messages

Reply

You can also tap the Reply To Sender command on the Compose menu or press CTRL+R to reply to a message.

Often you will want to respond to the author of a message. The Reply button provides a quick way to do this. Tap the Reply button while the message is open or while it is selected in the message list. The Inbox creates a new message, addressed to the author of the selected or open message. The Subject field contains the same text that was in the Subject field of the original message, prefixed by *RE:*. The other header fields can be filled in if you want them to be, as described in "Composing New Messages."

By default, the body of the message is filled in with the body of the original message, as shown here, so that you can easily refer to the message while you compose your response:

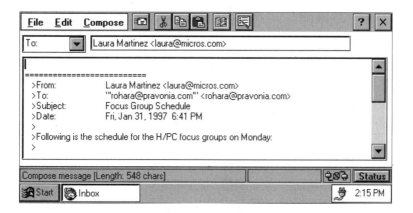

225

Type your response above the original message. You can control whether the body of the original message is included in the reply by changing an option, as explained in "Inbox Options," later in this chapter.

   IP   If you normally have the body of the original message included in your reply message but for this reply you don't want that, just press CTRL+A to select the entire text of the message, and then press DELETE to delete it. Now you have a clean slate on which to compose your reply.

Reply All

You can also tap the Reply To All command on the Compose menu or press CTRL+SHIFT+R to reply to all recipients of the original message.

You can tap the Reply All button, rather than the Reply button, to send your response to everyone who received the original message.

Finally, you can forward a message to someone else. Tap the Forward button to do this. As when you reply to a message, the body of the message is copied for you. The Subject field is filled in as in the original message, prefixed by *FW:*. The new message is not addressed; you must enter an address in the To field.

Forward

You can also tap the Forward command on the Compose menu or press CTRL+F to forward a message.

When you are done composing your reply or composing additional text for your forwarded message, tap the Send button. The message is moved to the Outbox folder and is sent immediately if you are connected to the mail server. If you are working off line, the message is sent when you next connect to the mail server.

Storing and Organizing Messages

To store and organize your messages, you can create additional folders. You can't create folders within folders, however. If you're tempted to create a lot of folders and store a lot of messages in them, remember that storage space on your Handheld PC is quite limited in comparison to that typically available on a desktop PC. For example, the stored messages on my desktop PC consume more than 25 MB of disk space, and that is only the messages I've received during the past three months! So I tend to use my desktop PC as a place to store messages, and I use my Handheld PC to work with messages while I'm away from my desk. I don't store many messages on my Handheld PC for very long.

You can also rename a folder by selecting it and then tapping Rename on the File menu.

To create a folder, tap the New Folder command on the File menu. A small dialog box appears. In the dialog box, type the name of the folder you want to create, and then tap the OK button. To rename a folder later, tap the folder name to select it, and then tap it again so that you can edit the name. After you've typed the new name, you can press the ENTER key to accept the new name, or you can press the ESC key to revert to the old name. You cannot rename the built-in folders.

The keyboard shortcut for the Delete command is CTRL+D.

To delete a folder, tap it to select it, and then press the DELETE key or tap Delete on the File menu. A dialog box appears, asking you to confirm the deletion. Tap Yes to permanently delete the folder and all the messages in it.

 ARNING When you delete a folder, you permanently and immediately delete all the messages in the folder as well. There is no Undo here.

The keyboard shortcut for the Move To command is CTRL+M, and the keyboard shortcut for the Copy To command is CTRL+C.

To move or copy messages from one folder to another, select the messages you want to move or copy, and then tap the Move To command or the Copy To command on the File menu. A dialog box pops up, displaying the folders in the Inbox program. Tap the folder to which you want the messages moved or copied, and then tap the OK button. If the messages you are moving or copying have not been downloaded, they are marked for downloading, as described in "Working Off Line," earlier in this chapter, and the move or copy operation takes place the next time you connect to the mail server.

ARNING Be careful when moving messages. If you move a message that has not been downloaded, when you connect to the mail server the message is downloaded and is permanently deleted from the server. If the message contained any attachments or embedded objects, they are lost. And if only the first 50 lines of the message were downloaded (the default), the rest of the message is lost as well.

You can also move and copy messages by dragging and dropping them. If the message you drag and drop has been downloaded, it is moved from its

current folder on your Handheld PC to the folder on your Handheld PC
that you drop it in. If the message has not been downloaded, a copy of the
message is downloaded from the mail server the next time you connect,
and this copy is then moved to the folder you dropped the message in. If
this seems a little confusing, don't worry. As you drag the message, the
status area at the bottom of the screen informs you whether a move operation or a copy operation is taking place. And of course you can always
drag the message back if you change your mind.

Inbox Options

*The keyboard
shortcut for the
Options command
is CTRL+T.*

The Inbox program has numerous options that let you customize how the
program operates. Try out different settings to tune the Inbox to your
needs. To open the Options dialog box, tap the Compose menu, and then
tap the Options command.

The "Setting Up a Mail Service" section, earlier in this chapter, described
the Services tab. Here I'll cover the options on the other three tabs.

The Compose tab has options that let you control how messages you
compose are formed and sent.

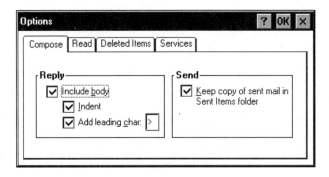

When you reply to a message, you can have the body of that message
included in your reply, for reference. Select the Include Body check box if
you want this to happen. You can choose to have the body of the original
message indented, prefixed by a character you specify, or both. The Keep
Copy check box controls what happens when a message you have sent is
transferred to the mail server. If this check box is selected, a copy of the

message is placed in the Sent Items folder. If not, no copy of the message remains on your Handheld PC.

When people are reading new messages, they typically work in the Inbox folder, opening unread messages and then moving them to other folders for storage or deleting them. The Read tab controls what happens after you move or delete a message.

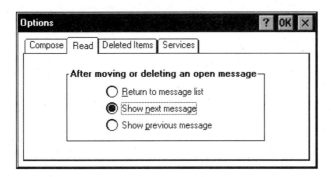

If you tend to jump around and read messages in a different order each time you look at new mail, tap Return To Message List. If you tend to read your new messages in sequence, tap Show Next Message or Show Previous Message, depending on whether you work the list from top to bottom or vice versa.

The Deleted Items tab controls what happens when you delete a message.

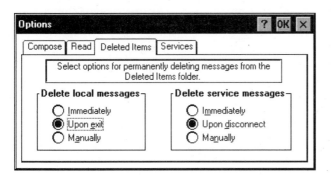

The group of buttons on the left controls what happens when you delete a message that is stored on your Handheld PC. The group of buttons on the right controls what happens when you delete a message that is linked to the corresponding message on the mail server.

By default, the options are set as shown in the previous illustration. When you delete a message, it is not immediately deleted. Rather, it is moved to the Deleted Items folder. So if, a few minutes later, you decide you don't really want to delete the message, you can move it to another folder. Messages in the Deleted Items folder are permanently deleted when you exit the Inbox. Linked messages are deleted from the mail server when you disconnect.

If you select the Immediately options, when you delete a message it is immediately deleted with no chance for recovery. If you select the Manually options, messages are deleted permanently only when you manually delete them from the Deleted Items folder. You can delete individual messages from the Deleted Items folder by selecting them and pressing DELETE, or you can clear all messages out of the Deleted Items folder by tapping Empty Deleted Items on the File menu.

Working with E-mail While Away from Your Desk

If you use Microsoft Exchange on your desktop PC, you can use the H/PC Inbox Transfer feature to download e-mail from your desktop PC to your Handheld PC. You can work with the e-mail on your Handheld PC—reading messages, composing replies, and composing new messages—and then when you return to your desk, you can upload any outgoing messages to your desktop PC. This feature lets you use your Handheld PC for e-mail even if you don't have remote access to your e-mail system or even if you don't have a modem for your Handheld PC. I have found the H/PC Inbox Transfer feature to be very powerful, as I often spend much of my day away from my desk.

H/PC Inbox Transfer does have some limitations. It only copies e-mail messages between the Windows CE Inbox program on your Handheld PC and Microsoft Exchange on your desktop PC. It does not synchronize the messages on both machines the way H/PC Explorer synchronizes your appointments, contacts, and tasks. So if you download an e-mail message to your Handheld PC and read it, the message is marked as having been read on your Handheld PC but is still marked as unread on your desktop PC. Similarly, if you delete a downloaded e-mail message on your Handheld PC, the corresponding message on your desktop PC is not deleted.

H/PC Inbox Transfer works even if you haven't set up a mail service for the Windows CE Inbox. You can use it as soon as your Handheld PC is connected to your desktop PC, without any further setup. So instead of playing Solitaire during meetings in which you are not paying attention, you can handle your e-mail instead.

To begin using H/PC Inbox Transfer, start Microsoft Exchange on your desktop PC, and click the H/PC Inbox Transfer command on the Tools menu in Exchange. The following dialog box appears.

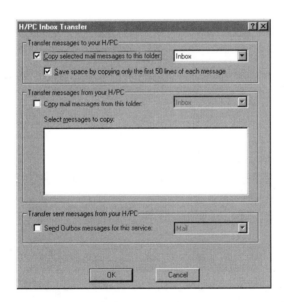

When this dialog box first appears, all the fields are disabled, and there is a progress bar at the bottom. This is because H/PC Inbox Transfer is communicating with your Handheld PC to determine which mail services, if any, have been set up and whether any folders have been created in the Inbox program. It will take 5 to 20 seconds before the dialog box appears as shown in the previous illustration, ready for your input.

This dialog box contains three groups of fields. The top group controls the transfer of messages from your desktop PC to your Handheld PC. The middle group controls the transfer of messages from folders you specify on your Handheld PC back to the Exchange Inbox folder. The bottom group lets you transfer messages you have composed and sent on your Handheld PC from the Outbox folder there to Exchange's Outbox folder so that they can actually be sent. I'll describe each of these three groups in turn.

Transferring Messages to Your Handheld PC

If you want to download some messages from Exchange on your desktop PC, select the messages before you click the H/PC Inbox Transfer command. You can select messages in any folder, and the messages can be read or unread. Remember that any attachments will be discarded. After you have selected the messages, click the H/PC Inbox Transfer command on the Exchange Tools menu. There will be a delay while H/PC Inbox Transfer gets folder and mail service information from your Handheld PC. After this is completed, select Copy Selected Mail Messages To This Folder.

Now choose into which folder on your Handheld PC the messages are to be copied. By default the messages are placed in the Inbox folder, but you can choose any folder in the Inbox program. You can also specify that only the first 50 lines of each message are to be downloaded. This is useful if the messages are large or if you intend to transfer many messages. If you clear the Save Space checkbox, the entire text of each message is downloaded.

Click OK, and the transfer proceeds. A status bar is displayed at the bottom of the dialog box to inform you of the transfer's progress. When the transfer is completed, the dialog box closes. If you have the Inbox program open on your Handheld PC, you might wonder what happened to the new messages. Unfortunately they are not automatically displayed; switch to a different folder, and then switch back to the Inbox folder (or whichever folder the messages are in). The transferred messages will then be visible.

The transferred messages are displayed in boldface, indicating that they are unread. This is done even if they were read on your desktop PC, because you have not yet read them on your Handheld PC. After you open the messages on your Handheld PC they will, of course, be marked as read. If you repeat the transfer operation with the same messages, you will have two copies of them on your Handheld PC.

Transferring Messages from Your Handheld PC

Perhaps you have created messages on your Handheld PC that you want to store in Exchange on your desktop PC. Or perhaps you started composing a message on your Handheld PC and you want to work on it further on your desktop PC before sending it. Regardless, if you want to transfer messages from your Handheld PC to your desktop PC, click the H/PC Inbox Transfer command on the Tools menu in Exchange. In the middle section of the H/PC Inbox Transfer dialog box, select the Copy Messages From This Folder check box, and then select the folder in the Windows CE Inbox program from which you want to copy messages. There is a delay while the message headers are retrieved from the Handheld PC, and then the messages in that folder are displayed in the Select Messages To Copy field.

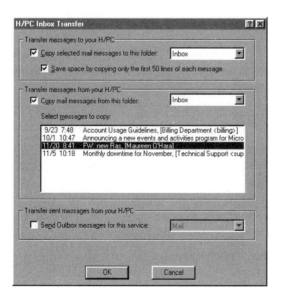

From the list of messages, select those you want to upload to your desktop PC. Initially all the messages are selected. If you click one message, only it is selected. You can select multiple messages by holding down the CTRL key as you click additional messages.

When you have selected all the messages you want to upload, click the OK button at the bottom of the dialog box. The following dialog box is displayed. It allows you to select to which folder in Exchange the messages are to be copied.

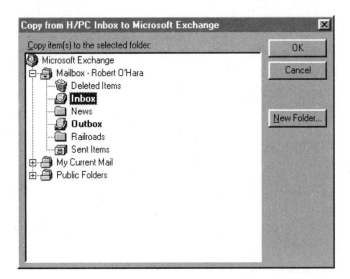

If you want the messages to be copied to a new folder, you can click the New Folder button. After you have selected the folder into which the messages should be copied, click the OK button, and the copy operation proceeds. The copied messages are marked as unread and are displayed in boldface on your desktop PC. This is because, as far as Exchange is concerned, they are new messages: you have not yet read them on your desktop PC.

Just as when transferring messages from your desktop PC to your Handheld PC, if you repeat the copy operation, you will get a second copy of the messages in the destination folder.

Transferring Sent Messages from Your Handheld PC

To transfer messages from the Outbox folder on your Handheld PC to the Outbox folder on your desktop PC so that they can be sent to their destinations, click the H/PC Inbox Transfer command on the Tools menu in Exchange. In the H/PC Inbox Transfer dialog box, select the Send Outbox Messages For This Service check box.

If you have not set up a mail service on your Handheld PC, ignore the field to the right of this check box. If you have set up more than one mail service on your Handheld PC, click the down-arrow at the right of this field to open a list of the set-up mail services, and select the service that was current when you composed the messages you want transferred. Click the OK button at the bottom of the dialog box.

The messages in the Outbox folder on your Handheld PC are transferred to the Exchange Outbox folder on your desktop PC. Even if you have chosen to have sent messages saved in the Sent Items folder on your Handheld PC, the transferred messages are not saved there, because they weren't sent to the mail server from the Handheld PC. If you have set the Exchange option to save sent messages in the Sent Items folder in Exchange, the transferred messages are saved there, since they were sent from Exchange.

Wireless Messaging

Several of these wireless communications devices and programs are described in Appendix B.

As mentioned previously, the mail service included with the Windows CE Inbox was designed for wired communications, in which you connect your Handheld PC to a telephone jack. Several companies offer devices and mail services for the Inbox that support wireless communications. With these you can send and receive messages without being tied to a telephone jack. I've used them while in a taxicab and while sitting by a hotel swimming pool. (You might or might not regard this as progress.) All the wireless devices described in this section have their own batteries, so they don't drain the batteries of your Handheld PC.

Sockets, Inc. markets a one-way-pager PC Card that you can use to receive messages. It slips into the PC Card slot of your Handheld PC, leaving a small "bubble" sticking out the end. This bubble holds the AAA battery that powers the device for a couple of weeks. The Sockets card has a small display on which you can read incoming messages without using your Handheld PC. Thus you can carry the PC Card alone and still receive your messages. When you plug the card into your Handheld PC, the messages are delivered to the Inbox folder. While the device is plugged into your Handheld PC, any new messages that arrive are immediately delivered to the Inbox folder. The Sockets one-way–paging PC Card is the most compact of all the wireless messaging devices, but it can only receive messages, not send them.

SkyTel's Messenger is a two-way pager: it can send messages as well as receive them. It is bulkier than a typical one-way pager, but it is still wearable. Its single AA battery powers the pager for a couple of weeks. The Messenger connects to the serial port of your Handheld PC via a short cable. Incoming messages are delivered to the Inbox. You can reply to them, or you can compose new messages to anyone who has a SkyTel one-way pager or two-way pager or anyone reachable via the Internet. Messages sent or received by using the Messenger are limited to 500 characters in length.

The Skytel Messenger is a real pager; it comes with a belt clip so that you can wear it. Also, with its little keypad, you can compose short messages even without connecting it to your Handheld PC. Its one disadvantage is that you have to carry a short cable with you to connect the pager to your Handheld PC.

The Megahertz Allpoints wireless modem is a PC Card that provides wireless connectivity to the RAM mobile data network. The card is powered by a 9-volt battery that provides about 30 hours of service, and it has a retractable antenna that must be extended when you are communicating. The "bubble" at the end of the card, which holds the battery and antenna, is somewhat bulky, but even so, the Handheld PC and modem combination is much smaller than the smallest notebook computer.

Several companies offer mail services for Windows CE that operate over the RAM mobile data network. I've used the products from Wynd and Zap-It. You can use them to send and receive messages of almost unlimited length to and from anyone reachable via the Internet. Another nice feature is that while you are connected to the RAM mobile data network server, new mail is delivered to you as soon as it arrives at the server. Because you don't pay for connect time, but rather only for data you send or receive, you can stay connected for extended periods of time.

Motorola offers three wireless PC Card modems that work with Handheld PCs. They provide connectivity to the RAM mobile data network, the ARDIS radio network, and the CDPD wireless network, and they are similar in size to the Megahertz modem. Mail services that work with these wireless modems are under development as this book is being written; they should be available by the time you read this.

All these devices and their mail services offer true wireless messaging. The modems are the bulkiest of the devices I've described here: when one of the wireless modems is inserted, the Handheld PC no longer comes close to fitting in any pocket. Unlike the built-in mail service in Windows CE, all these wireless mail services deliver mail messages to the Inbox folder and do not retain a copy of the messages on the mail server. The messages you view in the Inbox reside there and nowhere else.

You can also use a cellular telephone and a wired modem to connect to a mail server, an Internet Service Provider, or a remote network. This works just like connecting to a telephone jack. Of course, cellular telephone calls are more expensive than wired telephone calls, so watch how long you stay on line!

Advanced Topics

Windows CE in Action: Tips and Tricks

Here are a bunch of tips and tricks for using Windows CE. I've drawn some of these from my own experience, I've picked up others from my colleagues on the Windows CE development team, and some come from early users of Handheld PCs. I hope you'll find some of these ideas useful enough to incorporate into your own daily routine.

Automate your automobile maintenance

Keep track of scheduled maintenance on your automobile by creating a recurring event in the Calendar for periodic service needs. For example, you might create an event like "94 Taurus—change oil" that recurs every three months. Record the car's current mileage on the Notes tab so that you can keep track of how many miles you've driven between oil changes. Of course, after you set up a time to have your car serviced, create an appointment on your Handheld PC so that you won't forget!

Automatically synchronize notes

If you want notes you take in meetings to be automatically copied to your desktop PC when you synchronize, record them on the Notes tab of a new task instead of in a Pocket Word document. After you have synchronized your Handheld PC with your desktop PC, it's easy to cut and paste the notes into Word or another program.

Carry your H/PC in your old time-planner binder

Before I got a Handheld PC, I used a paper appointment and address book. It had a nice leather binder, which had room for business cards, a pen and pencil, and so on. Now that I have a Handheld PC, I don't need either the appointments section or the addresses section. When I removed all those pages, I found just enough room was left for my Handheld PC. I keep two extra AA batteries taped inside the ring binder, and on more than one occasion the binder's padding has protected my Handheld PC from damage during a fall.

If you don't have an old time-planner binder, don't worry. Binders designed specifically for Handheld PCs are available from some H/PC manufacturers.

Conserve the batteries when you won't be using your Handheld PC for a while

When you won't be using your Handheld PC for a while, if at all possible, plug it into its AC adapter. Or, follow these steps to ensure that alarms and appointment reminders don't drain the batteries.

1. In the World Clock, turn off all alarms.

2. On your desktop PC, in H/PC Explorer, click Synchronization Manager on the Tools menu. On the Databases tab, select the Appointments Database, and click Options. Choose Synchronize The Past, set 0 weeks of active tasks and 0 future weeks of active tasks, and then click OK. Do the same thing for the Tasks Database.

3. Synchronize, and your appointments and tasks are removed from your Handheld PC. Don't worry—they still exist in Schedule+ or Outlook on your desktop PC.

Now you won't have appointment reminders going off all the time, draining the batteries prematurely. When you are ready to use your Handheld PC again, restore your settings in H/PC Explorer, synchronize, and all your appointments and tasks are restored to your device.

Convert Web pages you've saved as favorites on your desktop PC

If you use Microsoft Internet Explorer on your desktop PC, you might have some favorite Web pages that you want to visit using Pocket Internet Explorer on your Handheld PC. To convert pages you've saved in the Favorites folder, follow these steps:

1. Check for favorite pages on your Handheld PC: Double-tap My Handheld PC on the H/PC desktop, and then open the Windows folder. When you save your first favorite page by using Pocket Internet Explorer, the Favorites folder is created at that time, inside the Windows folder. If you haven't saved any favorites yet, open Pocket Internet Explorer, save a favorite Web page, and then tap the Refresh command on the View menu to display the Favorites folder.

2. On your desktop PC, in H/PC Explorer, open the Windows folder and then open the Favorites folder.

3. On your desktop PC, in Windows Explorer, open the Favorites subfolder of the Windows folder. Select the .url file for each page that you want to convert, and then drag the file or files to the Favorites folder in H/PC Explorer.

Now you need to modify each favorite. Follow these steps for each file:

1. In Pocket Word, tap the Open command on the File menu. Open the Favorites subfolder of the Windows folder in My Handheld PC. Tap the drop-down arrow at the right of the Type box, and select All Documents from the list. Find the .url file you want to modify, and open it.

2. In the file, delete everything except the Web page address (URL). Be sure to delete the text *[Internet Shortcut]* and *URL=*. For example, if you're converting a file for the Windows CE Web page, leave only the text *http://www.microsoft.com/windowsce.*

3. Save the file, and you're ready to use it with Pocket Internet Explorer.

Don't get locked out

I have several combination locks: one for my gym locker, another for my skis, and yet another for my bicycle. I can never remember their combinations, so I created a contact called "locks" and stored the combinations on its Notes tab.

Don't ponder what to rent at the video store

In Tasks, create a project called "movies to rent." Whenever you hear of a good movie you might like to watch, add its name as a task. Then the next time you're at the video store you can check your list. Do the same thing for "books to read" or "CDs to listen to."

Use an alternative to double-tapping

Sometimes it is difficult to double-tap an icon to launch a program or open a document. I find this especially true when I am standing or walking with my Handheld PC or when I'm sitting in an airplane that's flying through turbulence. In these situations I don't double-tap—I tap and then I press the ENTER key to produce the same result.

Record driving directions

When someone gives you driving directions, enter them on the Notes tab of an appointment or contact so that they are always at hand. When you park your car in a large parking lot, record your location in a Pocket Word document.

Gather and use data on the run

I recently purchased a new car, and my Handheld PC was an invaluable tool in helping me figure out which of the autos I was considering was the right one for me. After perusing brochures and reading some articles in automotive magazines, I created a model document in Pocket Word. On each line I listed an attribute or criterion I wanted to compare, such as price, handling, and seat comfort. I ended each line with a tab. After test-driving a car but before I left the dealership, I opened my Handheld PC and recorded my impressions of each attribute on the appropriate line, right after the tab. I created a separate test-drive document for each car I drove.

I could have directly entered the information in Pocket Excel, but I found it easier to do so in Pocket Word. Use whichever program is best for you; it's easy to move data from one to the other.

When I had driven several cars, I selected the text of one of the test-drive documents and copied it to the clipboard. Then I opened Pocket Excel and pasted the information. Each line of text was placed in a new row, and because I had separated each line with a tab, the comments appeared in a different column from the criteria. I repeated this procedure for the other cars, each time pasting just the comments into a new column. Now I had all my comments in the same workbook so that I could compare my evaluations of the cars I drove.

At this point, the Handheld PC screen was just too small, so I used H/PC Explorer to upload the workbook to my desktop computer, where I used Excel to print out the file and more easily examine all the data I had collected.

And I really like my car.

Hear the voices of your loved ones when you travel

Get a personalized wake-up call from your loved ones while you're traveling by recording a greeting and using it for your wake-up alarm. Or just listen to it whenever you need to hear a friendly voice when you're far from home. To record the sound on your desktop PC, you'll need a sound card and a microphone. Once you've recorded the sound, use H/PC Explorer to download the recording to your Handheld PC.

Note   Handheld PCs can play only .wav files in 11-KHz, 8-bit, monophonic format, so be sure you record sounds in this format.

Download the sound you recorded to the Windows folder on your Handheld PC. Thereafter, when you set the notification options for an appointment or an alarm, the sound you have downloaded appears in the list along with the built-in sounds. You can also assign your new sound to an event in the Volume & Sounds program of the Control Panel, as described in Chapter 3.

Keep the kids quiet

Install the Microsoft Entertainment Pack for Windows CE on your Handheld PC before you set off on a long road trip with the kids. Give it to a bored child 10 years old or older, and it will keep your child occupied for quite some time. Warning: if you have more than one child, they might fight over whose turn it is, so you might need to take along two or more Handheld PCs.

Keep track of your frequent-flyer mileage

This will give you something to do on an otherwise boring flight. Create a workbook in Pocket Excel, and use it to reconcile your estimated miles against the statements you receive from your airline. Use the World Clock's Time Zone view to estimate how many miles you expect to earn from your current flight.

Use your Handheld PC as a negotiating tool

Take your Handheld PC along with you to the car dealer. In Pocket Excel, open the Amortize file. Decide the maximum amount you want to pay for the vehicle, and enter other pertinent information. Start dickering with the dealer, and each time the dealer proposes a price, enter it into the workbook. If you plan to finance the purchase, the Amortize program will show you your monthly payment. The Handheld PC can be an intimidating negotiating tool: it saved a colleague of mine several thousand dollars on the final price of his car.

Plug your H/PC into the AC adapter while you're at your desk or at home

This sounds silly, but it makes a very big difference in battery life. I bought a docking cradle with my Handheld PC, and as soon as I get to my desk at work in the morning, my Handheld PC goes into that cradle so that the batteries don't drain. At home, I always plug my H/PC into an extra AC adapter I purchased and keep at my desk. (Well, I do it most of the time.) In any case, plugging in your H/PC really helps make the batteries last for weeks instead of days.

Read a good book

When I suddenly find myself with some time on my hands (for example, at the airport when my flight has just been delayed for an hour), I don't always feel like working. Sometimes I prefer just to read a good book. Well, there is an ever-growing selection of good books available as text files that you can download to any computer, from an IBM mainframe to your Handheld PC, for no charge.

Project Gutenberg was started in 1971 with the objective of creating electronic editions of various works of literature that are in the public domain. Project Gutenberg is a volunteer group organized by Michael S. Hart at Illinois Benedictine College. Its online library contains works of fiction, nonfiction, and science fiction; Shakespeare, the Bible, dictionaries, and almanacs; and U.S. census data, famous speeches, and even large prime numbers. To find out which books are available, connect to http://www.promo.net/pg/ or use your Web browser to search for *Project Gutenberg*. For more information, send e-mail to hart@vmd.cso.uiuc.edu, or write to the Project Gutenberg Center at Illinois Benedictine College, Lisle IL 60532.

If you use Pocket Internet Explorer, you can download the files directly to your Handheld PC. Or you can download them from the Internet to your desktop computer and then use H/PC Explorer to transfer them to your Handheld PC. Keep in mind that you don't have to store a complete document. You can use a text editor on your desktop computer to split a file into smaller pieces so that it doesn't take up so much space on your Handheld PC. If you have a PC Card memory card, you can store the document on it, where you probably have more space available.

The keyboard short-cut for selecting an entire document is CTRL+A.

Once you have the files on your Handheld PC, use Pocket Word to view them. You can easily change the font to make reading easier by selecting the entire document and then choosing the font and font size you want from the command bar.

Record product warranties

Keep track of product warranties and product support information in Contacts. For instance, record your new answering machine purchase by creating a contact with the manufacturer's name, address, and product-support phone number. You can record the model number, purchase date, purchase location, and warranty information on the Notes tab.

Remember sources of good food and wine

Create contacts for restaurants you visit so that you'll always have the phone number and address at hand. On the Notes tab of the contact, you can type comments regarding things you liked (or didn't like) on the menu. Then, in the future, you can search for *good seafood* or similar phrases to find restaurants you liked.

You can use the same method to keep track of wines. When you enjoy a particular variety and vintage, record it on the Notes tab of your "wines" contact. The next time you are purchasing wine, you can search for words such as *Merlot* or *Chardonnay* to find wines you enjoyed.

Use the Run command to start programs

If you frequently use the Run command on the Start menu in Windows 95 or Windows NT to start programs, you might want to use it in Windows CE as well. The following table lists the filenames you type in the Run dialog box to start the built-in programs in Windows CE.

Program	Filename
Calculator	calc
Calendar	calendar
Contacts	addrbook
Help	peghelp
Inbox	pmail
Pocket Excel	pxl
Pocket Word	pword
PC Link	repllog
Remote Networking	remnet
Solitaire	solitare
Tasks	tasks
Terminal	pegterm
Welcome Wizard	welcome
World Clock	clock

Some of the filenames, such as peghelp and pegterm, stem from *Pegasus,* the original code name for Windows CE.

Here are some other actions you can take by typing commands in the Run dialog box:

To Do This	Type This	Example
Display a bitmap file	bmpview *pathname*	bmpview \windows\default.2bp
Play a sound file	sndplay *pathname*	sndplay \windows\alarm1.wav
Receive a contact from an H/PC via infrared transfer	irsquirt addr_recv:	irsquirt addr_recv:
Receive a file from an H/PC via infrared transfer	irsquirt	irsquirt
Send a file to an H/PC via infrared transfer	irsquirt *pathname*	irsquirt \my documents\letter.pwd

Save time packing for recurring trips

If you travel a lot, this tip will save you some time and frustration. Create a packing list for each trip in Pocket Word. When you create an appointment for a trip, copy the packing list from Pocket Word and paste it on the Notes tab of the appointment. Then you can refer to it when you're packing for the trip. While you are on the trip, if you find yourself thinking, "I should have brought an extra shirt," add a shirt to the packing list so that you'll remember it the next time. When you return home, if you find you never needed an item, remove that item from the list so you won't bring it on the next trip.

Squirt e-mail to another Handheld PC

Although the Inbox does not allow direct infrared transfer to an e-mail message, you can still forward a message to a colleague. Simply open the e-mail message, press CTRL+A to select all the text in it, and press CTRL+C to copy the text to the clipboard. Start Pocket Word, and press CTRL+V to paste the text into the new Word document that opens. Save this document, and then use Windows CE Explorer to squirt the document to your colleague's machine.

Store your documents on a flash memory or SRAM card

Although your documents are quite safe in the storage of your Handheld PC, they are safer on a flash memory or SRAM (static Random Access Memory) card. It is possible, although highly unlikely, that your Handheld PC could lock up to the point that you'd need to reset it, which would mean that any data you hadn't backed up would be lost. Or if both your main and backup batteries go dead, your data will join them. Flash memory cards require no power; they permanently keep the data stored on them. SRAM cards are powered by tiny lithium batteries, but they go for a year or more before losing their data.

You can keep only documents—such as those created by Pocket Word and Pocket Excel or other programs you install—on flash memory or SRAM cards. The databases used by the Calendar, Contacts, and Tasks programs and by the Inbox cannot be stored on a flash memory or SRAM card.

Take your Handheld PC with you while you shop

I use my H/PC to create shopping lists for projects I'm working on. For example, if I'm going to be working on my motorcycle, I make a list of the parts, tools, or other things I need in my "motorcycles" project in Tasks. When I'm in the store, I check off each item as I put it in my basket. Before checkout, it's easy to review the list and spot something that I might have missed. If I have to order certain items, I can add the pick-up date to the task as a due date so that my Handheld PC reminds me to return to the store to pick up the order.

You can do the same thing for other items that you purchase. For example, a colleague of mine has a large collection of compact discs. She entered a list of their names into a text file on her desktop PC and then downloaded that file to her Handheld PC. That way, when she visits a music store, she can avoid purchasing a CD that she already owns. Another friend uses the same technique for adding to his coin collection.

Type on the tiny keyboard

No, you are not going to want to write a 20-page report using your Handheld PC's keyboard, but there are some strategies you might employ to make the best of a small situation.

When I am standing up or walking around with my Handheld PC, I tend to use the "thumbs" method of typing. I hold the device in both hands with my fingers down, under the keyboard, and my thumbs on top. Then I use my thumbs to do the typing. With a little bit of practice, it works. In this position, I find tapping the screen somewhat clumsy, so I tend to use keyboard shortcuts (like CTRL+C for Copy and CTRL+V for Paste) much more often. Even though this book talks about tapping or double-tapping various items on the screen, usually I use the arrow keys to move the selection to them and press the ENTER key to open them.

At a desk or at a table in a meeting I place my Handheld PC on the surface before me as I would a laptop computer. Here I tend to use a more traditional touch-typing approach. One trick that seems to help is to hold my hands at an angle to the front of the device, sort of rotating my wrists apart while keeping my fingers over the home keys. The home keys (F and J) have raised ribs just like on a larger keyboard so that you can easily find them by touch. If your hands are not too large you can actually place your fingers on the traditional home row. My hands are a little too large for that, so I tend to keep my pinkies up in the air.

When I actually start typing, I find that what works best for me is to hold my hands a little higher over the keyboard than I would on a desktop keyboard. Then, when I go to press a key I move my entire hand a little bit so that the desired key is somewhat under my hand. If I try to hold my hands stationary and reach for a key, I often miss the key I want.

The best plan is to spend a little time practicing and getting used to the keyboard. Type some common words over and over again until you get the feel of your Handheld PC and until your fingers start to remember the small muscle movements needed.

One last tip: don't use the keyboard if you don't need to! If you are in your office or if you have your laptop computer with you, and if you have a lot of typing to do, use the desktop PC or the laptop to do the typing, and then download the text or data to your Handheld PC.

Use keyboard shortcuts

These keyboard shortcuts make using the keyboard quite effective.

Key or Keyboard Shortcut	Function Performed
ALT+CTRL	Displays a shortcut menu
ALT+ESC	Activates the next program on the taskbar
ALT+ENTER	Displays the properties of the selected item
ALT+H	Displays online Help in most programs and dialog boxes
ALT+TAB	Opens the Windows CE Task Manager so that you can switch between running programs
arrow keys	Select a file or folder
CTRL+ALT+=	Opens the calibration screen so that you can calibrate the touch screen
CTRL+arrow keys+SPACEBAR	Select multiple files that are not adjacent
CTRL+C, CTRL+X, CTRL+V	Copy, cut, and paste text or shortcuts to and from the clipboard
CTRL+ESC	Opens the Start menu
ENTER	Activates or opens the selected item
SHIFT+arrow keys	Select multiple files
SHIFT+BACKSPACE	Deletes the selected item and places it in the Recycle Bin
Windows key	Opens the Start menu
Windows key+SPACEBAR	Displays the Windows key shortcuts
Windows key+TAB	Displays the desktop

Use World Clock alarms
to keep a meeting on schedule

I don't know about you, but I hate meetings that don't stop when they should, or meetings in which 50 minutes is spent discussing the first item on the agenda and then 10 minutes discussing all the rest. I use the World Clock alarms to set reminders every so often during a meeting. When the alarm on my Handheld PC goes off, people realize that it's time to move on to the next item on the agenda. Somehow this seems to work much better than if I point to my wristwatch and mention that it's time to move on. The Alarm2 sound seems to be the most irritating and thus the most effective.

Use the World Clock even when you're not traveling

If you work with people who live in other time zones, the World Clock can come in handy even when you have not left home. Set the time zone for the visiting city in the World Clock to that of the person with whom you are working. This lets you easily keep track of the time in that person's city, making it easier to plan telephone calls, meetings, and so on.

And finally...

I've even used my Handheld PC to scratch that hard-to-reach spot in the middle of my back!

Chapter 10

Inside Windows CE

In 1990, Bill Gates, Chairman of Microsoft, gave the keynote address at the Comdex computer industry trade show. He named his address "Information at Your Fingertips" because that title "exemplifies the concept of making computers more personal, making them indispensable, making them something you reach for naturally when you need information." Windows CE is part of Microsoft's ongoing effort to deliver on that vision.

In this chapter, you'll learn how Windows CE went from idea to market-place; you'll also get a look at its inner workings and a guide to programming with this new operating system.

Windows CE: Where It Came From and Where It's Going

In this section, you'll find a brief history of Windows CE, a review of its design goals, an evaluation of how well it met those goals, a list of the attributes that set H/PCs running Windows CE apart from Personal Digital Assistants (PDAs), and a look at where Windows CE is headed.

A Little History

Windows CE began in late November 1994, as an outgrowth of two previous projects at Microsoft, WinPad and Pulsar. Both these projects were attempts to develop handheld products, but each of them took a different approach.

The WinPad project began in June 1992, in an effort to extend Windows to the then new class of mobile computers called PDAs. Apple had already declared Newton, its PDA, to be the next revolution in computing. (In the process, Apple raised unrealistic expectations for this class of computer.) Like Newton, WinPad did not have a keyboard, but instead it relied on handwriting recognition for data entry. It also supported untranslated "ink" (electronic handwriting) throughout its programs. WinPad was designed to be a companion to the user's desktop PC: when connected via a serial cable, WinPad would automatically synchronize its data (appointments, address book, e-mail, and so on) with data on the desktop computer. In fact, WinPad originated the concept of "Hot Sync," now popularized by the Palm Pilot. WinPad measured about 4" by 6" and looked like this:

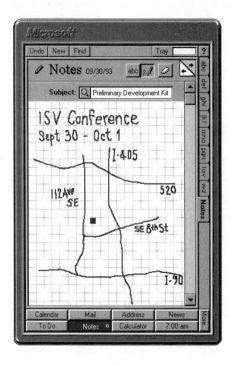

Like many software projects, WinPad didn't meet its original deadline, which required it to be ready by the end of 1993. The project didn't near completion until late summer of 1994. In the meantime, however, several things happened that cast doubt upon WinPad's prospects. To begin with, a substantial backlash developed against the Newton because its initial release did not measure up to expectations. This backlash poisoned not only the Newton but the entire category of PDAs. Then a series of Doonesbury cartoons portrayed the Newton as a laughingstock instead of a revolution. Also, other PDAs released in 1993 and early 1994, such as the Casio Zoomer and the Sony Magic Link, failed to sell. Hardware manufacturers working with Microsoft on WinPad estimated that their products would be priced at about $900, but it became clear that this was more than buyers would be willing to pay. Finally, the main computer chip, or CPU, on which WinPad depended was canceled in the fall of 1994, effectively terminating the WinPad project.

Microsoft started another project in March 1993: Pulsar was to be an enhanced pager, aimed at portable computer users. Its design called for a wireless connection via a two-way paging system to a network based on the then-forthcoming Microsoft Network. The Pulsar screen measured about 2.5" by 1.6" and looked like this:

In contrast to the WinPad computer, aimed partly at business users, Pulsar was to be strictly a consumer device. It featured what its designers called a "social interface," similar to that of General Magic's Magic Cap operating system. Because Pulsar was expected to be primarily used for viewing information broadcast over a network, it didn't have a true keyboard.

Instead, data was to be entered through an on-screen keyboard that featured a predictive mechanism as an accelerator. (The keyboard attempted to guess the word you wanted after a few keys were pressed, to speed up the typing process.)

In a series of focus group sessions held during the summer of 1994, the Pulsar team discovered that potential customers considered the device unnecessary and were unwilling to pay the proposed monthly subscription price. Focus group participants also thought the small size of the device and its lack of a keyboard were serious drawbacks. What's more, the wireless infrastructure on which the device depended was not developing as fast as anticipated.

Senior Microsoft management reviewed both the WinPad and the Pulsar projects in the autumn of 1994 and decided to combine the two teams to work on a new project—developing a mobile computer. The new Pegasus project inherited the WinPad vision: to build a device that would be a useful companion to a desktop PC. No WinPad software code was retained, but the WinPad design influenced Pegasus. The Pulsar team had developed a lightweight operating system that ran on a RISC (reduced instruction set computing) processor. This work continued uninterrupted during the reorganization and evolved into the Windows CE operating system.

Just What Does CE Stand For?

Consumer Edition? Consumer Electronics? Can't Explain? Well, the truth is that it doesn't stand for anything. During the naming of Windows CE, many suffixes to Windows were considered, including CE, CT, and CX. The suffix CE won. You can think of CE as you would the letters in a lot of automobile names (for example, the Ford Taurus GL).

Through the winter and early spring of 1995, the Pegasus team sorted itself out and developed a product design. By late spring, they had adopted the Windows 95 user interface and begun coding applications. The team held more focus groups during the summer of 1995 that validated the concept of Pegasus and its Microsoft Windows 95-like user interface. By spring of 1996, hardware manufacturers had produced prototype handheld devices, and a beta program helped to refine and finalize the design.

The team delivered the final software to hardware manufacturers in September, and Pegasus was announced to the world as Windows CE at the Comdex trade show in November 1996.

The Design of Windows CE

At the outset, the designers of Windows CE and the Handheld PC set the following five design goals:

Do not build a PDA.   The Windows CE team rejected the ambitious vision of PDAs such as the Newton and the Magic Link. No one on the team thought that Windows CE represented a computing revolution, nor did they believe that using a Handheld PC would change one's life. They set out just to create a product that people would find useful and would want to buy. So Windows CE was not marketed as an assistant or agent; instead it was billed as a tool that would make it easier for users to take critical data along with them wherever they went.

Create a companion to the Windows desktop.   The target customer for Windows CE was someone who already used Microsoft Windows 95. Thus it was essential that Windows CE leveraged users' knowledge of and experience with Windows and Windows-based programs. It was also critical that data could be moved easily between a desktop PC and the Handheld PC. Users should simply need to place the Handheld PC into its docking cradle to synchronize data on the two machines.

Deliver a device with a street price of $500.   Market research conducted by the Windows CE team in 1995 revealed $500 to be a critical price point. A product priced higher than this was predicted to face considerable consumer resistance, and indeed, PDAs then on the market priced above $500 had not sold well. To achieve this goal, the Windows CE team worked closely with hardware manufacturers to ensure that their designs could be delivered at or close to the desired price.

Create a platform for communications.   Windows CE should provide the key communications programs—e-mail and Internet access. This goal was abandoned and then readopted during the development of Windows CE.

Create an open development platform.   The incredible breadth of programs available from thousands of companies helped to make Windows so successful. The Windows CE team believed that for the Handheld PC to succeed, it must attract the efforts of independent software developers. Therefore it was considered critical that Windows CE support the Win32 API (application programming interface).

Does Windows CE Meet Its Design Goals?

The designers of Windows CE wanted the Handheld PC to be a portable computer that you would pick up and carry with you without even thinking about it, like your wallet or your car keys. Carrying an H/PC would mean you'd always have important information such as phone numbers, addresses, and reminders along with you when you needed them, as you would if you carried a traditional personal information manager.

What If You Don't Want to Be More Organized?

Some might argue that Windows CE was designed for all those type A personalities who keep extensive to-do lists, have all their appointments written down, and probably have neat desks too. Perhaps. But even if you don't want to be more organized, the communications capabilities (e-mail and Internet access), the note-taking capabilities (Pocket Word's outlining feature), and the entertainment capabilities (Solitaire and other games) make the Handheld PC worth considering.

Windows CE is more than just an electronic organizer, however. As the smallest member of the Microsoft Windows family, Windows CE implements the most popular programming interface, Win32, so hundreds of programs are available for your Handheld PC. Some of the first are described in Appendix B, and many more are under development.

The suite of programs built into Windows CE and described in this book is aimed at a broad range of users. As I write, developers are working on many other programs aimed at more specialized groups of users. So don't be surprised in the coming months to see a Handheld PC in a hospital or clinic, on a warehouse floor, in a real estate office, or in an investment office near you.

Finally, keep in mind that this is version 1 of Windows CE. Perhaps your H/PC doesn't do everything you want it to do. It doesn't do everything the Windows CE team wanted it to do. But if you evaluate it on what it does, I think you'll find the Handheld PC is a device that can make you more productive—one whose utility justifies its price. And building such a device is really what the Windows CE team set out to do.

Why Don't H/PCs Use Handwriting Recognition?

PDAs such as the Apple Newton and the Sony Magic Link do not have keyboards. Instead, they rely on handwriting recognition for data entry. When you use a Newton, you write or print with a stylus on a screen as you would with a pen on paper and the built-in software recognizes your electronic "ink" and translates it into text.

This feature is missing from H/PCs because the Windows CE team believed that the electronic "ink" feature wasn't ready for general usage, that it suffered from too much bad press, and that marketing studies revealed that potential customers wanted a real keyboard on a portable device. The most successful of the currently available handheld computers (for example, the HP 200LX, the Psion 3a, and the Sharp Zaurus) do not rely on handwriting recognition—they all feature keyboards as their primary (or only) data entry mechanism.

Will Handheld PCs Succeed?

As I write this, several handheld computers, PDAs, and pocket organizers are available. So far, none has been a great success, at least when compared to desktop or laptop PCs. Will Handheld PCs running Windows CE do any better? Perhaps—only the marketplace can answer that question. But here are some specific reasons why the creators of Windows CE at Microsoft believe it will succeed.

■ The Windows CE user interface is very similar to that of Windows 95, making it extremely familiar to the millions of people who are running Windows 95 on their desktop PCs. By leveraging people's knowledge of Windows, Windows CE lets users become productive immediately.

■ Windows CE is an active companion of Microsoft Schedule+ and Microsoft Outlook personal information management programs. People who use either of these programs to manage their contacts, schedules, and appointments can automatically transfer data between their desktop PC and their Handheld PC. Third-party programs provide synchronization with other popular desktop personal information management programs.

■ Pocket Word and Pocket Excel for Windows CE implement the features most people use in Microsoft Word and Microsoft Excel. So the programs for Windows CE are instantly familiar to those who use the corresponding Windows 95-based programs on their desktop PCs. Exchanging data between the handheld and desktop versions of these programs is straightforward.

■ By providing communications programs in the form of the Inbox and Pocket Internet Explorer, Windows CE allows those who need to stay in touch to do so with their H/PCs. They don't have to drag around a bulky portable computer.

■ Users are not the only ones who will find Windows CE familiar—programmers will as well. An experienced Windows programmer will find the learning curve for writing Windows CE-based programs very short, and many programs for Windows CE are already available less than six months after its launch.

- Unlike most other handheld computers, Handheld PCs running Windows CE are being marketed by several manufacturers. At the time this book went to press, Handheld PCs were available from Casio, Compaq, Hewlett-Packard, Hitachi, LG Electronics, NEC, and Phillips Electronics.

- With a street price as low as $500, H/PCs cost less than many competitive machines. They offer a high value-to-price ratio, giving them the kind of advantage desktop PCs have had when compared to more expensive workstations.

The Future of Windows CE

Windows CE is a new computer platform, and the Handheld PCs described in this book are the first of a new family of devices. The Windows CE team at Microsoft is hard at work on future versions of the Windows CE operating system, on new programs, and on new products based on Windows CE.

What are those products? At this point, one can only speculate. But by observing industry and technology trends, one can foresee many potential uses of the Windows CE technology. The four uses that are most interesting and most likely to be realized in the next few years are

Other form factors.   The Handheld PC is but one possible size for a small computer that is a companion to your desktop PC. The Palm Pilot PDA has demonstrated that a truly pocketable, inexpensive device can be popular. On the other end of the spectrum, many users of notebook computers complain that they are too large, too heavy, and that their batteries run out after only a couple of hours. Windows CE can easily shrink and grow to produce products in both of these areas.

Other types of devices.   For the first time, Windows CE makes the Windows operating system and the Win32 API available to embed low-cost operating systems in many devices. Thus in coming years you might see an onboard navigation and information system based on Windows CE in your automobile, or you might see Windows CE in your home, controlling temperature, lighting, security, your TV, and your VCR. Will you find Windows CE in your microwave? Probably not. But some future microwave might communicate with the Windows CE device that manages your house.

Wireless communications. Although the first wave of Handheld PCs can communicate wirelessly by connecting to cellular phones, two-way pagers, or wireless modems via cable, or by making use of rather bulky radio transceivers inserted in the PC Card slot, such communication is still a somewhat clumsy affair. As electronic components continue to shrink, and as the wireless communications infrastructure improves, future Handheld PCs might have more completely integrated two-way wireless communications.

Electronic commerce. Imagine an ATM "beaming" a cash advance to your Handheld PC, or perhaps your getting a cash advance wirelessly even when you're nowhere near an ATM. And then imagine beaming the money to the clerk at the grocery store. These features might turn future versions of the Handheld PC into a Wallet PC—a device that replaces your credit cards and cash.

At the moment, of course, these future applications of Windows CE are just dreams, yet each of them is based on a technology that works today. I suspect that all these potential applications will be realized to some extent by the end of the decade.

Windows CE Architecture

Much as you can drive your automobile without really understanding how it works, you don't really need to understand how Windows CE works in order to drive it. But you might find that learning a little about what goes on inside Windows CE will provide you with useful insights as you use it on a daily basis.

The Windows CE operating system is the smallest member of the Windows family of operating systems. Like Microsoft Windows NT, Windows CE is a fully 32-bit, multitasking, multithreaded operating system that runs on multiple CPU architectures. Its user interface looks and feels like Windows 95, and it exports Win32 APIs to programs. Yet it is an extremely lightweight operating system: Windows CE runs on systems that have only 4 MB of ROM and 2 MB of RAM, including built-in programs.

The first two processor families on which Windows CE runs are the MIPS and the Hitachi SH3. There are two versions of the MIPS processor: the NEC R4100 and the Phillips R3000. In addition, support for the Strong-Arm processor and the Power PC RISC processor, as well as for the Intel 486 and Pentium family of processors, has been announced.

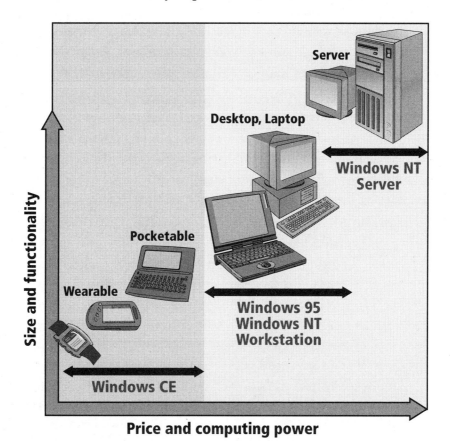

Communications facilities were designed into the system from the beginning so that Windows CE can connect to your desktop PC, to the Internet, and to other Handheld PCs. Another important system feature—unobtrusive power management—allows Handheld PCs to run for weeks on a pair of AA batteries.

Windows Compatibility

Windows CE is compatible with the rest of the Windows family, both on the outside and on the inside. On the outside, the user interface looks like that of Windows 95. All the key user interface elements of Windows 95 are supported: the taskbar with its Start button and status area, the Recycle Bin, Windows Explorer, shortcuts, ToolTips, dialog boxes, and controls. Context-sensitive Help is there, as are Windows 95 operations such as drag and drop. When most Windows 95 users see a Handheld PC for the first time, they say "Oh, I already know how to use that!"

On the "inside," the other Windows interface is seen not by the end user but by the programmer. Again, Windows CE provides a high degree of compatibility with Windows 95. It supports the multithreaded Win32 programming model, where executable code resides in .exe and .dll files and where application processes can spawn multiple threads. More than 500 of the Win32 APIs are supported by Windows CE.

The Win32 APIs that are missing from Windows CE are mostly contained in the subsystems that Windows CE does not support. These "missing" APIs include OLE, COM, and ODBC; ActiveX; printing APIs and those that support multiple device contexts; MAPI; DDE; and multimedia APIs—beyond those needed for maintaining a low level of multimedia support. Other Win32 APIs not supported by Windows CE are those that support security, Help, named events, and interapplication synchronization. Because Windows CE does not support the overlapped window model of Win32, APIs that support that model are missing (such as those that support topmost windows) or modified (such as those that support minimizing and maximizing windows). Also missing are Win32 APIs provided for compatibility with old, 16-bit programs.

The C runtime library (supporting operations such as file I/O, console I/O, and process support) is also largely missing, although the string functions are mostly present. Of course, most of these missing APIs have functional equivalents in the Win32 API set. Most of the function definitions in math.h are missing as well, and functions that are included, such as scanf and printf, lack support for floating-point numbers.

APIs specific to Windows CE are provided to support the capabilities of Windows CE that are not present on other Win32 systems, or to support the functions of Windows CE that are simplified versions of full Win32 functions. These APIs provide access to Windows CE-specific user interface controls—the Windows CE database, the notification mechanism, the Help system, the address book, and the e-mail client application. Additional APIs available on a desktop PC running Windows 95 provide remote access to Windows CE functions and allow construction of additional file filters for replication.

An overview of the Windows CE software architecture is shown in the following illustration.

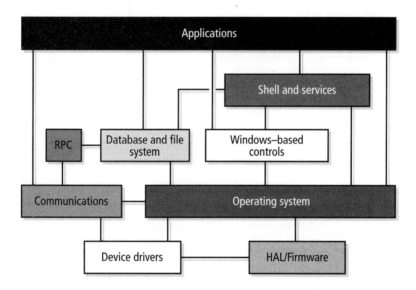

Small Memory Footprint

The Windows CE operating system is built to provide high performance on small devices. The kernel itself occupies only 64 KB of ROM. The complete operating system and all the built-in programs reside in 4 MB of ROM. The system and multiple programs can run in less than 400 KB of RAM. The illustration on the next page shows the Windows CE operating system architecture.

Win32 API

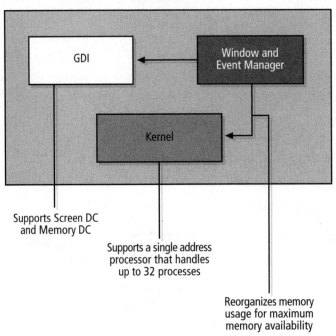

Supports Screen DC
and Memory DC

Supports a single address
processor that handles
up to 32 processes

Reorganizes memory
usage for maximum
memory availability

The kernel supports a single address space, with process protection. Up to 32 concurrent processes are allowed, and each process can have as many threads as memory permits. The kernel is designed to have a very low RAM overhead for process and thread management. Likewise, interrupt service routine overhead is kept to a minimum.

The window and event manager provides the support for the Win32 API subset of Windows CE. With a couple of exceptions (Help and the Calculator), Windows CE-based programs use the entire screen, and only one program is visible at a time. Thus the support for overlapping windows is quite limited, and there is no support for owned or topmost windows. Also, system events (for example, keypresses) cannot be hooked as they can in Win32.

The Windows CE graphics device interface (GDI) supports two kinds of device contexts (DCs). The screen DC is a 2-bits-per-pixel grayscale bitmap. GDI supports memory DCs at either 1 or 2 bits per pixel. Printing DCs are not supported.

The operating system is cleverly designed to hide low-memory conditions from the user. When the remaining available memory reaches a critical threshold, all running programs are sent a message requesting that they free up all possible memory. Because only one application is visible at a time, the others can free most of their memory. If all this sounds rather limiting, in practice it is not. The richness and depth of both the built-in applications and the early third-party programs testify to the completeness of the Windows CE operating system implementation.

Built-in Communications

Windows CE provides built-in support for communicating with other Handheld PCs, with desktop PCs, and with the Internet. Communication between two Handheld PCs is supported via an infrared beam using IrDA protocols. Sockets, TCP/IP, and PPP protocols give access to the Internet and to a desktop PC when it is connected to the Handheld PC via a cable. The Win32 serial interface is provided for direct serial connections. Windows CE provides subsets of the Windows 95 TAPI and Unimodem interfaces to support dial-up communications.

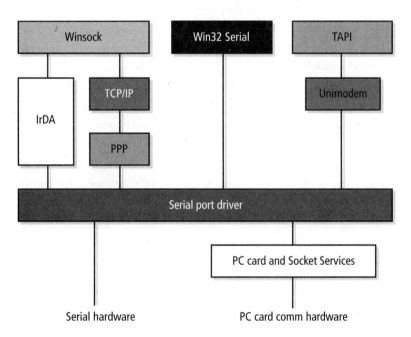

Windows CE also provides a subset of the PCMCIA card and socket services for modems. In addition to these services, Windows CE provides support for installable client drivers. These drivers are PCMCIA card-specific and can be configured to be loaded automatically when the card is inserted. The client driver implements the Windows CE device driver interface for application use. This interface is not the Windows NT device driver model but is rather a simple interface to the small client drivers written for Windows CE.

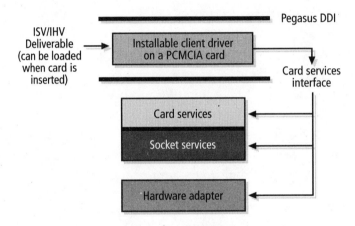

Unobtrusive Power Management

One of the design goals of the Windows CE team was to make sure battery life for Windows CE devices was comparable to that for other handheld computers—that is, measured in weeks. Because the processors used in Windows CE devices are much more powerful than those in other handheld computers and thus consume more power, achieving this goal was quite a challenge. Therefore, the Windows CE operating system shuts the processor down whenever possible. This happens without affecting running programs, and it is done as soon as the CPU becomes idle—even between keystrokes while you are typing. You don't notice this suspension of the CPU because the screen and other hardware remain active.

When you press the Off button (or when the automatic power-off time-out is reached), the CPU is suspended and external devices such as the screen, touch panel, modem, PCMCIA card, and infrared port are powered down. The CPU state and memory are preserved so that when you press the On button your Handheld PC is immediately ready for use. You never boot Windows CE the way you boot Windows on your desktop PC. The only time you will probably ever boot your Handheld PC is when you turn it on for the first time. But if things go awry (if an errant program hangs the device, for example) you can reboot it by inserting a pointed object into the "reset" hole located somewhere on the device.

Communications programs are notified when Windows CE is about to shut down, and they can prevent the shutdown if necessary to keep communications from being disrupted. Alarms can wake the device as needed, so even if your Handheld PC is shut down, the wake-up alarm you set for 6:00 a.m. will sound.

Database and File System

Persistent data can be thought of as information that you want to keep. Windows CE allocates RAM for persistent storage and uses a backup battery to ensure the information is not lost.

To store persistent data, Windows CE implements an object store that is optimized for storage of many small objects and that is designed to use minimal memory while running. Since the storage medium is RAM, little caching of data is done. All data in the object store is stored in a compressed format. Compression and decompression are done by the system and are completely transparent to the application. The object store is accessed by programs through three interfaces: the Windows CE database, the file system, and the registry.

Several Windows CE-based programs needed a high-performance, lightweight database, and to meet this need, the Windows CE database was created. Although this database is similar to others available for Windows 95, it and its APIs are specific to Windows CE.

A Windows CE database is a collection of objects, each object consisting of properties and values. The objects in a database can be sorted on any of four properties and can be searched on the primary sort property. Objects cannot be linked, and the database is flat: hierarchies of objects are not supported. Also, there is no support for transactions like journalling, commit, and rollback. The database is tuned to support large numbers of small (less than 4-KB) objects. Because critical personal information is stored by programs in databases, the Windows CE database is robust: power failure during any database operation will not corrupt the database.

The Windows CE-based programs that store information in databases are Contacts, Calendar, Tasks, and the Inbox. Contacts and the Inbox provide additional APIs for accessing their application-specific data, but Calendar and Tasks do not.

As noted previously, the Windows CE file system is implemented as a second API on top of the underlying object store. It supports all the common Win32 file system APIs. The C runtime file APIs are not supported. The directory structure is similar to that of Windows 95; there is, however, no device-name prefix such as C:. Instead, the file system is rooted at \ (symbolizing the root directory). Because Windows CE does not have a command prompt, there is less need for the concept of a search path: most programs are invoked from H/PC Explorer or via shortcuts. Instead of searching a path, Windows CE looks only in the \Windows directory if no explicit path is given.

For more information on converting file formats, see Chapter 6.

Windows CE also supports removable FAT volumes on PCMCIA flash and static RAM cards. The file system on the card is rooted at \pc card. Because the standard FAT file system is supported, cards can be used to transfer data with other Handheld PCs or portable computers. Of course, the files you transfer to the card must be in a format usable by the programs in Windows CE. (If you simply copy Excel or Word documents to the PC Card and then place the card in your Handheld PC, Pocket Excel or Pocket Word will not be able to read the documents because their file formats differ from those of their desktop PC counterparts.) One restriction in this support is that only files (including programs) can reside on the flash or static RAM card: databases are restricted to the Handheld PC's main memory.

The Win32 registry APIs are also supported on Windows CE, and the registry is used for much the same purposes as it is on a desktop PC. All string data stored in the registry is in Unicode format.

Remote Procedure Call APIs

Windows CE provides a set of Remote Procedure Call (RPC) APIs that allow programs on a desktop PC to communicate with a those on a Handheld PC when the two devices are connected via a serial cable. Through this interface, a program on the desktop PC has access to the

Windows CE database, file system, and registry calls, as well as a few other miscellaneous calls such as GetSystemInfo. RPC runs over the Sockets, TCP/IP, and PPP protocols. RPC calls can be initiated only from the desktop PC. Several of the Windows CE development-environment tools use the RPC interface, as do the desktop PC-based Setup programs.

Programming for Windows CE

One of the goals of the design team was that Windows CE become an attractive platform for development; that is, that companies other than Microsoft would want to develop software for it. To reach this goal, they designed Windows CE to be as compatible as possible with the most widely used personal computer operating system on the planet— Microsoft Windows.

The Windows CE Development Environment

The Windows CE development environment is the same as the Windows 95 and Window NT development environment. To develop an application for Windows CE, you use Microsoft Visual C++ Developer Studio and you code in C or C++, just as you would when developing an application for Windows 95 or Windows NT. Well, that's almost true. As described in "Windows CE Architecture," earlier in this chapter, the programming APIs provided by Windows CE are a subset of the Win32 API set.

The Windows CE Software Development Kit (SDK) is an add-on product to Microsoft Visual C++ that provides a development environment that installs as an extension to the Microsoft Visual C++ Developer Studio. You do your editing, compiling, linking, resource editing, and debugging on a desktop computer running Windows NT version 4.0. You can do most of your development right on the desktop PC using the Windows CE emulation environment, which reproduces the Windows CE shell in a window on your desktop computer. Of course, hardware-specific features and the performance characteristics of the actual devices can't be emulated.

When you are ready to execute on the actual handheld device, a cross-compiler produces code for either the MIPS or the SH3 processor. The resulting executables, DLLs, and other files are automatically transferred to a Handheld PC attached to the desktop PC via a serial cable. Your program runs on the Handheld PC, and you can remotely debug it using the Visual C++ interactive debugger. So from the single desktop PC development environment, you can develop for Handheld PCs running either processor. The development environment also handles the conversion of bitmaps and icons from desktop PC resolution (8 bits per pixel) to Windows CE resolution (2 bits per pixel).

Included in the Windows CE SDK are a set of remote tools that run on the Handheld PC and display their user interface on the desktop PC. Several of them are adaptations of familiar Windows SDK tools, while others are specific to Windows CE. They include the following items:

- The Object browser, which lets you examine and edit Windows CE databases and files. You can examine and alter records and their properties.

- pZoomIn, which is an adaptation of the familiar SDK tool. It lets you copy part or all of the Windows CE screen to the desktop PC, where it can be copied to the clipboard and then pasted into another application. This is the tool used to produce most of the screen illustrations in this book.

- RegEdit, another SDK tool adaptation. It allows the Windows CE registry to be remotely manipulated.

- Spy, one of the most useful SDK tools. With it you can remotely monitor messages being sent to specific windows on the Handheld PC.

- MemView, an essential performance tool. It allows you to track application resources and is invaluable in finding memory leaks.

- pView, a tool to let you view and control Windows CE processes.

Although Windows CE is the newest operating system for handheld computers to enter the market, because it uses the established Windows development environment, it has the most mature and comprehensive tools. Feedback from independent software developers who had early access to the Windows CE development environment was very positive; they agree that there is only a very small learning curve for experienced Windows programmers.

Developing Programs for Windows CE

You can write programs for Windows CE in C or C++, with or without the Microsoft Foundation Classes (MFC). Other languages, such as Java and Visual Basic, are not supported as of this writing. Check the Windows CE Web site for announcements in this area.

Part of writing a program for Windows CE is discovering just which APIs that you wanted to use aren't available, and working around that situation. As you get more comfortable with the limitations inherent in a small computer such as the Handheld PC, you will probably hit these API "potholes" less often.

You should consider several issues when developing programs for Windows CE, because a Handheld PC is not a desktop PC. First of all, both memory and storage are at a premium. A 300-KB application is large by Windows CE standards, although a typical application for Windows on the desktop PC might be 10 times that size or larger. Secondly, the Handheld PC is not a 200-MHz Pentium screamer, so it is not the right device on which to perform complex mathematical operations. And because H/PCs will be used in on-the-go situations, it is essential that programs for them be quick and responsive. A 3-second response time that might be acceptable on a desktop PC is a big problem on a Handheld PC.

Beyond performance and memory issues are user interface considerations. Although Windows CE does a good job of evoking the Windows 95 user interface, there are a lot of small differences needed to make it work on the small Handheld PC devices. Desktop PC programs that are blindly ported to Windows CE will be clumsy indeed.

Where Windows 95 features multiple overlapping windows, on Windows CE each application runs in a full-screen, nonsizeable window. You can see an example of the impact this has on an application by contrasting Excel or Word on a desktop PC with its counterpart under Windows CE.

On the desktop PC, each open document gets its own child window; on the H/PC, each document uses the full screen, and when you close the last document you close the application. Although the application window is not sizeable by the user, you should not code static layouts if at all possible. Future Handheld PCs will have differently sized screens, so it is best if your application will be able to adapt to them.

The Calculator and Help are two programs included in Windows CE that choose to violate the full-screen model: both offer pop-up views because each program is useful in the context of another program visible below. Unlike its Windows 95 counterpart, the Help application in Windows CE is not a topmost window; when the underlying application is activated, the Help window is covered. This happens because there is no topmost window support in Windows CE.

Unlike Windows on a desktop PC, Windows CE does not support cursors, so you can't reveal active targets by changing the cursor's shape. To see an example of this, compare Pocket Internet Explorer with Internet Explorer. Also, when you touch the H/PC screen with the stylus, it's as if you pressed the left mouse button. There is no direct support for simulating a right-mouse-button press; by convention, it is achieved by holding down the ALT key while tapping the screen. Because this is somewhat clumsy, you should use it more sparingly than you would on the desktop PC.

The whole point of the Handheld PC is just that—it is handheld. Therefore the screen is small and the keyboard is tiny. The screen is not a nice, bright CRT—it's a 4-level grayscale LCD that is not backlit in most H/PCs. Screen contrast is much less than that of a desktop monitor or that of any modern, backlit, color, laptop LCD. Consider also that unlike a desktop PC used in a well-lit office, the Handheld PC will be used in many places where the lighting is dim, making the screen even harder to read. So use black text on a white background whenever possible.

Another application design consideration is that the Windows CE user will frequently be on the run. Your application will be used while the user is standing or in a moving vehicle, meaning that selecting on-screen objects with the stylus will be difficult. So ensure that your application has adequate keyboard shortcuts to facilitate control and navigation in these situations. The typical usage pattern for many programs will be "open it, use it, close it." Thus it is important that the user be able to quickly access the desired information without wading through multiple menus or screens.

Finally, keep it simple. Don't attempt to overload your application with functions. Instead, implement the 20 percent of features that 80 percent of your users need. Don't pack the screen with information; instead, keep your screen layouts light and clean. Make the application's functions easily accessible to the user who wants to quickly get information. Keep in mind that users will want to read information more often than they'll want to write or enter new information.

Today's business world demands quick access to information—I think you will find the Windows CE development environment to be a very practical and productive place in which to develop your programs.

Handheld PCs

During the development of Microsoft Windows CE, Microsoft worked closely with hardware manufacturers who planned to produce Handheld PCs. By the time you read this, Handheld PCs should be available from Casio, Compaq, Hewlett-Packard, Hitachi, LG Electronics, NEC, and Philips Electronics. More manufacturers are expected to produce H/PCs in the future, so you can choose the one that best suits your needs, just as you can when you shop for a desktop or laptop PC.

The first generation of Handheld PCs have more similarities than differences, for two reasons: Microsoft specified the minimum requirements for the device design, and only Casio and Hewlett-Packard had experience producing H/PCs before. Because Microsoft had done a great deal of market research, most of the manufacturers decided to follow the design specifications closely. You can expect differences to emerge in future generations of H/PCs as both Microsoft and hardware manufacturers gain confidence and experience.

Choosing a Handheld PC

All the first generation Handheld PCs are similar in some ways: all have a clamshell design and a touch screen, weigh a little under a pound, and have about the same dimensions. Yet each manufacturer has distinguished its device with features that set it apart. In choosing an H/PC, you should consider the criteria shown on the following page.

- The exact dimensions and shape. There are differences in size and weight among H/PCs. If you intend to carry one of them in your pocket, make sure it fits and, because some slide in and out of a pocket more easily than others, check that out as well.

- The feel of the keyboard. Some keyboards have hard, plastic keys, while others have soft, rubbery keys. Be sure to try out different keyboards to find the one that feels best to you and on which you can type with maximum accuracy.

- Whether the screen is backlit. Backlighting is nice, but of course it helps to drain the batteries. Make sure that backlighting makes the screen more readable in the lighting situations in which you'll actually use the machine. Unfortunately, the fluorescent lighting found in most stores is the best type of light for reading an LCD, making accurate comparisons difficult. The most challenging test I've found is trying to read the screen at night when it's illuminated only by the map light of my car.

- The dot pitch of the screen. Although Windows CE specifications call for a .26 mm dot pitch, many of the devices use a .24 mm dot pitch. This might not sound like much difference, but a larger dot pitch improves readability considerably.

- The screen resolution. Most devices have a screen resolution of 480 by 240 pixels, but the Hewlett-Packard machine displays 640 by 240 pixels. The HP's wider screen is especially nice when you're working with Pocket Excel workbooks or Pocket Word documents.

- Device speed. Although I haven't actually measured device speed, some of the units seem somewhat faster than others. You should evaluate the unit you are considering to be sure it is fast enough for your needs.

- Industrial design. Do you find the machine easy to grip when it's closed and easy to hold when it's open? Can you access the stylus conveniently? Does the power supply cable interfere with the PC Card slot? Does a light notify you of alarms even when the cover is closed? Is the PC Card slot built in, or does it clip onto the device? These are some of the questions you should ask when evaluating the overall "feel" of the unit.

■ Additional features. Some units feature built-in modems, which are nice because they free up the PC Card slot for other uses such as additional storage. The Philips Velo 1 comes with a microphone and a built-in voice memo program. The Philips Electronics and Hewlett-Packard devices have compact flash slots for greater memory expansion. The Hewlett-Packard Handheld PCs have limited printing support.

 OTE Battery life in all H/PCs is shortened considerably by the use of a PC Card modem or any other high-power-consumption PC Card.

■ Bundled software. Each manufacturer includes programs for Windows CE that add to the utility of the device.

■ Service and support. You are probably going to use your Handheld PC a lot, and some day it might need service. Consider the manufacturer's warranty and service policy before you purchase.

My descriptions of some models are based on preproduction prototypes. As changes and improvements are made, what I've written here may become out of date. Be sure you compare the units themselves. The Windows CE Web site (http://www.microsoft.com/windowsce) is a great starting place to find information you can use to make comparisons. The Handheld PCs described here are listed in alphabetical order by manufacturer.

My Honest Opinion

At conferences and trade shows, whenever people find out that I work on the Windows CE team, they ask which machine is my personal favorite. The truth is, I like all of them—I don't think any one machine stands head and shoulders above the rest. Each has features I like and problems I can criticize.

Casio Cassiopeia

Cassiopeia is a constellation in the night sky and a play on the Casio company name. This H/PC comes in two models: the A10, with 2 MB of RAM, and the A11, with 4 MB of RAM. Optional features include rechargeable batteries and two styles of docking stations. The Cassiopeia also connects to the Casio QV-10 digital camera so that you can transfer images between the two devices.

The Cassiopeia was the first Handheld PC to reach the market—it was in stores the day after the launch of Windows CE in November 1996. Its keys are hard plastic with a concave surface, and its case has a slightly rubbery feel that makes it easy to grip. The overall design of the Cassiopeia is clean and straightforward. You can find Casio's Web site at http://www. casiohpc.com.

Specifications

- Models: A-10, A-11

- Display: 480 by 240 dots, .24 dot pitch, FSTN LCD, 4 grayscale monochrome with backlight

- CPU: Hitachi SH3

- Memory: 2 MB RAM (A-10), 4 MB RAM (A-11), 4 MB ROM

- Speaker: Built in

- Interfaces: RS-232C: 115.2 Kbps, data communication jack, PC Card slot, infrared port (IrDA standard)

- Main power supply: Two AA alkaline batteries, rechargeable battery pack (not included), AC adapter (not included)

- Main battery life: 20 hours (in Pocket Word, continuous cycle of 1-minute input and 10 minutes input standby)

- Rechargeable battery-pack battery life: 14 hours (in Pocket Word, continuous cycle of 1-minute input and 10 minutes input standby)

- Backup power supply: One CR2032 lithium battery

- Backup battery life: 5 years when main battery is replaced immediately after appearance of low battery message, 1 month when unit is left without a main battery

- Dimensions: 1" high, 6.9" wide, 3.6" deep

- Weight: 13.4 oz with batteries

Accessories

- Docking station

- MiniDock (a more modest version of the docking station)

- Rechargeable battery pack, which operates the Cassiopeia for 20 hours; it requires the charger to recharge the battery

- Charger for the rechargeable battery pack

- Docking Station Set, which includes the docking station, an AC adapter, the charger, and the rechargeable battery pack

- MiniDock Set, which includes the MiniDock and an AC adapter

- Data communications cable to connect your Casio QV series digital camera directly to the Cassiopeia

Compaq PC Companion

Compaq sells three models of their PC companion: the C120 and the C120+, both with 2 MB of RAM, and the C140, with 4 MB of RAM. Compaq's H/PCs are manufactured by Casio. As a result, units from the two companies differ only in their colors and labeling. You'll find Compaq's Web site at http://www.compaq.com/us/common/prodinfo/handhelds.

Specifications

The Compaq PC companion's general specifications are the same as those of the Casio Cassiopeia.

Accessories

- 2-MB memory expansion

- 10-MB, ATA-compatible flash RAM on a Type II PC Card

- 14.4 LP PC Card modem, which is a "battery-friendly," 14.4-Kbps modem; you can use it for up to 1 hour on AA battery power

- Combo Pack, which includes an AC adapter and the Quick Connect (a mini port replicator that provides serial, AC adapter, and battery charger ports) for connection to your desktop PC

- Power Pack, which includes the Quick Connect, an AC adapter, a NiMH battery pack, and a battery charger

- Convenience Cradle (a docking station), which connects to both Auto-Sync cable and battery charger ports; it also includes a stylus holder

- Stylus 3-Pack

- Carrying case, which provides cushioned protection for your PC companion and has room to store PC Cards, notes, business cards, and credit cards

- Slipcase, which provides protection for your PC companion

Hewlett-Packard 300 Series Palmtop PC

The Hewlett-Packard (HP) 300 series Palmtop PCs are distinguished from other Handheld PCs by their wider screen: 640 pixels instead of 480. There are two models, the HP 300 LX and the HP 320 LX, with the 320 LX featuring a backlit display. The HP machines use a bolder font than the other Handheld PCs, making information displayed on the screen more legible.

The keys on the HP machines are hard plastic, they don't rock from side to side, and they are the largest on any of the Handheld PCs. HP Palmtop PCs have two other unique features: you can print directly from the device either via serial cable or IR port and you can back up appointments, contacts and tasks to flash memory cards or CompactFlash cards and then restore the data directly from the card.

Compare the following screen illustration to similar illustrations in Chapter 4, and you'll see how much more information the HP Handheld PC can display.

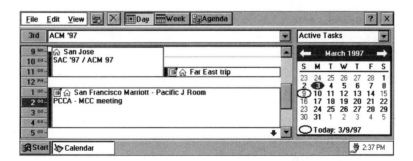

Hewlett-Packard's Handheld PC Web site is located at http://www.hp.com/handheld.

Specifications

■ Models: HP 300 LX, HP 320 LX

■ Display: 640 by 240 dots, .24 dot pitch, FSTN LCD, 4 grayscale monochrome, backlit on 320 LX

■ CPU: Hitachi SH3, 44 MHz

■ Memory: 2 MB RAM (300 LX), 4 MB RAM (320 LX), expandable via miniature card slot on 320 LX only; 5 MB ROM, upgradable

■ Speaker: Built in

■ Interfaces: RS-232C: 115.2 Kbps, data communication jack, Type II PC Card slot, infrared port (IrDA standard), one miniature card slot on 320 LX only

■ Main power supply: Two AA alkaline batteries, AC adapter included, rechargeable NiMH AA batteries also supported

■ Main battery life: 20 hours

■ Backup power supply: One CR2032 lithium battery

■ Dimensions: 1.1" high, 7.2" wide, 3.67" deep

■ Weight: 15.6 oz with batteries

■ Other: Pocket Internet Explorer version 1.1 is installed in ROM so that you don't have to install it, saving RAM space. Bundled software includes utilities for translating data from other HP Palmtop PCs

Accessories

■ Docking cradle (included with HP 320 LX)

■ AC adaptor

■ Leather case

■ Spare styluses

Hitachi Handheld PC

Hitachi's devices are manufactured by LG Electronics. The Hitachi Handheld PC model HPW10E2 and the LG GP40M differ physically only in their color and labeling. Hitachi makes the processors for all the Handheld PCs except for the NEC and Philips devices. Hitachi's Web site address is http://www.hitachi.com.

Specifications

Hitachi's machine is made by LG Electronics, so its specifications are the same as those for the LG Electronics GP40M.

Accessory

A 14.4/9.6 Kbps low-power FAX/modem. The modem, when added, becomes built in and does not occupy the PC Card slot—a big advantage.

LG Electronics GP40M

The LG GP40M is distinguishable from other Handheld PCs by the larger dot pitch of its screen, .26 mm instead of .24 mm. This seemingly small difference makes the screen surprisingly more readable. The LG Handheld PC also features an optional built-in modem.

The keyboard on the GP40M has hard, plastic, calculator-type keys, more widely spaced than those on some of the other Handheld PCs. The case is not stylish, but it has a straightforward design. The LG Electronics Web site address is http://www.lge.co.kr.

Specifications

- Model: GP40M

- Display: 480 by 240 dots, .26 dot pitch, LCD, 4 grayscale mono-chrome

- CPU: Hitachi SH3

- Memory: 2 MB or 4 MB RAM, expandable to 16 MB; 4 MB ROM

- Microphone and speaker: Built in

- Interfaces: RS-232C: 115.2 Kbps, data communication jack, Type II PC Card slot, infrared port (IrDA standard)

- Main power supply: Two AA alkaline batteries, AC adapter included, rechargeable NiMH AA batteries also supported

- Main battery life: 20 hours

- Backup power supply: One CR2032 lithium battery

- Dimensions: 1" high, 6.45" wide, 3.76" deep

- Weight: 11.35 oz without batteries

Although the GP40M comes with a built-in microphone, none of the Microsoft-supplied programs make use of it. I suspect third-party programs will soon be available to take advantage of this feature.

Accessory

A 14.4/9.6 Kbps low-power FAX/modem. The modem, when added, becomes built in and does not occupy the PC Card slot—a big advantage.

NEC MobilePro HPC

The NEC MobilePro HPC uses the NEC VR4101 MIPS RISC processor. NEC claims that this processor has the best performance per watt ratio of the current crop of Handheld PC processors, and it does seem to have an advantage in battery life.

MobilePro™ HPC

NEC's Handheld PC has a sleek, nicely rounded case, which fits most easily into a hip pocket. The widely spaced keys have a soft, rubbery feel. NEC's Web site can be found at http://www.nec.com. Search the site for *mobilepro*.

Specifications

- Model: MobilePro HPC

- Display: 480 by 240 dots, .24 dot pitch, LCD, 4 grayscale monochrome

- CPU: NEC MIPS Vr4101 processor optimized for Windows CE

- Memory: 4 MB RAM, 8 MB ROM

- Speaker: Built in

- Interfaces: RS-232C: 115.2 Kbps, data communication jack, Type II PC Card slot, infrared port (IrDA standard)

- Main power supply: Two AA alkaline batteries, AC adapter (not included)

- Main battery life: 30+ hours

- Backup power supply: One CR2032 lithium battery

- Dimensions: 1" high, 6.89" wide, 3.74" deep

- Weight: 12.8 oz without batteries

Accessories

- Docking cradle

- Direct connection cable

- AC adapter

- NiMH rechargeable battery and battery charger (does not recharge in the device)

- Stylus pack

- Carrying case

Philips Electronics Velo 1

The Philips Velo 1 has won several awards for its design. It features a built-in modem and microphone and a unique PC Card slot in a separate module that clips onto the bottom of the unit. In the future, Philips plans to release other modules that will clip onto the unit in a similar fashion.

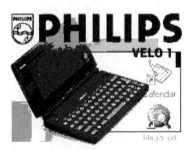

The Velo 1's keyboard has small, oval, hard, plastic keys. It looks cool with its blue coating, which has a rubbery feel and makes a secure grip easy. A silver shield on the case highlights the product name. The Velo 1 always gets stares when I pull it from my pocket. Phillips implemented the modem in software so that it doesn't drain additional power, and the phone jack pivots out from the case to the left of the screen.

A microphone is built into the cover, along with a button that allows you to record spoken notes while the machine is closed—just pick up the H/PC, press the button, and start talking. Phillips' Web site is located at http://www.velo1.com.

Specifications

- Models: Velo 1 with 2 MB RAM, Velo 1 with 4 MB RAM, and Velo 1 with 4 MB RAM and a rechargeable battery pack

- Display: 480 by 240 dots, .24 dot pitch, LCD, 4 grayscale monochrome with backlight

- CPU: Philips MIPS V3101 processor

- Memory: 2 MB or 4 MB RAM, expandable via miniature card slot; 8 MB ROM

- Speaker: Built in

- Interfaces: RS-232C: 230 Kbps, data communication jack, Type II PC Card slot in clip-on module (not included), infrared port (IrDA standard), two miniature card slots

- Main power supply: Two AA alkaline batteries, AC adapter included

- Main battery life: 15 hours

- Backup power supply: One CR2032 lithium battery

- Dimensions: 1" high, 6.7" wide, 3.65" deep

- Weight: 13.8 oz without batteries

- Other: Docking station is included. Microsoft Pocket Internet Explorer version 1.1 is installed in ROM, so you don't have to install it, saving RAM space. Also, a database program that lets you create and manage lists and forms is included in ROM

Accessories

- Flash and DRAM miniature memory cards; the Velo 1 supports 100 MB of total memory

- Type II PC Card slot in a clip-on module

- NiMH rechargeable battery pack

- Carrying case

Programs for Windows CE

As I write this book, new programs for Windows CE are being announced almost daily. In this appendix, you'll find brief descriptions (and illustrations where appropriate) of a sampling of commercial programs that are available for Windows CE. I've chosen programs from several categories that I think you'll find useful, including communications programs, databases, games, handwriting recognizers, maps, notetakers, and personal information managers. Within these categories, I've selected programs somewhat randomly.

As usual, the World Wide Web is the best place to locate, and in many cases to purchase, software for your Handheld PC. I haven't listed the numerous freeware and shareware programs that you can download.

The programs described here are just a few of the hundreds available for Windows CE. They demonstrate that Windows CE has truly become a new computing platform. For the latest information on these and other programs for Windows CE, check the vendor's Web site, or visit the Windows CE Web site (http://www.microsoft.com/windowsce).

Communications Programs

See Chapter 8 for information about using the Inbox.

The communications category includes e-mail programs, fax programs, pager programs, and remote-access programs. Because most of these programs use the familiar Windows CE Inbox to display messages, I've only included one screen illustration in this section.

bFAX Pro

bFAX Pro, from bsquare development, lets you send and receive faxes using a standard PC Card fax modem over an ordinary telephone line or via a cellular phone. It allows you to manage multiple and recurring faxes, fax multiple documents in different formats, create distribution lists, send text and bitmap images, and receive and view faxes. bFAX Pro can automatically use names and fax numbers from the Windows CE Contacts program. Here's an example of a bFAX Pro screen:

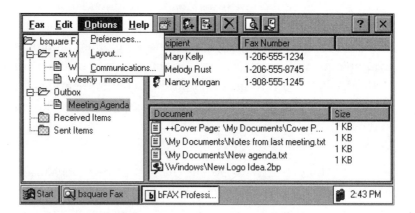

bsquare development
Phone: 888-820-4500; 206-644-9970
Fax: 206-644-8057
Web: www.bsquare.com/development

Mail on the Run!

See Chapter 7 for information about setting up a Remote Networking connection.

Mail on the Run! provides you with direct and remote access to the world's most popular e-mail systems for local area networks (LANs), including Lotus cc:Mail, Lotus Notes Mail, Microsoft Exchange, Microsoft Outlook, and Microsoft Mail. You install Mail on the Run! as a mail service in the Windows CE Inbox. Mail on the Run! lets you keep your existing LAN mailbox and password so that people don't know you are communicating remotely. You can communicate over the telephone using a Remote Networking connection or over ARDIS and other wireless networks using a PC Card wireless modem.

An agent is a program that prepares and exchanges information between computers on a network.

The Mail on the Run! agent runs on either Microsoft Windows 95 or Microsoft Windows NT version 4.0 with Remote Access Service (RAS) installed. The RAS server provides security functions for people using Windows CE. The agent can support multiple concurrent users, and it must be connected to the LAN on which the e-mail system post office resides.

River Run Software Group
Phone: 203-861-0090
Fax: 203-861-0096
E-mail: info@riverrun.com
Web: www.riverrun.com

PageSoft for Windows CE

Socket Communication's PageSoft for Windows CE turns your Handheld PC into a sophisticated "data pager" that can receive both conventional pages and wireless data. You can use PageSoft to download messages from the Socket PageCard alphanumeric pager to the Windows CE Inbox, making it possible for you to receive and store wireless e-mail, stock quotes, sales leads, and other time-critical information in time to make effective responses. The PageCard is a PC Card pager that slides into the PC Card slot in your H/PC. A small "bubble" sticks out on the end, which houses the AAA battery. Because the PageCard is self-powered, it does not drain the batteries on your H/PC.

PageSoft is for receiving pages only—the PageCard does not allow you to send pages directly from your Handheld PC. It's easy, however, to send a page using Pocket Internet Explorer—just connect to the Internet and access your paging service provider's Web site.

You install PageSoft as a Windows CE Inbox mail service. PageSoft automatically places new pages in the Inbox folder, and it allows you to specify how you are notified of incoming pages.

An interesting feature of PageSoft is its ability to reconstruct long messages that have been divided into multiple pages using Socket's Page Descriptor Footer (PDF) format. Since many paging services have rather short message-length limits (sometimes as low as 80 characters), Socket created the PDF format to allow a longer message to be segmented and reconstituted at the receiving end.

> **Socket Communications**
> Phone: 510-744-2700
> Fax: 510-744-2727
> E-mail: info@socketcom.com
> Web: www.socketcom.com

SkyTel Messenger for Windows CE

SkyTel Messenger for Windows CE is another mail service for the Windows CE Inbox. It allows you to send and receive messages up to 500 characters long by connecting your Handheld PC to the SkyWriter 2-Way pager with a short cable. The pager itself is 3-3/4 inches wide, 2-1/2 inches high, and only 7/8 inch thick.

You can send and receive messages to and from any Internet e-mail address, to and from any other SkyTel 2-Way pager, or to any SkyTel one-way pager. Of course, you can also use the pager independently of your Handheld PC.

> **SkyTel**
> Phone: 800-395-8930
> Web: www.skytel.com

Virtual Courier

Virtual Courier, from MicroBurst, allows you to exchange e-mail messages between your Handheld PC and your Lotus cc:Mail, Microsoft Mail, or Microsoft Exchange client on your desktop PC. Virtual Courier is an SMTP/POP3 server that extends your Handheld PC's e-mail functionality by giving you access to your desktop PC inbox from the Windows CE Inbox on your Handheld PC. You don't have to install any software on your Handheld PC to use Virtual Courier.

The Virtual Courier server allows connection via modem using Dial-Up Networking on Windows 95 or RAS on Windows NT. Virtual Courier supports POP3 and SMTP Internet protocols, and it can work over a phone line, across a network using TCP/IP, or via a direct cable connection. It provides built-in security by using your e-mail user ID and password to validate the connection.

You can configure one computer as a dial-up messaging server for many Handheld PC users. Registered users can log onto Virtual Courier and exchange mail with their e-mail accounts. Virtual Courier comes in two versions: Lite, for a single user, and Enhanced, which supports up to 20 users. It also includes a utility to download addresses and a utility to Uuencode/decode files, which lets you add attachments to your messages.

MicroBurst, Inc.
Phone: 301-330-2995
Fax: 301-330-8609
E-mail: 71660.3416@Compuserve.com
Web: www.virtualcourier.com

WyndMail CE

WyndMail CE, from Wynd Communications, is another mail service for the Windows CE Inbox. Using WyndMail CE, you can wirelessly exchange e-mail messages with anyone on the Internet, send faxes worldwide, send messages to any alphanumeric pager in the United States, send e-mail messages to telephones, and filter and automatically forward messages to another e-mail address.

WyndMail uses the RAM radio packet network, which is specifically designed for sending and receiving data. Since there are no phone calls involved, there are no long distance charges, cellular roaming charges, or long log-on procedures. The RAM radio packet network is a nationwide service that covers 92 percent of the metropolitan U.S. To use it, you need a US Robotics AllPoints Wireless PC Card, which slides into the PC Card slot of your Handheld PC and which you can purchase or rent from Wynd.

The message header preview feature lets you see the message subject and sender before you pay for transmitting the message, keeping you in control of your wireless bill and the information flow to your Handheld PC. You can also sign up for delivery of filtered news and information to your Handheld PC.

If you run Microsoft Exchange on your desktop PC, you can use its Inbox Assistant to forward selected mail from your LAN system to your Wynd account. You can specify that replies to your messages are sent to your Exchange Inbox.

Wynd Communications
Phone: 800-549-9800
Fax: 805-781-6001
E-mail: info@wynd.net
Web: www.wynd.com

ZAP-IT

ZAP-IT Wireless Service, from DTS Wireless, another mail service for the Windows CE Inbox, lets Handheld PC users receive and respond to e-mail, faxes, and phone messages without the hassle of locating a phone jack.

ZAP-IT offers a single 800 number for incoming faxes and phone messages, gives you the ability to preview e-mail message headers before downloading them, and lets you redirect incoming faxes to print on any fax machine. You can also send messages to fax machines, most alpha pagers, and even telephones; fax documents using letterhead and fax attachments you have stored; and access the Web and download pages in text mode.

ZAP-IT service, which uses the RAM packet radio network, is available in more than 8000 cities and towns across the U.S. and covers 92 percent of the urban business population, including metropolitan areas, airports, and transportation centers.

DTS Wireless
Phone: 888-2-GET-DTS; 908-602-1144
Fax: 908-602-0990
E-mail: info@dts.net
Web: www.dtswireless.com

Databases and Programs for Recording Time and Expenses

You can use the programs in this section to send data collected on your Handheld PC to a desktop PC for further processing.

AllPen Mobile Forms Database

AllPen Software has developed AllPen Mobile Forms Database for Windows CE. This program allows you to design your own customized database and associated data collection forms that run on your Handheld PC. You can easily define field types and preset default responses, so you save time when entering repetitive data. Field types supported include text, notes, and numbers (integer and floating point); available controls include pop-up menus, option buttons, and check boxes.

The database resides on your Handheld PC so you can easily collect important data while you're away from your desktop PC. Import and export functions make exchanging data with your desktop PC easy.

Here is a sample form showing several different types of fields:

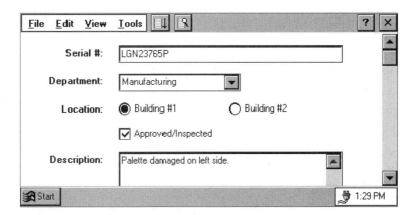

The form is not constrained by the screen size. This database program is included in the Philips Velo 1's ROM.

AllPen Software, Inc.
Phone: 408-399-8800
Fax: 408-399-4395
E-mail: info@allpen.com
Web: www.allpen.com

TimeReporter for Windows CE

TimeReporter is a time-tracking and expense-tracking program from iambic Software. It is designed to make it easy for lawyers, consultants, and anyone else who bills by the hour to record time and expenses. Because of Windows CE's portability, TimeReporter is available everywhere you are. Entries made on the go are stored digitally, eliminating errors and the necessity to rewrite client names, descriptions, and so on. TimeReporter is based on the familiar time-sheet format, and it works hand-in-hand with your desktop PC to eliminate retyping data. Here is an example of a TimeReporter screen:

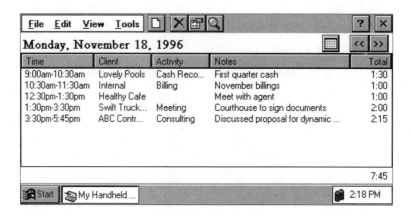

TimeReporter comes with Access database forms that match one-to-one with the TimeReporter forms on Windows CE. You don't need a copy of Microsoft Access on your desktop PC because TimeReporter comes with a run-time license for the forms. The program fully synchronizes data you enter on your Handheld PC with data in the Access database on your desktop PC. You can also put data in tab-delimited format for export to other desktop PC time and billing programs.

iambic Software
Phone: 408-882-0390
Fax: 408-882-0399
E-mail: sales@iambic.com
Web: www.iambic.com

Games

Remember, it's important to play as well as work.

Microsoft Entertainment Pack for Windows CE

I had to include the Microsoft Entertainment Pack because my group at Microsoft created it. Also, it's the first retail Microsoft program for Windows CE.

The Microsoft Entertainment Pack for Windows CE is a collection of 10 games that might amuse you, puzzle you, challenge you, or just distract you for a few minutes. Some of the games are designed for two-person play: you can play against the computer or use infrared communications to play against a friend using another Handheld PC. The following games are included:

- Blackjack: Test your card sense and luck at this classic casino game.

- Chess: Play the game of the ages against the computer or against your favorite opponent, sharing the same Handheld PC.

- Codebreaker: Try to crack the secret code in this great brain-teaser.

- FreeCell: Even with all the cards on the table, it takes skill and practice to win this version of solitaire.

- Hearts: Play this classic four-person card game against the computer or against an opponent over an infrared connection, with the computer playing the other two hands.

- Minesweeper: Clear the minefield using skill and speed.

- Reversi: Just when you think you've won, your fortunes reverse. Play against the computer or against an opponent over an infrared connection.

- Sink the Ships: Sink your opponent's ships before yours end up at the bottom of the sea. Play against the computer or against your favorite opponent over an infrared connection.

- Space Defense: Defend your space station and its life pods from enemy attack. You need quick reflexes if you want to survive. Here's a screen from Space Defense:

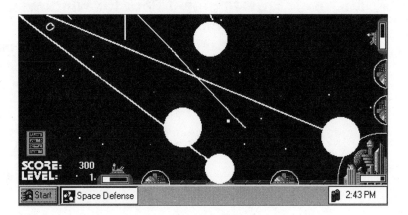

- Taipei: Match the tiles in this ancient favorite.

To save disk space on your Handheld PC, you can uninstall one or more of the games in the Entertainment Pack without losing your preferences, high scores, or other settings. Then, of course, you can reinstall the games from your desktop PC at any time.

Microsoft Corporation
Phone: 800-358-3952
Web: www.microsoft.com/windowsce

Handwriting Recognizers and Data-Entry Programs

Although Microsoft did not include a handwriting recognizer with Windows CE, several companies have stepped into the breach. InScribe is not a handwriting recognizer, but it offers an alternative entry method.

CalliGrapher

ParaGraph International's CalliGrapher 4.0 recognizes both cursive and hand-printed letters at a level of accuracy that makes it the industry leader in both categories. These capabilities are seamlessly integrated into the most effective mixed-recognition system available.

This program is a "universal" recognizer, recognizing cursive, mixed cursive and print, and print handwriting—the way people normally write.

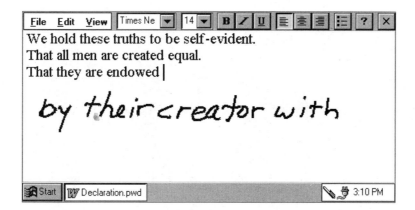

CalliGrapher does not require you to memorize special symbols or change your writing style. Based on principles of fuzzy logic and neural networks, it recognizes dictionary and nondictionary words and symbol sequences, and it contains algorithms that adapt to your writing style. CalliGrapher can be customized for a particular user, if desired, and it currently supports English, French, German, and Swedish.

CalliGrapher operates either in transparent mode, in which you write directly in the window of the program into which you want to enter data, or in notetaker mode, in which you write in a simple note-taking program. It also recognizes a set of gestures to make editing easier.

> **ParaGraph International, Inc.**
> Phone: 408-364-7718
> Fax: 408-374-5466
> E-mail: info@paragraph.com
> Web: www.paragraph.com

InScribe for Windows CE

InScribe, by Ilium Software, offers an alternative method of text entry designed to make Handheld PCs easier and more fun to use. It lets you enter text and numbers by dragging your stylus from character to character across a grid, moving your hand the way you do when writing or drawing—not by tapping characters but by connecting them with a natural, easy, comfortable gesture.

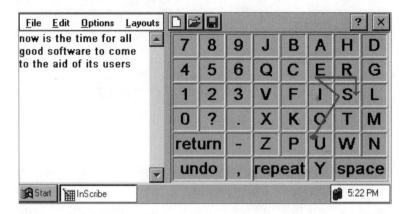

InScribe's patent-pending algorithm recognizes the character you "mean." The program gives you a fast, accurate, and intuitive way to take notes, draft documents, and record ideas on an H/PC without having to use the keyboard. You can enter information as fast as you can write and then save it to a file or move it to another program to edit or manipulate it.

InScribe's character table is fully configurable, so you can arrange it in a way that's comfortable for you—use one of the defaults, or design your own.

Ilium Software
Phone: 888-632-5388
Fax: 313-207-9358
E-mail: info@iliumsoft.com
Web: www.iliumsoft.com

Jot

Communication Intelligence Corporation's Jot is specifically designed for easy input of handwriting on Handheld PCs. It is user-independent and combines a natural character set with a patented user interface for accurate, fast, and modeless input. (Modeless input means that you don't have to switch between writing and tapping with the stylus.) Jot allows handwriting input at maximum speed but requires a minimal amount of memory—less than any other handwriting recognition system available for Windows CE.

Jot recognizes your handwriting one character at a time and does not use a dictionary, which provides very good performance and requires much less memory usage.

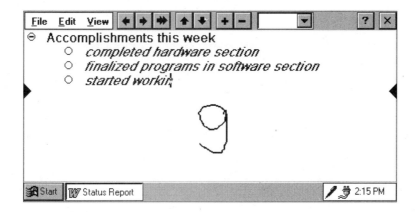

To get the best accuracy, you must write your letters in certain areas of the screen. Mentally connect the two triangles at either side of the screen to form an imaginary line. Jot interprets letters written below that line as lowercase and letters written across the line as uppercase. Write numbers and equations above the line. You can use Jot to write all the standard keyboard characters, and Jot gives you a way to enter special Western European language characters such as accent marks, something you can't do from the Handheld PC keyboard.

Jot also supports gestures such as space, carriage return, and cut and paste, letting you edit with the pen so that you don't have to put it down and type on the keyboard. Although no training is required to use Jot, the Training Wizard lets you customize Jot's recognizer to maximize accuracy. In addition, Jot features a macro editor that lets you define frequently used phrases and actions to speed up text entry and editing.

Communication Intelligence Corporation (CIC)
Phone: 415-802-7735
Fax: 415-802-7777
Web: www.cic.com

smARTwriter

smARTwriter, from Advanced Recognition Technologies, is a handwriting system that adapts to your style. It features a training mode that lets you "tune" the recognizer to the way you write. smARTwriter combines a patented shape recognizer with a unique linguistic layer that matches any set of written words with combinations of letters that are common in a specific language and grammar rules for that language.

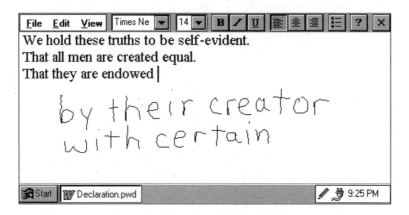

You can also configure smARTwriter as a character-based recognizer that uses the Graffiti character set or one of your own, such as shorthand. You can define additional symbols to stand for words or phrases, and smARTwriter supports gestures to facilitate editing with the pen.

Advanced Recognition Technologies, Inc.
Phone: 408-973-9786
Fax: 408-973-9787
Web: www.artcomp.com

Maps

If you install one of these map products on your Handheld PC, you'll have no excuse for getting lost!

Microsoft Pocket Automap Streets Plus

Microsoft Pocket Automap Streets is a companion to Microsoft Automap Streets Plus, which runs on your desktop PC. Streets Plus enables you to pinpoint virtually any street address in the United States. If you're planning a trip, it helps you plot and highlight your route by giving you access to millions of updated street segments. It also includes many points of interest, addresses, zip codes, and thousands of hotels and restaurants. In addition, Streets Plus provides a powerful mapping framework that helps you build unique, practical maps that are really useful. For example, you can use the Pushpin Wizard to add customer, supplier, or personal information to your maps. Pushpin maps can be annotated with travel directions or integrated with other databases.

Pocket Automap Streets makes the maps included in Streets Plus portable. You can take maps of any 40 cities in the United States that you select along with you on your Handheld PC.

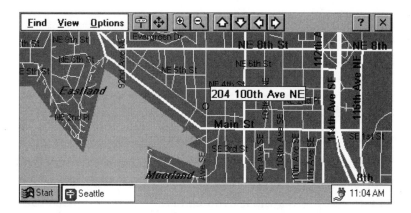

Each Pocket Automap Streets map shows you a whole city at a glance and lets you zoom in to see the details you need, right down to street level. You can quickly locate a specific location by entering its name or street address in the Find Address dialog box. Or, you can use the Find Places feature to locate a specific city or point of interest. The Zoom and Pan buttons on the command bar let you display just the information you want to view.

Microsoft Corporation
Phone: 800-358-3952
Web: www.microsoft.com/automap/pstreets/

Pocket Survey

Pocket Survey, from Agri-Logic, turns your Handheld PC into a flexible tool for navigating, mapping, and gathering geographically-referenced data. When your H/PC with Pocket Survey installed is connected to a GPS (Global Positioning System) receiver, you can see your current location, heading, speed, and altitude displayed in real time. In addition, you can enter data that is linked to a location, and you can perform distance and area calculations.

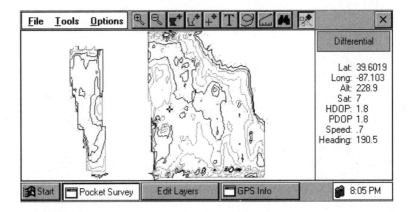

Zoom out to see the outline of North America, or zoom in to your own backyard. When you return to your desk, connect your Handheld PC to your desktop PC and upload the data in any of a number of common map and database file formats. You can edit, view, and print your maps and field-collected data using the Pocket Survey Desktop Companion program for Windows 95 or Windows NT.

Agri-Logic, Inc.
Phone: 800-444-8214
Fax: 812-442-8214
E-mail: info@agrilogic.com
Web: www.agrilogic.com

Teletype GPS

Don't you hate that feeling you get when you realize you're lost? Where are you? Where are you going? When you install Global Positioning System (GPS) technology on your Handheld PC, it acts like a precise digital compass to help you avoid the frustration and wasted time of getting lost.

TeleType GPS, from the TeleType Company, is moving map software for your Handheld PC. It allows you to display your location on a moving map while driving, flying, biking, or trekking. Using the precision of global positioning satellites, it shows your current position in relation to nearby cities and towns.

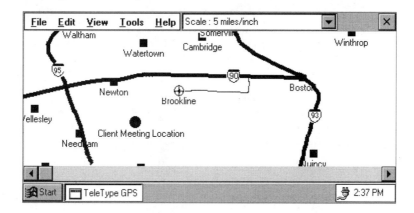

The TeleType GPS moving map software is controlled by a powerful yet small and lightweight GPS receiver that you connect to your Handheld PC's serial port.

TeleType Company
Phone: 617-734-9700
Fax: 617-734-3974
Web: www.teletype.com/gps

Note Takers

Note taker products provide an alternative to using Pocket Word and your H/PC's small keyboard to take notes. Instead, you can jot down your notes with the stylus as if you were using paper and pencil.

QuickNotes

QuickNotes, from CIC, is an electronic writing pad that collects all your handwritten notes and organizes them by date. It makes recording your thoughts, ideas, and drawings as easy as scribbling them on a notepad.

QuickNotes does not translate your notes or drawings; it stores them in a highly compressed form to save memory—each page uses an average of only 1.5 KB of space.

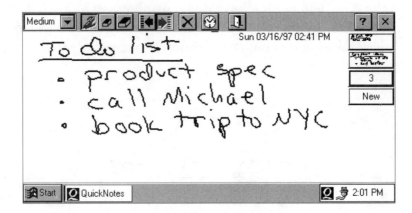

QuickNotes enables you to take notes, draw pictures, or just doodle. You can write and erase just like you can with paper and pencil, and you can stamp your notes with the current date and time. QuickNotes also is ideal for jotting down information when you're on the telephone.

Communication Intelligence Corporation
Phone: 415-802-7735
Fax: 415-802-7777
Web: www.cic.com

smARTscribble

Advanced Recognition Technologies' smARTscribble is a drawing program that lets you draw strokes of electronic "ink." After you draw the strokes, you can select them, perform basic editing actions, and then add text to your drawings. smARTscribble lets you create document pages of unlimited size; each document can include one or more pages. You can select all or a portion of a smARTscribble document, copy it to the clipboard, and paste it into other programs for Windows CE, such as Pocket Word.

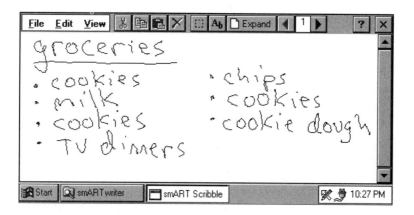

Advanced Recognition Technologies, Inc.
Phone: 408-973-9786
Fax: 408-973-9787
Web: www.artcomp.com

TakeNote!

TakeNote!, from Landware, transforms your Handheld PC into a multi-functional electronic notepad with different types of "stationery" for different purposes. You can capture ink notes for "back of the envelope" inspirations or use the Currency pages to convert currency or calculate loans. The Plane Trip pages let you keep track of travel information, and the Phone Memo pages let you easily capture the details of your calls.

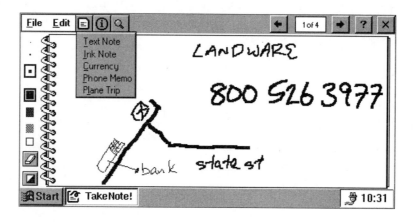

You can also add stationery types and export your notes to your desktop PC.

> **LandWare, Inc.**
> Phone: 800-526-3977
> Fax: 201-261-7949
> E-mail: sales@landware.com
> Web: www.landware.com

PIMs and Synchronizers

Personal Information Managers (PIMs) and synchronizers are quite different types of products. PIMs provide an alternative to the built-in Windows CE Contacts, Calendar, and Tasks programs. Synchronizers let you use these three built-in programs with desktop PIMs other than Microsoft Schedule+ or Microsoft Outlook.

ACT! for Windows CE

From Symantec Corporation, ACT! for Windows CE is a version of the popular desktop contact manager for your Handheld PC. Now you can take your ACT! contact database with you so that it's always available for immediate reference. ACT! for Windows CE looks and works just the same as ACT! 3.0.

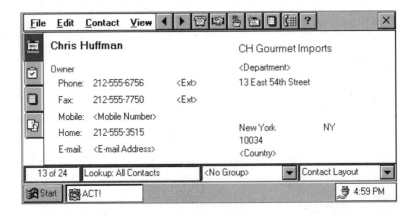

Just as you can on your desktop PC, you can manage your contacts on your Handheld PC by individual contact or by group. The program can store thousands of contacts on your H/PC.

One neat feature of ACT! for Windows CE is that it will generate the tones needed to dial a phone. When you want to call a contact, just hold your Handheld PC near the telephone and ACT! dials the number for you.

Besides handling contacts, ACT! for Windows CE is a full-function calendar program, with daily, weekly, and monthly views. Like the built-in Calendar in Windows CE, ACT! lets you choose to be notified of upcoming events by an audible alarm. The big difference between ACT! and the built-in Calendar is that ACT! integrates the contacts database with the calendar—you can associate appointments and to-do's with a contact.

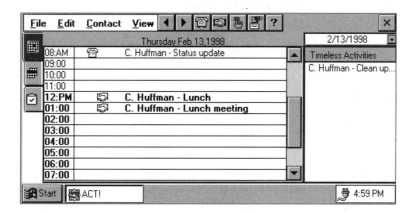

For example, when you create an appointment that refers to a contact, it is automatically added to the history of that contact. Likewise, any notes created for that contact are date-stamped. When you view the contact, you can display the history of your activities regarding that contact. And you can do the same for groups.

ACT! for Windows CE is also integrated with the Windows CE Inbox. When you want to compose e-mail, just type the name of one of your contacts, and ACT! retrieves the appropriate e-mail address from its database.

Symantec Corporation
Phone: 800-441-7234
E-mail: custserv@symantec.com
Web: www.symantec.com/pcanywhere

Desktop To Go for Windows CE

Desktop To Go, from DataViz, increases the number of programs that can synchronize and share data with your Handheld PC. It supports a variety of desktop contact managers, group schedulers, word processors, and spreadsheets. Desktop To Go is not a separate program, but it installs additional file converters and options as part of H/PC Explorer. It provides synchronization for Lotus Organizer 97, Symantec ACT! 3.0, and Starfish Software Internet Sidekick. The file converters it installs let you download data to your Handheld PC from the following programs: Lotus Organizer 2.1, Symantec ACT! 2.0, Starfish Software Sidekick 95, and NetManage Ecco 3.x. Here is an example Desktop To Go screen:

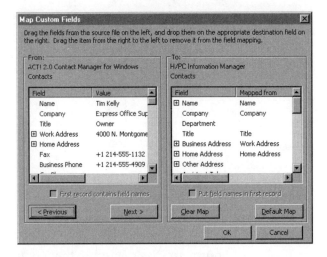

Desktop To Go also broadens the set of desktop programs that can exchange files with Pocket Word and Pocket Excel on your Handheld PC. As you can see, you can control the mapping of data between your desktop PC and your Handheld PC at the field level. These programs include Microsoft Word 97; Microsoft Excel 97; Corel WordPerfect 5.x, 6.x, and 7.0; Corel Quattro Pro 1.0, 5.0, 6.0, and 7.0; Microsoft Works 4.0; Lotus Ami Pro 3.x; and Lotus 1-2-3 Wkx.

DataViz, Inc.
Phone: 203-268-0030
Fax: 203-268-4345
Web: www.dataviz.com/desktoptogo

IntelliSync for Windows CE

IntelliSync for Windows CE, from Puma Technology, enables you to synchronize your Handheld PC directly with your favorite desktop PC personal information management, contact management, and group-scheduling programs all in one easy step.

When your desktop PC and Handheld PC are connected, IntelliSync for Windows CE automatically links your desktop PC contact and scheduling programs with their counterparts on your Handheld PC, ensuring that scheduling and informational data is accurately reflected on both devices. You can decide whether to synchronize your Handheld PC data with a single desktop PC program or with multiple programs. Synchronization is direct and comprehensive. Here is an example IntelliSync screen:

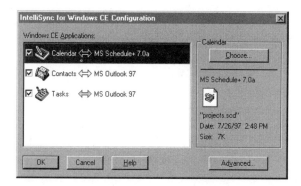

IntelliSync for Windows CE works with Microsoft Schedule+ for Windows 95, Microsoft Exchange Address Book, Lotus Organizer 2.1 and 97, Sidekick for Windows and Windows 95, NetManage ECCO 3.03, Now Up-to-Date for Windows and Windows 95, DayTimer Organizer 2.0, and other programs. It runs under both Windows 95 and Windows NT.

You might have one desktop PC program for personal information or contact management, a second for scheduling appointments, and perhaps a third for keeping track of to-do items and notes. With IntelliSync for Windows CE, you can synchronize your Handheld PC programs with multiple PC programs at one time. For example, you can bring the Handheld PC contacts into conformity with Lotus Organizer 2.1 and the calendar into conformity with Microsoft Schedule+ for Windows 95 all in a single step. You can let Intellisync handle conflict resolution automatically, or you can ask it to prompt you to confirm any changes before they are made.

Puma Technology
Phone: 800-248-2795; 408-321-7650
Fax: 408-433-2212
Web: www.pumatech.com

Pocket On-Schedule

Odyssey Computing's Pocket On-Schedule for Windows CE is a companion to On-Schedule 97 for Windows 95 and Windows NT. On-Schedule 97 is a versatile, network-ready contact and information manager that allows you to organize information efficiently.

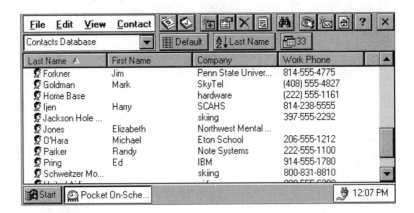

It has interlinked phone books, calendars, and to-do lists, and it is customizable. The program features phone call tracking, mail and fax merge functions, direct e-mail and Internet support, comprehensive contact history, and integration with many other popular programs.

Pocket On-Schedule provides its own contact manager for your Handheld PC but makes use of the H/PC's built-in Calendar and Tasks programs to display appointments and to-do lists. Unlike the built-in programs, Pocket On-Schedule supports multiple databases for contacts, appointments, and tasks, as well as custom views for contacts. It also provides direct dialing and speed dialing support from its contacts lists.

Odyssey provides synchronization support, including conflict resolution, between Pocket On-Schedule and On-Schedule 97. Like H/PC Explorer, On-Schedule 97 controls synchronization from the desktop PC, but it has additional capabilities beyond those in H/PC Explorer. For example, the filtering mechanism shown here controls which contacts are synchronized with their counterparts on the Handheld PC:

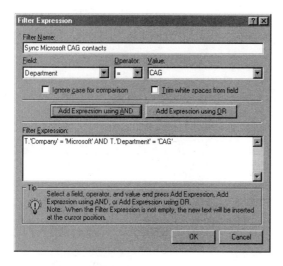

Odyssey Computing, Inc.
Phone: 800-965-7224
Fax: 619-675-1130
Web: www.odysseyinc.com

Other Programs

To illustrate the breadth of programs available for the Handheld PC, I've listed in this section some other interesting products that don't fit into any of the previous categories.

pcAnywhere CE

Symantec's pcAnywhere CE lets you remotely control your desktop PC, workstations, and servers right from your Handheld PC. Using pcAnywhere, you can remotely access files and information on your desktop PC so that when you're away from your desk and suddenly realize you forgot that important file, you can retrieve it.

pcAnywhere for Windows CE lets you run programs just as you would on your desktop PC.

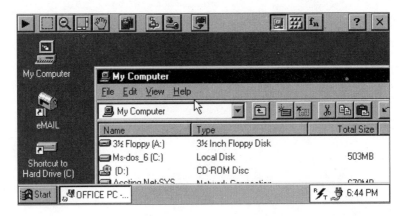

You can use your desktop PC's e-mail program to send and receive e-mail, including messages with attachments. pcAnywhere displays the desktop PC's large program window on the smaller screen of your Handheld PC, so it provides three tools, ezZOOM, ezSCROLL, and ScreenScale to make working with the differently sized displays easier.

pcAnywhere is particularly useful to Help Desk managers and network professionals who need to respond to problems immediately. pcAnywhere connects to a desktop PC, workstation, or server via a modem or, under Windows NT, through TCP/IP Dial-Up Networking.

Symantec Corporation
Phone: 800-441-7234
E-mail: custserv@symantec.com
Web: www.symantec.com/pcanywhere

PocketChart

PocketChart, from Physix, is an electronic medical record. It enables physicians and their care teams to fully document patient encounters and to access important medical information at the point of care.

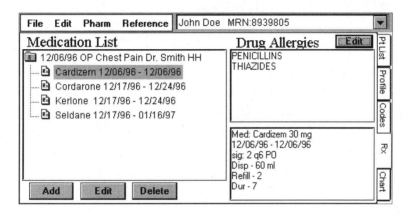

PocketChart is designed to minimize typing: mostly you just tap. You can use it to complete an entire patient note, send prescriptions to the pharmacy, collect billing information, and access a wealth of medical reference information.

Physix, Inc.
Phone: 800-749-2585
E-mail: sales@physix.com
Web: www.physix.com

ProCalc

LandWare offers proCALC cx, a much more serious calculator than the one that comes with Windows CE. Designed for technical professionals who need the flexibility of RPN or algebraic input logic, proCALC cx enables you to tackle the most sophisticated calculations.

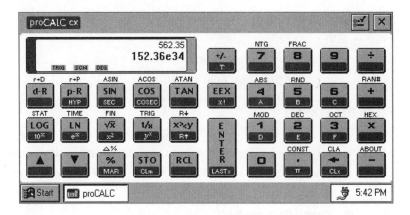

The proCALC cx calculator includes the following features:

- **Powerful functions at a keystroke.** The built-in Science, Statistics, Finance, Trigonometric, and Date/Time function libraries give you keystroke access to more than 100 functions, including hyperbolics; trigonometrics; one-variable or two-variable statistics; linear regression; rectangular to polar, radian to degree, and base conversions; time value of money; and many others.

- **A fully configurable environment.** You can choose display settings, date modes, Input logic, and more.

- **A multiline display.** This display provides detailed feedback of calculator status and the contents of the X and Y registers.

LandWare, Inc.
Phone: 800-526-3977
Fax: 201-261-7949
E-mail: sales@landware.com
Web: www.landware.com

Symbols and Numbers

A

B

About the Author

Robert O'Hara is Development Manager in the Microsoft Mobile Electronics Product Unit. His team is responsible for the Information Manager and Inbox for Windows CE, and they also produced the Microsoft Entertainment Pack for Windows CE. Robert has participated in the design of Windows CE and its applications since the inception of the Windows CE project. His personal contribution was porting Solitaire from Windows 95.

Robert has worked in the software industry since 1973. Before joining Microsoft, he worked at Lotus Development Corporation, and before that, at IBM's Thomas J. Watson Research Center.

On weekends during the winter, Robert works as a certified ski instructor at Crystal Mountain Resort; in the summer he tries to ride his motorcycle as much as possible. He and his two sons, Michael and David, and wife, Maureen, live near the Microsoft campus in Redmond, Washington.

The manuscript for this book was prepared and submitted to Microsoft Press in electronic form. Text files were prepared using Microsoft Word 7.0 for Windows 95. Pages were composed by Frog Mountain Productions using Adobe Page-Maker 6.01 for Windows 95, with text in Melior and display type in Frutiger Condensed. Composed pages were delivered to the printer as electronic prepress files.

Cover Graphic Designer
Gregory Erickson

Cover Illustrator
Gregory Erickson

Interior Graphic Designer
Kim Eggleston

Interior Graphic Artist
David Holter

Principal Compositor
Frog Mountain Productions

Indexer
Maro RioFrancos